Luther M. Siler

Searching for Malumba

Why Teaching is Terrible.. and Why We Do It Anyway

PROSTETNIC
PUBLICATIONS

While *Searching for Malumba* is a work of nonfiction to the best of my recollection at the time the pieces were written, all names of human beings other than elected public officials have been changed.

SEARCHING FOR MALUMBA: WHY TEACHING IS
TERRIBLE… AND WHY WE DO IT ANYWAY

Searching for Malumba is dedicated to all of the hard-working, talented educators I have known and worked with throughout my years, and specifically to some of those who had to put up with me in class:

Dr. James Ackerman
Dr. Scott Alexander
Dr. William Ayers
Dr. Quinton Dixie
Mrs. Ruth Gates
Mr. Gerald Kline
Dr. Bernard Levinson
Mrs. Babette Maza
Dr. Susan Panzica
Dr. William Schubert
Dr. Mary Jo Weaver
Dr. Stephen Weitzman
Dr. Beverly Wills

The techniques are all theirs. The profanity is mine.

Table of Contents

Foreword: What this Book Is, and What it Isn't

Searching for Malumba is my fourth book as an independent author. It's also as close to a vanity project as I'll likely ever get. I've been teaching since leaving graduate school in 2000, and I've been writing about teaching for nearly that entire time. You will, I'll admit, notice a gap here and there, because there were a couple of points in my life where I wasn't writing as much as others, but overall the narrative is pretty continuous. The book's subtitle is *Why Teaching is Terrible... and Why We Do It Anyway.* At first glance, there will be rather more from the first half of the title than the second, but I hope that the second part comes through here and there as well.

You can think of this book as a Best of Luther Siler on Teaching, if you like. Let me be perfectly clear: if you've been following my various blogs (the material in this book is culled from four of them, along with a few other sources) over the past fifteen years, there is not much here new to you, and a good chunk of it is available on the web *now*. But a lot of it is not, and I think there is enough new material for everyone to find something interesting.

(Let's be honest. No one other than my mother and my wife has actually been following my blogs for the last *fifteen years*. And they *have* to read this.)

Two things, before you start: First, a fact that was already on the copyright page, but which I feel compelled to repeat anyway, because none of you read the copyright page: *every single name in this book* that does not belong to an elected official is a pseudonym, whether I explicitly mention that in the text or not. In some cases I have altered genders, ages, and/or races too. There may be a couple of composite characters here and there, too, although I don't think I did that more than once or twice.

Second: my language is salty. Saltier, perhaps, than one might expect from one who spends his career working with young children. If that offends you, well, there's a reason this is at the *front* of the book and not the end. You can expect there to be many, many bad words and perhaps a bit of name-calling here and there. I will not be upset if that bothers you and you choose not to read this. I don't cuss *at* the kids, just *about* them. So do most of the other teachers I know, but still: we'll call this book 18 and over anyway, okay?

Thank you to my beta readers: Holly Bland, B.D. Cavet, L.S. Engler, Gene'O Gordon, Elizabeth Langley, Jessica O'Bryan, Suzanne Seidel, Jennifer Strahl, Eudora Struble, and Tracy Zahl. Special thanks to my wife Becky, who red-penned the entire manuscript and has been forced to live with me through the majority of the writing process as well.

All jokes and caveats aside, the main goal of this book, and of all my writing about teaching throughout my career, has been to be honest and to help myself process my story. I write for catharsis and for understanding; you may be able to tell, reading through this book. I hope you enjoy reading through my journey. Thank you.

Yours,

Luther M. Siler
Somewhere in Northern Indiana
October 10, 2015

(PS: Wondering about the title? You'll have to wait until the end of the book. I put it there for a reason; try and resist the urge to skip ahead— then again, it's not like I can stop you.)

Part One: Catholic School, Grad School, & Student Teaching

2000-2005

I started as a Catholic school teacher, a fact that still surprises me. I still don't know how I lucked into the job, but more details on that in a page or two. I would be there for three years, then get laid off and head to grad school to actually get certified as a teacher. This section covers those few years at the Catholic school, plus a couple of grad school pieces and a handful from student teaching— sixth through eighth grade Language Arts in a school where my smallest class had 40 kids in it.

That's not a typo.

Kids' Appreciation Day

JUNE 2001

So today was Kids' Appreciation Day at the elementary school
I teach at.

The idea of such a thing seemed absurd, putting me in mind of
the old joke about why there is a Mother's Day and a Father's Day
but no Kids' Day: *every* day is kids' day, right? The same principle
applies here. There had actually been a Teacher Appreciation Day in
early May, and I have the cards from my kindergartners on my wall
to prove it, but the notion of a "Kids' Day" at a *school*, of all places,
initially felt silly.

The day worked something like this: Starting at around 10:00 in
the morning, our school board and a whole slew of parent volunteers
set up a gigantic inflatable obstacle course called the "Adrenaline
Rush" in the school parking lot. A makeshift basketball court was
constructed. Massive quantities of hot dogs and bratwurst were
grilled. Chips and Fritos and what seemed to be a small lake of
carbonated beverages were consumed. The weather, for the most
part, cooperated, hitting us with fifteen minutes or so of rain in the
late afternoon but staying dry for the rest of the day. The Adrenaline
Rush occupied most of the kids' attention. They were required to
scale a four foot wall, make their way under, around, and through a
bunch of inflated obstacles, then climb a seven or eight foot wall
using footholds and a rope, before tumbling down a slide at the
end. The whole thing was basically a gigantic vinyl balloon, making
it all very bouncy and making keeping one's footing a hazardous
task. My job, starting around 11:30, when I foolishly offered to spell
one of our parent volunteers, was to help the smaller students climb

the first wall. Often "helping" meant physically lifting them over the thing or, when I was in the mood, just tossing them.

Being able to actually *throw* one's students can be remarkably cathartic. This went on for around two hours, until the aforementioned burst of rain shut the Adrenaline Rush down.

In between tossings, I took several rolls of pictures. This was the first time I'd brought my camera to work all year, and I wanted some physical evidence of my first year. Now, sitting at my laptop and looking through the photographs, I'm starting to understand exactly why we have a "Kids' Appreciation Day." Or, at least, I'm making up a rationale I can live with.

A little background: I am still a little mystified as to exactly how I ended up teaching elementary school. I don't look like an elementary teacher— I'm 24, male, 5'10", and I weigh around 235 pounds. I shave my head. I have a vandyke. I wear a black trench coat (horrors!) when it's cold. And I'm tattooed, although nowhere the kids can see.

As one of my more charming seventh graders put it once, I "look like a psycho killer."

There's more. I graduated from Indiana University in 1998 with a triple major in Religious Studies, Jewish Studies, and Psychology. I minored in Near Eastern Languages and Cultures and was a class away from a second minor in Afro-American studies. I'm not religious, Jewish, crazy, Eastern, or black, but don't let that worry you. I followed that up with an MA from the University of Chicago in Biblical studies.

All of this was excellent training for realizing that I was sick to death of college, but perhaps not the most obvious way to end up as the computer teacher at a Catholic school.

I'm still not sure why they hired me. I'd spent my two years of graduate school as a part-time TA in the computer lab at a public school in Chicago's south side, where I live, and I'd spent some summers in high school and college teaching summer computer classes in high school, but I wasn't certified, wasn't trained, and certainly didn't have any bloody idea how in the world I was going to handle teaching computer classes full-time, especially considering that my school goes from preschool through eighth grade.

That's ten different grade levels, if you're counting.

On top of everything else, I was to be the school's first ever full-time computer teacher. So, in other words, I didn't have any

6

previously existing computer program to fall back on. My job? Create one from the ground up. I must talk a good game or something, because despite my numerous drawbacks (and my distinct lack of Catholicism) I got the job.

I spent the summer before the school year started in a bit of a haze. What in the world did I think I was doing? A Catholic school? A *Catholic school?* My boss was going to be a priest. And they wore *uniforms*, for crying out loud! With the exception of graduate school, all of my previous educational experiences had been with public schools and I didn't have any idea what a private elementary school was going to be like. I wasn't sure if my less-than-entirely-orthodox religious beliefs were going to get me ostracized or, worse, fired. The thought of entire rooms of kids dressed exactly the same was creepy. And then there was the whole "Mr." thing. At my previous school, all of the kids had called me by my first name. Mr. Siler was somebody else— somebody with, like, responsibility and a job or something like that. Certainly not me. No way should an eighth grader, someone only a scant ten years younger than me, be calling me *Mr.* anything. On top of that, the school seemed to be primarily Hispanic, a community I hadn't had much experience working with in the past. My Spanish can charitably be described as rusty, and I wasn't sure how much of a cultural difference I should expect.

And then there was the thought of the preschoolers. Dear God, the preschoolers. One of my less well-kept secrets is that I'm scared to death of babies. As far as I'm concerned, very small children only exist to give me the opportunity to make terrible, life-altering mistakes. You can't *drop* a sixth grader. Babies can't talk and they look funny and they have to be carried places and they do horrible smelly naked things to their clothing that adults have to take care of. Preschoolers, having only recently been babies and not quite having kicked the habit yet, couldn't possibly be much better. They cry, don't they? Crying children terrify me.

This wasn't going to work. I was the worst kind of charlatan, and I was going to be found out, and I was probably going to utterly ruin a few dozen innocent children along the way. Whee!

Luckily, it turns out to have not quite worked out that way. I'm one day away from no longer being a first-year teacher, and to the best of my knowledge I have yet to ruin any lives or destroy any young minds. Despite my initial fears, I have the creeping suspicion

7

that I might have actually educated someone at some point during the last ten months. Whether this can be directly attributed to my efforts or was simply a by-product of the increased exposure to computer technology that the kids enjoyed this year is still up in the air, but I'm arrogant enough to take the credit.

It took "Kids' Appreciation Day" to really get me thinking about all of this, and that's the odd genius involved in the event itself. It happened sometime in the first half-hour or so of kid-chucking, when the kids were playing and laughing and shouting and generally having a blast and I was working my butt off and thinking to myself *my body will make me pay, yes, pay dearly for all of the lifting I'm doing this afternoon*, that it occurred to me: I can't *believe* I actually get *paid* for this.

Hi. I'm Luther Siler. I'm a teacher. I have the best damn job on the planet.

So many things have happened in the past ten months that I never want to forget. At the beginning of the year, I spent most of my energy just getting acclimated. Phrases like *my classroom* felt strange coming out of my mouth. I actually got a little choked up the first time I saw the little "Mr. Siler" nameplate that sits next to the door of the computer lab in the hallway. I said "Good Morning" to my first ever class, the second graders, on the second day of school, and the little buggers responded "GOOD MORNING, MR. SILER!" in unison, which nearly led to a runaway case of the giggles on my part. In retrospect, their response should have been obvious, but it took me completely by surprise at the time.

The third grade teacher brought her students in and told them that we were going to start the day by going over the rules for the computer lab.

Rules for the lab. Yes, that would have been a good idea. I had no rules for the lab. I had known that I was going to be teaching computer classes for about five months at that point, and I had spent exactly zero seconds thinking about the rules for the lab. I improvised. Quickly. The third grade teacher, several years more experienced than I, realized that I was floundering and helped me out with a few rules of her own, including the wonderful trick of asking the students what *they* thought the rules for the lab should be, but the overall effect was humbling.

The first time I uttered the phrase "Perhaps you'd like to share the joke with the rest of us?" I had to excuse myself into the hallway a few moments afterward. The fact that I'd *actually said that* seemed so unbelievable that I had to go laugh about it for a minute or two.

The first time one of them started crying on me was rather traumatic, too. Luckily, I figured out something essential fairly quickly: even though it seems counterintuitive (or, alternatively, sick and wrong and cruel), sometimes the best response to a crying kid is to completely ignore the tears. See, they're sneaky, the little ones: they know that opening up the waterworks is a great way to get what they want. One must be able to recognize the difference, and respond appropriately.

After a while, though, I managed to get myself settled, and got down to the business of attempting to make people learn things. I had a few days where we took computers apart and put them back together again, which worked out pretty well. We did units on word processing and spreadsheets and other things like that. A parishioner was wonderful enough to donate a high-speed cable modem and Internet access through his cable company, and we took the school online for the first time. The Science Fair, which can only be described as a holy crusade of our science teacher and our middle school students, hit in mid-November and kept me extremely busy for nearly two months.

Relating to my kids was one of the more interesting things about my job. For the first time, literally, in my entire life, I was *popular*. I think I have a pretty good rapport with most of my students. There's a danger to this, though. As much as I wanted to be friends with my kids, I couldn't be. I'm not a friend. I'm a teacher. There's a difference, and sometimes discerning exactly where that line is proved to be a complicated affair. Rehashing the events of the most recent episode of "Buffy the Vampire Slayer" (the best show on TV, and yes, I'm serious) with several of my eighth graders occasionally swallowed perhaps more time than it should have. And once the kids figured out my email address and that they could find me on AOL Instant Messenger at pretty much any hour of the night, all sorts of odd, boundary-shattering things started happening. More than once I'd look at my watch to realize I'd spent an hour conversing electronically with my kids. Messages from people with such lovely monikers as "DigitalPimp" and "Thumptress" started showing up. Use our real names? Why would we do that? The percentage of seventh and eighth-grade boys who think using the word "pimp" in their handles is clever is stunningly, depressingly high.

They'll grow out of it, hopefully.

There's plenty more to talk about, of course. During the course of a single week in September I had both my most hectic day and one of my best days nearly back-to-back. One Tuesday morning, in one of the more brilliant moments of my life, I managed to accidentally get a computer speaker to catch fire internally by plugging the wrong kind of power source into it. As I was holding the heavily smoking speaker in my hand, panicking just slightly and wondering what I would do if it exploded, one of my kindergartners informed me that he'd just wet his pants.

There's nothing in the teacher handbook on how to deal with this situation, just in case you're wondering. The fact that this story is funny now is no consolation.

Then, two days later, I had my concerns about both the preschoolers and my Spanish abilities resolved in rather stunning fashion. I was attempting to demonstrate how to use the mouse to one particular little girl, who had clearly never laid eyes on such a thing before, and was getting absolutely nowhere. After a couple of weeks of school, she had yet to say a single word to me. Feeling a little desperate, I switched to Spanish. Watching her eyes light up was an amazing, uplifting experience. She wasn't shy, as I'd thought— she simply understood my Spanish a lot better than she did my English. By the end of the year, far from wondering how to get her to talk, I'd be busy inventing ways to keep her quiet— in English *or* Spanish.

My single finest moment as a teacher came in March, during "Spirit Week", which we held just after a week of Terra Nova testing. We had a variety of events during that week, and Wednesday was Teacher Swap Day. I spent an hour or so in the afternoon teaching a religion class (finally, something I was genuinely qualified for) to the eighth graders. The Class of 2001 was truly an amazing group, and going back and forth with them for an hour on my lecture ("Was Jesus Black?") was a thrilling, invigorating experience. I was dealing with challenging material— I'd given the exact same lecture to college-age audiences before with far less success in getting them to follow along— to say nothing of the sensitive racial aspects of the lecture, which began with my hanging a picture of a white, blond, blue-eyed Jesus on the blackboard and vigorously mocking it for several minutes. I was expecting resistance; I was expecting anger; I was expecting annoying amounts of apathy from some of them. What I got was an incredibly energizing conversation— I was sweating by the end of the hour— and I came away with a tremendous appreciation for the abilities of my students. I'll never again be able to listen to someone denigrating the skills of American students without reflecting on that hour and smiling. There are plenty of brilliant students out there. They just don't get enough attention.

I watched our sixth grade, suffering from the inattentions of a substandard (and luckily now departed) teacher the previous year, develop from a class that I dreaded meeting with at the beginning of the year into one of the most inquisitive, lively groups in the school by the end of the year; kids I genuinely enjoyed working with. Our sixth grade teacher is one of the most dedicated educators I've ever met, and she, along with the other middle school teachers (our sixth through eighth graders switch classes for English, Science, and Math), absolutely worked wonders with that class.

I found myself adopted by three of my third graders, who spent most of their waking hours during the last two months of school devising innovative and enterprising ways to drive me insane. The horrifying thing is that I'm going to *miss them* this summer.

I spent four hours after school with our Student Council officers at the end of Spirit Week, wrapping and packaging shamrock-shaped suckers for our Sham-O-Gram sale. I'll be taking over as the faculty sponsor of the Student Council next year (insert odd, I-can't-possibly-be-talking-about-myself-can-I feeling here), so I have more of these kinds of evenings to look forward to.

I attended a Mass for the first time ever as part of our eighth grade graduation, and had to fight to hold back tears. Most of the class seemed to be doing the same, with varying degrees of success. I'm really, *really* going to miss those kids next year.

I've spent most of the year alternating between an odd, quiet sort of confidence in my abilities and the absolute conviction that I'm wasting everyone's time. Frankly, I hope to *never* be at the point where I stop doubting myself; where I am certain that I know exactly what I am doing; that I can't improve myself or come up with a better way to get my point across. My theory is that so long as I keep thinking that I suck, I'll keep trying to get better.

After all this, it seems that Kids' Appreciation Day makes sense after all. I'm grateful for the reminder— a subtle pointer to the fact that, whatever I may have given to my kids over the course of the last ten months, what they have given me is infinitely more valuable and, ultimately, more lasting. Twenty years from now, many of my current students will have stopped thinking of me. Some, I hope, will not have, but many— perhaps most— will. I will not forget them. They were my first group of *my kids*, that odd voluntary possessive that all teachers use. I love every damn one of them.

And I can't wait for next year.

On Bitches, and the Location Thereof

SOMETIME IN 2002, I THINK

Turns out I don't speak preschooler. Who would have guessed?

Fun fact: my computer lab is just across the hallway from the bathrooms. This means that whenever the kids need to go during class (which doesn't happen as often as you might think) I can just wave at the door and off they go, because there's really nowhere for them to go other than directly across the hall to the bathroom. I can keep an eye on them out of one of the doors (there are two) if I need to and everything is fine.

Unless the kid needing to go to the bathroom is a preschooler, which sorta short-circuits all of my rules. They're supposed to be potty trained, but... hell, *I* don't know anything about preschoolers. Am I supposed to go with them? I can't very well leave the rest of them in the room. I can't tell them to *hold it*. Previous practice has been to call the preschool teachers, who are generally happy to come grab the kid in question and take him down to the appropriately toddler-sized bathroom in their room at the other end of the hallway.

Unless they're not *in* the room for some reason. And the kid's dancing, so...

Shit.

Okay, dude. Can you go to the bathroom across the hall by yourself? Because if you can't, I dunno, I gotta call the *secretary* or something, and I really don't wanna do that.

His head bobs up and down. I look up and down the hall. No adults nearby. As far as I can tell, me and these fourteen or fifteen four-year-olds are the only living humans in the building.

Okay. You can go across the hall.

He goes. I wait anxiously.

An appropriate-seeming period of time later, he comes back out. He doesn't appear to have any stains or wet spots or anything. There's some water on his shirt; I take that to mean he washed his hands, because if he peed *on his shirt* there would surely be more somewhere else.

He smiles at me.

"There's bitches in there!"

Um.

A lot of the time I can't understand them. The good news is that frequently it doesn't matter. But... *What?*

"What did you say?"

He *enunciates* this time.

"There's."

"Bitches."

"In."

"There."

Okay, so, I appear to have two problems here? One, there appear to be girls in the boys' bathroom. Two, I apparently have a *preschooler* who has a home life so fucked up that he uses *bitches* as a collective noun for girls already. I mean what the *hell*, universe.

Maybe I misheard him.

Twice.

Exactly the same way.

"Who's in there?"

Big, sunny smile again.

"Bit-ches!"

Okay.

"Go siddown."

He goes and rejoins his friends. There's BusyTown to be played, after all.

A couple of eighth-grade boys come out of the bathroom. They have sneaky looks on their faces. They head upstairs without saying anything.

Oh, *hell.* They're not... no way. There's no *way* there were *couples* in there. But I can't go check because that means leaving the kids alone. So I have to stand awkwardly in the doorway, watching the bathroom in case anyone else comes *out*, until the teachers get here to pick the kids up.

I run through twelve thousand possible things the kid could have said. He *slowed down*. I know the word "bitches" when I hear it!

I wait.

The preschool teachers show up. I explain the situation and check the bathroom.

The bathroom's empty. But— holy *hell*— the *window is open*. Wide open. Wide enough, perhaps, that a girl could have climbed out, had she been so inclined.

And it hits me that there's a sub upstairs with the eighth graders. A sub who may be less adept than an actual teacher at policing the location of all of his current students.

The preschool teachers, meanwhile, are conferring with the kid. He's *singing* "Bitches, bitches, bitches, bitches!" now. It's not helping, because this situation is both really serious and *completely hilarious*, and I'm having trouble hitting the tone properly. We're trying to decide whether we need to go grab the principal when it hits one of the teachers.

Not "bitches." There were no girls in there.

Big kids.

There were big kids in the bathroom. The eighth graders.

Christ.

Like I said, I don't speak preschooler.

The Can Crusher

December 7 2002

This essay was written as part of an application for...
something. I no longer remember what, and I don't think it did
whatever it was supposed to do for me, but I enjoyed writing it.

"Miss Sanchez, for *exactly how long* have you known you
needed a can crusher?"

I'd never said that sentence before. It's entirely possible that in
the entire history of English-speaking people *no one* had ever said
that sentence before. I said it to one of my seventh graders yesterday
afternoon.

Science Fair was today, you see.

The middle school Science Fair is the dominating element in
the academic lives of our 6th, 7th, and 8th graders, as well as several
of their teachers, from late October until late January of every year.
Science Fair is a holy crusade and an unholy nightmare and a
tremendous learning experience and a giant, unmoving pile of *work*
all at the same time, and we have to do it every year. As the
Computer teacher, I'm right in the thick of things, as the students—
who would start living in my computer lab starting in January or so
every year if I would let them— complete significant portions of
their research and nearly all of their 10- to 15-page written projects
in my room. This year our Science Fair was an Invention Convention
(the broad outlines change every year or two) and a complete project
included a fully constructed, working invention, a board detailing the
creation and testing of the project, and a massive writing project—
the largest that the students will see before entering high school, and
probably the largest they will see for a year or two after that—

17

involving no less than ten separate parts, all of which must be approved individually by either the science teacher or myself before receiving full credit. We demand rewrites. Lots and lots of rewrites. One hapless eighth grader from last year needed *twenty-six drafts* to get his hypothesis written and formatted correctly. The record for most rewrites this year was sixteen, for a seventh grader's procedure section.

Pulling off an event of this magnitude, as one might imagine, is a complicated affair, involving large amounts of careful planning in advance and very clear instructions to the students about what is expected of them and when each individual piece of the project is due. Presentations for the judges must be rehearsed. Judges must be recruited— my friends all know to avoid me in January— and floor space and tables must be reserved and set up for the projects. The sixth graders in particular require large amounts of hand-holding and coaching, as they've never been through the process before, so we often assign 8th grade mentors to them to help us guide them through everything.

All the careful planning and forewarning in the world, however, didn't stop a good twenty kids from descending on my lab after school yesterday to finish things at the last minute. That would be impossible. Previous years had taught me to not allow the kids into the lab on the day of Science Fair in order to preserve my own sanity, and the words "THE LAB WILL BE CLOSED ON THE DAY OF SCIENCE FAIR!!!" have been printed on my blackboard in foot-high, intimidating-looking letters since November. The night before Science Fair, though, is still fair game. Over the past three years, I've stayed at school for an average of three and a half hours after the end of the school day on the night before Science Fair, moving from student to student as fast as I can, solving problems and putting out fires.

This all brings me back to Miss Sanchez and her can crusher. She had just come to me and informed me that I had a problem. That's not a typo— *I* had a problem, not her. She needed to prove that her custom can-crushing contraption could crush cans quicker than a common can-crushing contraption could crush cans (go ahead, say it five times fast), but there was a problem. She didn't *have* a common can-crushing contraption. She just had the special one she'd built. And, oh, she didn't have any extra cans lying around, either. What was I going to do about it?

18

I resisted the strong urge to laugh in her face. I want to be a good teacher, and I think I read somewhere that good teachers generally avoid laughing in faces. But I couldn't help this: "Miss Sanchez, for *exactly how long* have you known you needed a can crusher?" This was something she and Mom were going to have to work out, and it had a good chance to involve yelling and weeping and gnashing of teeth. Sorry, kiddo, nothing I can do right now.

Her completed project, by the way, looked great. The kids have a way of pulling everything together and making me proud once the chips are finally down, even if they drive me half-insane with stress and worry along the way. Science Fair has taught me several things about my job: One, it is *work*. I will not sleep the week before Science Fair. There's too much to do. Two, it is *challenging*. Thinking on my feet and improvising are absolutely essential skills for what I do. So is time and resource management. I qualify as a scarce resource to my students in the last few days before the Fair, because there is only one of me and all of them have questions. I have to learn how to focus, to deal with each individual student as quickly and carefully as I can before moving on to the next member of the pack of crazed hyenas all shouting my name. I have to notice when a student is *not* shouting my name and make certain that he or she isn't sitting there quietly confused and desperate while I deal with more assertive, vocal kids. I have to restrain the urge to bellow, to be sarcastic, to bark out the same answer to the same question I've heard thirty times in a row, not noticing that it's not being asked in quite the same way and it wasn't that student who asked the last twenty-nine times and I need to help her or she's going to tune out and give up. They are *all* going to finish. They are *all* going to do a good job.

And they do. No matter what. They always make me proud of them in the end. Which brings me to Thing #3 That Science Fair Has Taught Me: The kids are me. I am the kids. I'll be honest right now: I really, really, really want to be in bed. I'm not in bed because I'm writing this essay, which is due ... um ... tomorrow. I've put it off long enough that I'll have to hand-deliver it, because the mail can't be trusted at this point. I need to be understanding to the Ms. Sanchezes of the world, because I can't pretend I don't know exactly what they were thinking. I've been there. I'm there right now. Say it with me: "Mr. Siler, for *exactly how long* have you known you had essays to finish?"

19

A Brief Introduction to No Child Left Behind

September 7, 2004

This is the only piece I'm including about graduate school, because it contains some stuff that you'll probably need to know about education law. There is a lot of griping about NCLB in this book, believe it or not.

You may note that my predictions came true, if not the way I thought they would. Once everyone realized that the law was impossible, a fact that should have been clear from the beginning, the federal Board of Ed started handing out waivers to NCLB like they were candy.

They should have been reading my blog.

One of the classes I'm taking this semester is SPED 410, Introduction to Special Education. The class is required; I could have taken it at any point in the past three semesters, but I decided to wait until my last semester of coursework before I actually did it. It was the right decision.

See, SPED is the scary class. SPED is the class that reminds me (as if I need to be reminded) about just how fucking hard this job is and just how much bullshit one has to wade through while attempting to actually educate people. And that's the part *before* we get around to actually discussing learning disabilities. This is just the part with the *lawyers*. This is a good thing; I've spent most of the last year and a half in this lovely little wonderland where I was forgetting about how goddamned *hard* teaching is and was instead reveling in the idea of my little magical classroom where everybody will know all sorts of stuff and my students will go forth from my lessons enlightened and encouraged and we will all save the world together.

I know better, and a little dose of reality is definitely nice. Teaching is *work*, not happiness and flowers. Well, okay, it's work, and *sometimes* it's happiness and flowers— maybe even a lot of the time— but it's *never* not work.

We spent tonight's lecture on special education law, which is complicated and scary even though ultimately it really is to the benefit of the students. It isn't hard to be both, unfortunately, especially since the teachers are the ones that bear the brunt of the punishment if we happen to stray afield of any of the innumerable federal or state laws governing special education. What got me writing, though, was our discussion of President Bush's No Child Left Behind act.

NCLB is one of those laws that, on its face, sounds good. I'm for all the goals of the law, and am even growing to like standards-based education now that I'm reaching the point where I *understand* it. It's the implementation of NCLB that drives me insane, though, because the law as it stands right now doesn't make any goddamned sense.

Here's how it works: The states were asked to put together a standards-based description of what an average— *average,* mind you— student at each grade level might be expected to know. "A fourth grader can write a five-paragraph essay," "A kindergartner knows not to drink gasoline," "The President of the United States can pronounce the word *nuclear*," that sort of thing. So far, perfectly reasonable and therefore so good, right? There are nods to local control, since each state set their own set of standards, so it's not like the feds are imposing any sort of national educational system or anything like that. (Part of me feels like even state control is too big, but it's a small part, and that's another story anyway.)

Here's where the problem comes in: NCLB mandates that all students will meet or exceed those state-set standards by twelve years after the law was signed. *All* students. Which means that by 2014, 12 years after NCLB became law, all students must be *at least* average.

Those of you who understand basic math should be shaking your heads, and those of you lucky enough to understand both math *and* irony should be either chuckling or horrified. Possibly both. I'll accept both as an answer.

So, let's say that in 2002 64% of the students in your school met or exceeded standards. All good, right? Nearly two-thirds of your kids are above average. You've got twelve years to get those other 36% up to snuff.

This means that next year, you need to get one-twelfth of that 36 percent, or another three percent, at or exceeding standards. The year after, that, another three percent. Then another three percent, and another three percent, and so on and so forth.

If you fail on any of those benchmarks, which are not only calculated by your school as a whole but also calculated along other lines— race, ethnicity, gender, and socioeconomic status among them, so 3% more of your poor kids and your black kids and your Hispanic kids and your boys all have to pass the tests too— your school goes on the watch list. Four years on the watch list and the bitchslapping begins. People get fired, schools get closed, that sort of thing.

Urban schools, which have enough problems already, are starting to panic. Those schools are the ones with the kids who were *already* having trouble meeting benchmarks and passing standardized tests, which means that not only do they have farther to go, but they have to get there *faster*.

Here's the thing, though: In a few years, ugly mathematical reality is going to begin slapping around even the "good" schools, the rich suburban enclaves where Mommy and Daddy buy Lexuses for their kids on their fourteenth birthdays so that they have something to *practice* driving on.

You see, even in the "good" schools, it's still gonna be pretty damn difficult to get one hundred percent of the kids above average.

Y'know, seeing as how it's mathematically fucking impossible, and all.

The standards are supposed to have been based on what AVERAGE students at a certain grade level SHOULD BE able to do. And now the NCLB law says that ALL kids MUST be able to do those things.

Madness. Sheer madness.

Twelve years from now, according to this law, virtually every school in America is going to be failing. And it won't be anyone's fault except for the innumerate morons who passed the law.

Luther M. Siler

Whee.

Student Teaching: Meet the Kids

January 22 2005

I met the kids in the next couple of essays during student teaching.

Meet Luther. Luther has a thick accent and his English can be hard to understand sometimes. He's got a list of acronym diagnoses as long as my arm— LD, BD, ADHD, LEP, BDSM, you name it. He's special education, but full-inclusion. He has a habit of slipping into Spanish midsentence without realizing it. He needs to be kept occupied *constantly* or bad things happen— he's a good bathroom monitor, for example, because a lot of the time giving him responsibility helps keep him on track. He can barely read at all, in either language. I'm not sure what the precise reasons are, and they may be connected to his disabilities; I haven't listened to him read enough yet to discern any patterns to his mistakes.

Luther is one of my favorite kids, because he's funny and he's completely freaking unpredictable and he has a way of sometimes being frighteningly insightful about what's going on in my head or in the classroom. He was the second kid whose name I knew. He told me that he was famous; everybody in the whole school always remembered his name within thirty seconds of meeting him. I told him the other day that my goal was to understand every word he said by the end of the semester. He immediately began trying to teach me Spanish, mostly by asking me to repeat phrases insulting his friends in the classroom. My Spanish vocabulary remains stubbornly unenlarged.

He's also got a protective, caring streak that is a mile wide but still only shows when he wants it to. There used to be a child with

25

autism in the classroom who was the butt of a lot of teasing from some of the other kids until Luther, more or less singlehandedly, put a stop to it. He decided that he didn't like the way the other kids were treating Ricky, so he took him under his arm and started defending him whenever the other kids were picking on him. It stuck. Within a couple of weeks not only was Ricky not being abused by the other kids in the class, but the rest of them picked up on Luther's protective behavior and started defending Ricky, no questions asked, whenever he ran into trouble with anyone else in the school.

Meet Tomás. Tomás grew up in Mexico, a trait he shares with a good number of the kids in the room. His father was murdered in front of him in a drug deal gone bad when he was seven years old, and he spent the next three years homeless and alone on the streets of Mexico City. His grandfather went down and got him, somehow, and brought him back to Chicago when he was ten. I have no idea why it took so long, and I suppose it's possible that there's a good reason. His teachers at the time (this was less than three years ago) tried to get him referred for psychological help immediately (my mentor teacher described him, without a trace of rancor or sarcasm, as "an animal" when he first got to America— you can imagine why, given his circumstances) but nothing actually got done until he was caught huffing *hairspray* by another teacher.

Three years later, he's doing fine. He is, in fact, a perfectly average kid, which strikes me as an unqualified, towering triumph. I would have had no idea of his story at all had I not asked an idle question about his parents to my mentor teacher. His academic abilities aren't good by any means, which shouldn't be surprising, but he's trying. He's a quiet, industrious kid, and has never presented any sort of discipline problem of any kind since I've been in his classroom. Given what he's gone through, I can't even imagine how he sleeps at night. His strength and resilience in the face of experiences that would have shattered stronger men than myself is astounding. I don't know him very well yet— like I said, he's quiet, and he's still in bilingual classes for part of the day as well, so I don't see him as much as the other homeroom kids. But I probably think about him more than all but one or two of them. I picked him as the second one to talk about, after all.

26

Student Teaching: Meet the Kids 2

January 26, 2005

Meet Joseph. Joseph is nearly fifteen, and due to an arcane set of rules governing how old one must be to graduate 8th grade from a regular CPS school, he will have to spend next year in some sort of special transition school for students who have aged out of the regular schools. Joseph is my class's second most prominent Child of the Acronym, behind Luther. He's almost as interesting, but in different ways. Joseph is a gangbanger and, I discovered today, an amateur rapper. He's also an excellent dancer, an ability he tends to demonstrate whenever possible in lieu of standing still. I attempted to keep him relatively motionless in line for a while, only to realize that the dancing was basically just a way to get a rise out of me and that not noticing it was probably a better idea.

Luther's learning disabilities are real. I'm less convinced about Joseph's. He seems pretty goddamned bright, frankly, although I shouldn't draw any conclusions because I really haven't had a chance to examine much, if any, of his work. He gets pulled out of class a lot, and I don't think I've had the chance yet to listen to him read out loud. He's a little more confrontational and a little less deferential than Luther as well. He's also a playboy, which is actually one of his more endearing traits.

We went on a field trip last week to the Field Museum. I spent a fairly healthy chunk of my time keeping Joseph and another student from wandering away from the group to score phone numbers from pretty girls in other groups. This was an interesting way to spend the day; Joseph was clearly enjoying the fact that I was chasing him around, and I think after a while he was less interested in the numbers than in making sure I had something to do. (This is a

27

pattern with him. At least half of his misbehavior that I've witnessed has been minor rule violations apparently designed for nothing better than to get somebody to look at him.)

I finally decided that if the kid was gonna spend so much energy on fucking around with me I was going to have some fun at his expense as well. He gave me a chance soon enough; he and the other kid found a gang of girls and started throwing game around like it was going out of style. The other student, Jorge, saw me coming, read my mind, and sort of slunk away, leaving Joseph to his fate.

I waited for an opportune moment, walked up behind him, threw an arm around him, and said "Sorry, ladies, Joseph's a lovely young man, but *he has to go now.*" And half-dragged him off. Jorge, who had been watching, cracked the hell up, as did the girls.

Joseph's reaction was pretty damn funny as well, to tell the truth. As soon as we'd gotten out of line-of-sight from the girls, he whirled away, shot me a fake glare, and said, fairly loudly, "DAAAMN, NIGGA, I WAS ABOUT TO HIT THAT SHIT!!"

Never been called "nigga" before, at least not by anybody who wasn't *white*. That's a new one.

Now, I had a decision to make here. Joseph was clearly guilty of a couple of relatively major violations. I'm pretty sure calling a teacher "nigga" is against a couple of rules, not to mention the secondary swearing later in the sentence. What to do?

I suspect I could have gotten him suspended if I'd wanted to. I didn't. No money in it. I shot him a you-musta-done-gone-and-lost-your-GOT-damn-mind look, he started laughing, and I let him get away clean. The whole thing was kind of risky, but I think I made the right call, because I think he's decided to stop testing me now. He was fine for the rest of the trip, and since then he's been coming to me a lot for help and advice. The kid's got a temper— hell, he's got a mean streak, from some of the stories I've heard— but twice *just this week* he's come and blown off steam with me rather than lashing out at somebody he thought deserved it.

Good kid, that Joseph. He's trying. Now if I can just get some homework out of him...

On Snowball Fights

JANUARY 26, 2005

I was walking back to my car yesterday soon after the end of the school day when I encountered one of my sixth-grade students, who I'll call Gregg (if only because his real name also contains superfluous letters, to the point where I question his parents' spelling ability), along with a few other kids I didn't recognize, energetically throwing snowballs and iceballs at one another.

Were they on school grounds? No. They were, in fact, across the street. Not that I care, mind you. As I explained to them, patiently and carefully, I don't give a damn if I catch you messing up at the *mall*. If I recognize you, you belong to *me*, and you're bloody well going to act right, particularly when you're doing something dangerous.

The other day the principal had begun the day with a rather angry morning announcement regarding snowballs, and specifically referencing a younger student who had been hit in the forehead with an iceball during a fight. I reminded them of the story. A little girl, who had been a bystander to the snowball fight, piped up. "That was me!" She pulls off her hat to reveal a healed, but still visible, scar across her forehead. *Great*. As it turns out, this was Gregg's *sister*.

Quit throwing the goddamn snowballs, dumbasses. This is why.

Now, I'm not stupid. I know damn well that snowball fight started up the second I drove away. The point is that they were warned, and I stopped it for a *little while*, not that I expect these kids to hear my voice in their head when they participate in what is usually a harmless childhood activity, even though it's usually safer with fresh country snow and not the icy shit that clogs the sidewalks

29

in the city. Okay, that's not true, I *do* expect them to hear my voice in their heads, I just don't expect them to listen.

When I saw Gregg the next day, he *immediately* put his face down on his desk, covering up with his hands. Didn't want me to look at him.

Not a chance. Lemme see your face, kid. Dozens of little scratches, most less than half an inch long, all over the place. Did you perchance decide to wash your face with *gravel* last night, my friend? Because I don't remember you looking like that yesterday afternoon.

Guess what? He got hit in the face with an iceball. Now *both* of Mr. and Mrs. Cantspell's kids have facial wounds from snowball fights. And this one they can't blame the school for.

Children are silly creatures.

A Talk in the Library

January 31 2005

I cashed in in my promise to visit the library class sometime (sans Luther, who was banned from the library for a week the last time he went, for— get *this*— speaking Spanish, and is currently serving out said sentence) and, true to my word, followed my class in and dutifully presented myself to the librarian. I hadn't met her previously and I figured I should let her know who I was and that I was gonna be in her room.

From the look she gave me when she noticed I was standing next to her counter (which she never left once in the entire period) I initially thought that I was going to get the same shitty treatment she provides to the kids. Luckily she caught herself before she barked and settled for merely nodding curtly at me.

Nothing fucking happens in library. The librarian yells— *loudly*— at the kids for any number of real or imagined offenses, they get books, they may or may not read them, they talk, then they leave. I never witnessed any instruction of any kind, formal or otherwise, not so much as a "Hey, maybe you would like this book..." Nothing. Just lots of yelling.

I gave up on any pretense of "observing" after a few minutes, when it became clear that nothing important or useful was going to happen, and sat down with four of my kids— Hector, Darnell, Amber, and Moné— and ended up falling into a conversation that lasted for the rest of the period about the Constitution and the federal penal system. It started with Amber asking why torture was illegal (not in a moral sense, but a Constitutional sense) and kinda went from there. Turns out three of the four kids knew someone (two of the four had family members) currently in jail. We got into the

31

concept of institutionalization, recidivism, the punishment vs. rehabilitation concepts of criminal justice, all sorts of shit. Fucking fascinating. Under ordinary circumstances I'd have been worried that I was boring the hell out of them, but they all kept firing questions and comments at me and seemed interested, so what the hell.

Oh, at one point, Darnell asked me how old I was, and when I told him (I'm 28) he went "Oh, cool! That's how old my mom is!"

Seventh-grader. Do the math.

Eek.

'Twas a good day.

Suicide

February 3 2005

I'm writing this a full six days after the events described in this story. Thursday was an *incredibly* stressful day, zooming back and forth repeatedly, from utter insanity to a sort of sublime peace that comes around sometimes when we realize that some particular kid in our classes is Actually Learning Something.

Amber, of the capital punishment library conversation, tried to kill herself this morning. I will not speculate as to whether the event was related to the fact that report cards came out yesterday— her grades aren't great, but they aren't *that* bad. She apparently has a horrible home situation, and had been fighting with her mom for most of the preceding evening *and night*. She came into school sobbing, disheveled, wearing, I suspect, the same clothes she'd changed into when she got home from school the day before. My mentor and I tried to talk to her, but she was entirely incoherent. She'd obviously come to school so that she could talk to someone, but hadn't gotten control of herself to the point of being able to *do* it.

She'd just swallowed about a half a bottle of aspirin, you see.

We didn't find this out for a while. We sent her downstairs to talk to the school counselor, and it was the counselor who managed to calm her down enough to find out what had happened. She was packaged off to the hospital immediately, of course; we only found out about it when one of the special ed teachers, a family friend, got yanked out of our class (in a big goddamned hurry, as you can imagine) to accompany her to the hospital— it's apparently a legal requirement that some school personnel accompany a child sent to the hospital if no parent is available, and this person was the clear

33

first choice. I've never seen a teacher *running* before. It's rather unnerving.

Now, on one level, the fact that her method of choice was *pills* is rather comforting. Pills are generally reversible, even more so when you immediately go to school after taking them and tell people you did it. Amber's fine now, if any of you have been worried about her. DCFS was called about the situation, and she's been moved into her grandmother's custody for the time being. She was back in school the next day, and has seemed fine since then. Then again, had I written a "Meet Amber" piece prior to her suicide attempt, I would have described her as a happy kid, and probably wouldn't have even thought to mention her problems at home, since as far as I'd been able to tell they hadn't been affecting her at school any.

Clearly that would have been a substantial mistake.

I kinda had to put the whole thing on autopilot for processing while I got through the rest of the day, as thinking about it would have pretty much wrecked me. There was also the minor consideration of keeping the situation utterly secret from the kids. As far as they'd known, Amber had just gone home sick; luckily, nobody thought to connect the special ed teacher's abrupt departure from the room to her early dismissal. And while I'm sure a number of them know about it by now, nobody seems to be talking about it.

I'm gonna save the good parts of the day for later. There were several, which just made the day more surreal— little glimpses into my kids' heads that made it clear just how bright some of them are and just how easy it is to underestimate even the kids I see every day. Amber's okay, which is the important thing.

All the same, I'd prefer not to have a day like last Thursday again anytime soon.

Thinking Like a Lawyer

February 8 2005

I fucked up yesterday, and it took me until today to get it fixed. The discipline system at my school is a variant of the system that I and likely many of you probably grew up with. It's pretty simple— all of the teachers keep a clipboard handy with a class list on it. You fuck up, where "fuck up" is defined by the teacher's will, you get a check mark next to your name. Three check marks from a single teacher in a week gets you a Friday detention.

Obviously some things are beyond the scope of the check-mark system; fighting or serious disrespect will earn you a quick trip to the principal's office. But it works well enough, and does so without the stigma of having your name on the blackboard. I can *still* remember the single time I got my name on the board in fourth grade (yes, I was that much of a goody-goody as a little kid,) because I was burning with shame for the rest of the afternoon. Granted, I suspect the feeling would subside with repeated exposure, but you still get the idea.

I don't give check marks that often. I haven't had to, for the most part; I simply haven't encountered many discipline problems that require them. I also have a somewhat visceral dislike of tally-based discipline systems, but that's another story.

You can get check marks for silly things, like chewing gum in class. Everyone's best friend Luther managed to get popped *twice* for it before lunch yesterday. My mentor teacher's ability to detect gum is fucking inhuman; I've seen her nail a kid for it from *across the room,* when the kid in question *had her back turned.* I shit you not. They don't bullshit around with this gum thing.

35

Anyway, this meant that Luther had two out of his three checks on Monday afternoon, with five long days left to go. This is trouble. Adding to the complication was the fact that there's a dance Friday after school. The dance is giving the teachers a nice bit of leverage— if you get detention on Friday, you ain't going.

Cue us walking back to class after library. You'll remember that Luther has issues with the librarian, something I'm just recalling right now as I'm typing this, and something that makes me feel *even stupider* about the entire situation. The kids are normally a little rowdy on the way back from library, as they've been under the thumb of an evil, iron-fisted despot for forty minutes.

Luther walks in the front of the line. This has several benefits: a) it keeps him away from other kids who might distract him, b) it keeps him near the teacher, c) it lets *him* be the decision-maker about whether the boys are in a straight-n-quiet enough line to proceed through the hallways from time to time. He takes this seriously; he's tougher on them than either of us teachers are. The trouble is, when he *is* being loud, he's right next to you and it's hard to ignore. And he was especially loud on the way back from the library.

Note: Never, ever, say "Do you want a third check mark?" or "Do you want to miss the dance?" to a kid with a behavior disorder, because it's not going to work out the way you want it to, particularly when the kid's already in a bad mood. The answer will be "yes," and then you'll have to *do* it, even though you meant it as an idle threat, something to get the kid back on track for two damn minutes to give you enough time to get the class back to the room.

Grr.

What I *should* have done: Congratulated the kid for not getting kicked out of library, for one, something I can't believe I forgot to do. Allow the brief flush of pride from the compliment to take hold, then ask if he can keep up the responsibility thing for a couple more minutes until we're back in the classroom. It woulda been *gold*, and he probably would have gone right into marshalling the rest of the line like he often does. Instead, he and I are *both* pissed off at *me*, and I have to write a detention because of three relatively minor transgressions of the rules: gum twice, and some hallway talking.

Shit.

I'll skip a full discussion of the events of the next couple of hours. Luther, naturally, soon realized that he didn't want to miss the dance after all, and apologized to me for making noise and asked if I could reconsider. My mentor teacher and one of Luther's special ed tutors both told me (gently) that they thought I fucked up, an assessment I agreed with entirely, although the MT said the punishment ought to hold (for obvious reasons: I can't be backing off of punishments all the time; my word needs to mean something) and the tutor was coming from the "oh, come on, be nice" sort of angle.

I can see both sides. What I *couldn't* see was a way out of the mess, until I took a look at the discipline code for the school the next day, after spending most of the evening thinking the thing over.

Three check marks from *one teacher*.

I didn't remember giving out any check marks for gum. Those weren't from me, even though they were put on the same sheet as my check mark for line misbehavior. So ... if no one teacher didn't give Luther three check marks, than Luther doesn't have a detention, now, does he? I hadn't sent the paperwork home yet because we had needed to make more copies and there hadn't been time at the end of the day. So the detention wasn't *official* yet. But the check mark— the actual "punishment" I applied— could still stick. I wasn't taking anything away, I was just wrong about the ramifications for the mark. Victory!

I presented the situation to Luther and he promised he'd behave for the rest of the week. So far, he's kept up his end of the bargain; he hasn't been any trouble at all for either of us since.

Sometimes thinking like a lawyer is a good thing.

On Bad Ideas

April 7, 2005

Today was my school's annual student-faculty basketball game. Apparently early in the school year the girls play the teachers in a volleyball game, and in the spring the boys play the teachers in a basketball game. I played. I didn't want to, but the gym teacher, who runs the thing, is a devious bastard— he asked me if I was interested, I said "No, not really, but I'll play if you can't find enough people to round out the team."

He then *told the kids I was playing*, guaranteeing that there was no damn way I was going to be able to back out.

Lemme say this right now: this tradition? Is a *bad idea*. Student-faculty competition is fine if it's all in fun. I participated in some similar events (including a volleyball game) when I was at my previous school. But the game, as it was put in practice at this school, is just not that smart, and sure as hell wasn't all in fun. Trash-talking has been *epidemic* over the last few weeks. From the kids *and* the teachers— well, the non-me teachers, I guess, since I've been consistent and clear about the fact that I suck at basketball and the students should expect *nothing* from me in terms of production or contribution to the game.

Let's take a look at this, shall we? Take seven 7th and 8th grade males, several of whom have gang connections and none of whom are particularly good students (Joseph, incidentally, is on the team) and put them in a *contact sport* competition with their teachers, who are not only larger than them, but as it turns out *considerably* outnumber them.

This was apparently the first time in a couple of years that an ambulance didn't have to be called during the game, and even then

39

we had a student injured, landing on his wrist at an awkward angle and thus eliminating himself from the rest of the game. The kids don't really bother being nice for the most part, either— if they're not trying to kick your ass (one of the faculty players is the permanent sub for the school, and the students *hate* him— they were knocking him around for the entire game) they're trying to grab a handful of ass or tit from the younger female teachers. The teachers, for their part, are generally not being much more mature— the 80-year-old special ed teacher spent the *entire game* talking shit from the bench, loudly, and directed at *specific* students; students who he should know damn well have trouble with anger management and don't really need this sort of abuse from a grown-up.

We won, of course. It's grown-ups against a bunch of adolescent kids. It's not as if they had a damn chance. The kids, who, as I've said, were *really* into the game, were upset— one of them was *crying* at the end of the game. As I was walking to my car after the game, one of the kids spotted me from the playground and came racing over, hollering about how we were "hackers" and brandishing a large, rather nasty-looking scratch on the underside of his forearm as evidence. I couldn't really say anything about it other than to point out that it wasn't me that did it. I was on the court for maybe six minutes, barely touched the ball, and sure as hell didn't hurt anybody.

This is bullshit, and we don't need it. I understand the *principle* behind the game, but surely there are better ways to do something like this. At my last school, there was a coed volleyball game— which, incidentally, isn't a contact sport— and then a 3-point and freethrow-shooting contest. Which, incidentally, the kids *won*. The kids are *never* going to win a straight-up contest like a basketball game with adults. We're too damn tall and there are too damn many of us. Why do the competition if it's just going to piss them off? What the hell is the point?

Gah.

Part Two: Chicago Public Schools

2005-2007

I needed only a single interview to get my first job as a certified teacher. They actually called and offered me the job while I was driving home: seventh grade language arts and social studies. I was at that school for two years, eventually leaving to move back to the town I grew up in and get married. Two things you should know: first, if I had stayed in Chicago, I would currently be making somewhere in the neighborhood of ninety thousand dollars a year. Second, the money would not be remotely worth it.

Are We Still Black?

October 18 2005

I start each day off with a "bell-ringer", usually in the form of an essay question posed on the board for the students to answer on a sheet of paper. Today was a Social Sciences day, so the question was "Imagine that you are a colonist in Jamestown. What is your day-to-day life like?" I wanted to hear things about daily life, jobs, technology, stuff like that. (Mental note: research toothpaste; my kids are obsessed with dental hygiene for some reason.) The question's on the board, I'm not dealing with it yet, busy with attendance and lunch money and collecting progress reports and such. Not, in any way, thinking about the bellringer.

Student puts his hand up. I look up from what I'm doing and call on him.

"Are we still black?"

In the context of the bell-ringer, mind you, this makes sense and even shows some pretty good thinking. However, it wasn't in context. I didn't have the *tiniest idea* what the fuck he was talking about, and in fact assumed that I had to have heard the question wrong. There were a couple of comical moments where I tried to figure out what the hell he was talking about. About half the class got the question and was laughing at me and the other half was on my side, not having the vaguest idea what the hell was going on or why one of my students would suddenly begin questioning his racial affiliation.

It kinda started the day off strangely.

Reading Counts, or Something
November 7 2005

Friday was Staff Meeting and Get Your Grades Done day.

Several weeks ago the kids took a standardized test. It's called Reading Counts or Life Counts or Read for Life because It Counts or some shit like that, maybe the word "counts" wasn't in there at all, hell, I don't know. It was presented to the teachers as a low-stakes thing, no big deal, just a diagnostic tool that we could use to target our reading instruction. Frankly, I was glad to give it, because I really don't know how the hell to teach reading (*no, really, I don't*) and I'll take any advice, suggestions, or instructions I can get.

Well, today we talked about that little low-stakes, no-big-deal standardized test in our faculty meeting. And my brain is boiling as a result.

Turns out, by *low stakes* they meant *wrap your entire goddamn curriculum around getting the scores up on this thing.* They also meant "reading groups," which ... hell, I don't even want to *think* about it. I cannot handle my class in *one* group, and I don't have any novel sets, and I'm sure as hell not making enough money to go buy them myself. I try to think about doing leveled reading groups *in a basal reader* and keeping them on track with these kids and ... Christ, it makes me want to *cry*, it's such a miserable, unworkable idea.

That's not why I'm writing about it, though.

I asked some questions and discovered some interesting things. When I got the scores, I was surprised to discover that there were only *raw* scores reported. Anyone who spends any time looking at standardized test scores should be surprised by that, as raw scores are basically meaningless numbers. There's a reason these things are *standardized*; the point isn't whether a kid missed a specific question, but whether a *whole lot* of kids missed a specific

45

question. Or, to phrase it more coherently, it might not be my kids that are the problem— the test might just be really hard, or unclear somehow, and without comparing my kids' scores against a whole lot of other kids, it's not remotely clear who to blame for bad scores. It's why you get a 1400 on your SAT and not, say, 29/30.

There are only raw scores because the test hasn't been normed. At *all*. So they have *no idea* whether the test is remotely useful as a diagnostic tool.

They have, however (and by "they" I mean "the test people," not, say, my administrators) determined, by all available evidence *entirely arbitrarily*, that any school, class, or kid scoring below 70% on the test is "in need of remediation." Needless to say all but, like, *five* of my kids were below 70%, most by a substantial margin.

Is this the place where I point out that the test is produced by a *fucking textbook company*, which also produces and sells the very materials "needed" to "remediate" a school for poor performance on their worthless test? It might be. Also: We need to write out a plan describing precisely how we're going to get our kids up to snuff. The plan requires us to concentrate on our two "problem areas" (out of five, and my kids didn't hit target on any of the five.) One of my two problem areas was determined based on *three test questions.*

Three. That's an entire subgroup on the test. Three. Goddamn. Questions.

Sure. This makes sense.

The Menstrual Pad

December 21 2005

This has been kind of a rough week. I have just *two more days* until glorious winter vacation, and I am hoping beyond hope that those two days go somewhat more easily than the last three days have. Monday and Tuesday were behavioral nightmares. Today the behavior was more on-track, but...

...well, lemme just start the story.

I'm in the hallway having a conversation with a parent, a parent who has apparently (heh) spent the *entire morning* observing in my partner teacher Mr. Irish's classroom. Her son is one of my paper-throwers, so I'm glad she's in the room, but all the same I'm kinda feeling the need for my kids to be nicer than normal since I've got somebody watching me.

So I'm talking to her as my classes switch and my homeroom kids file into my room. All the sudden I hear a chorus of *piercing screams* from inside my classroom. I walk into the room to pure bedlam. The boys, mostly, are in their seats looking sneakily amused. The *girls* are literally climbing over each other and shrieking their damn fool heads off trying to get away from the pod of desks in the corner of the room where, normally, five or six of them sit.

I start bellowing immediately, because, really, the best thing to do when the classroom has suddenly gone completely batshit bonkers and you have a parent watching you is to *add to the noise*. What's the problem? Rat? Cockroaches? Somebody eviscerate a goddamn cat and stick it inside one of the desks?

They don't say anything. I mean it— they wouldn't tell me what was inside the desk. One of them just *points*, a comically horrified look on her face.

Hm. Menstrual pad.

Menstrual pad covered, I shit you not, in *red lip gloss*.

Points for creativity, I suppose.

I remove the thing and throw it away, causing more horror and screaming because *oh my god he touched it*. I wouldn't have been surprised if the *boys* had been freaking out, but the girls? Come the hell on. You're in 7th grade, ladies, it's probably about time that you got used to these goddamn things. They will be with you for a while, knaamean?

A few minutes later, I decided to send a note downstairs to the assistant principal— which I literally labeled an "FYI"— telling him that somebody in my other room had an intriguing sense of humor, but that I had no real suspects. Nearby seats had all been occupied by boys in the previous class, and I kinda doubt they were responsible. I then proceeded to forget about the note.

After lunch, all hell broke loose. The principal, who was absolutely *livid*, pulled *all the 7th grade girls* and piled them into the library for ... well, *something*, I don't know what, I wasn't allowed in the room, while the boys were packed off to gym. When the girls came out forty minutes later they all had sour looks on their faces and were carting letters to their parents in their hands, which have to be returned tomorrow, signed, on pain of death or some damn fool thing like that.

And who did they take those sour moods out on? Me, of course, since the whole damn thing was *my* fault apparently. It *destroyed* my afternoon, because every time I turned around for the rest of the day I had another pissed-off thirteen-year-old girl giving me That Look. You know what I'm talking about. And, man, was *that* fun.

Will anyone be bothered if I go to bed now?

I am Not a Rapper

January 10 2006

The school I teach at is part of a program where periodically black entrepreneurs come by to give inspirational pep talks to the seventh and eighth graders. This is both a good thing and a bad thing for me as a teacher, because I never get any warning that these things are coming— which means some days I'm glad that an hour of my schedule is filled by someone else and the speaker is engaging enough that I don't have to worry about discipline and other days I have to reschedule a *test* at the last second and the speaker sucks.

I had a speaker today. It was ... interesting. I didn't mind the interruption; I had plenty to do but wasn't especially interested in actually doing it, so ... whatever, bring in a speaker, fine, I don't care. Unfortunately, the poor guy kinda backfired. He introduced himself as a businessman and a rapper. The kids perked up a bit at "rapper" and began firing questions at him, at which point he revealed that he'd been on stage with ... wait for it ... Chris Bridges!

The kids were unimpressed, because none of them knew who the hell Chris Bridges was. I *do* know who Chris Bridges is— it's Ludacris' real name— and sorta cringed on the inside. See, unbeknownst to him, the guy was sort of heading into a minefield. I use Ludacris as my example every time I want to talk about lazy, boring rap music, which happens more often than you might think. In the process, I've managed to more or less extinguish any Luda fandom that may have been going on in the room. So when the guy dropped "You might know him as Ludacris!" on the class, clearly expecting hoots, hollers, and impressed stares, he got an audible "pfft" from one corner of the room and a fair number of skeptical glares.

49

It didn't get better. While our last speaker was really energetic and engaging, if a bit of a huckster, this guy ... not so much. I had to work on keeping the kids respectful and under control or they would have run over him. Things never really got better, though— the kids kept that mix of skeptical and ever-so-slightly scornful through the entire presentation.

Then it happened. He asked if there were any questions at the end of the presentation, and was asked, predictably, if he'd rap for them. Naturally, he pretended to not want to for a while, but then relented and dropped a couple of verses on them. Verses that, unfortunately, were not very good. I tried to keep the wince off of my face, because the kids were already conditioned to dislike him because of the Ludacris thing. What I *wasn't* expecting was what actually happened.

The guy finishes. A moment or two of total silence.

"Maan, Mr. Siler, take this fool out."

Followed by a loud chorus of claps and cheers. Twenty-four heads turned to the back of the room. They actually *wanted me to battle this guy*. And, most entertainingly, despite the fact that he had a CD out, *thought I was going to win*.

Obviously it didn't happen. Because, despite anything that might happen in poetry readings from time to time, I'm, well, *not a rapper*. And they got a bit of a lecture on how to respect people who take their time to come talk to us. A lecture that was, I admit, a bit half-hearted. Because, really, whenever your kids randomly decide to call you out against an *actual rapper with a CD*, especially when you're a fat white guy, well ... that's kinda cool. :-)

That's all.

Say it Loud!

FEBRUARY 22 2006

Interesting day today. I accomplished *absolutely nothing* at work, because we had our Black History month assembly today and it totally ruined my shit. I knew about it, for once having had the sense to at least *glance* at a calendar before doing my lesson plans, so it's not like I overplanned for the day or anything, but it's amazing how much a two-hour assembly can totally destroy an entire school day.

I kinda feel bad about Black History month. Between the standardized testing on Language Arts days and my unwise placement of the Constitution test in the 3rd grading period (we're doing it *first* next year) I have paid just about no attention to it at all. This is made worse by the fact that I teach at an entirely black school (incidentally, if you notice that the phrase "African-American" seems to have dropped from my vocabulary, it's because my students have forcibly removed it) and ameliorated somewhat by the fact that I try to weave black history into *everything* in some way or another. Whatever; the Con test is on March 9th, most of them will pass on the first try, and I've already told them that the rest of March is Black History month for the seventh grade. I think they'll forgive me.

So. The assembly. It was, if you don't mind me saying so, exceptionally awesome, and all the kids who had spent *weeks* bitching about having to bring in $4 to pay for an assembly *in their own school* were silenced. I've Googled around for an acceptable webpage for "By a Black Hand" and haven't really been able to find one; calling it a hip-hop musical and slide show sorta covers it. The thing you need to know is that one of the women in the play was a

51

goddess. My current life challenge is figuring out how to track down a woman who I only know by her stage name (the rather un-googlable "Mystery") who is political enough to dress as Angela Davis in her spare time and find a way to convince her to marry a white guy. The deck is stacked against me, I think, but then again it always is.

Note that I *fully* participated in the performance, including (at the kids' prodding) screaming along in "Say it Loud/ I'm Black and I'm Proud" cheers and a couple of minutes of everyone bellowing "Black Power!" at each other. They only notice that I'm white when it suits their purposes, I think. The kids were hollering at me to join in with them and nobody so much as looked at me cross-eyed once I started in.

(My euphoria was spoiled somewhat at the gym later in the afternoon when I caught myself getting dirty looks in the locker room that I'm more or less convinced were caused solely by the Martin Luther King Black History Month t-shirt that I was wearing. Almost all the teachers wore Black History Month shirts today, found cheap at South Side Walgreens stores across the city, and apparently I'm not *allowed* to have such things on outside of work— much like the Public Enemy hat I had in high school.)

Context is funny, ain't it?

Of course, the event ran crazy late, and by the time we were done we were *over an hour* late for lunch, and they all had to *pee*, and all of this was my fault somehow, and the care and feeding of middle schoolers and their various body functions took damn near the entire rest of the day. Perhaps tomorrow there will be time for the acquisition of cheap, tasty knowledge. We'll see. They'd also missed gym, which they were trying to be pissed about until I reminded them that they were going to miss gym *anyway* on account of their wild, untamed assholery of the previous few days.

Example: leaving huge ink puddles on no less than *seven* different desks during the time (and by "time" I mean "about a minute") I was in the hallway supervising class switching, an accomplishment that required either Flash-level speed or the coordination of several students. Do we get to use pens in class any more? No, we do not. Yes, that's right. I have banned *pens* until they learn how the hell to use them.

And if there's one more goddamned paper-ball fight when I have my back turned we're going back to writing on shovels with coal.

Oh, and, also? Got a new kid today. New Kid seems terrified. This makes sense, as he chose the *absolute worst day possible* to begin attending my school. He flunked every class last semester at his other school(*) but got an A on the spelling test I made him take this afternoon— the one thing I did manage to get done today— without seeing the words for more than 10 minutes beforehand. Am I a monster for making him do that? I told him it wouldn't count unless he did well. He did. And, given that the Constitution test is in two weeks and he's seen none of the material, what the hell am I going to do with him in Social Studies for the next two weeks? Bah.

(*) Previous teacher's sole comment on report card: "XXX is a pleasure to have in my class." Am I right in thinking that if he fails *everything* one might want to put at least *one more* sentence on his report card???

On Mr. Irish

MARCH 4 2006

I have had an absurdly long week, and have two more absurdly long weeks ahead. I got home yesterday and died on the couch for four hours. And then I got up half an hour early today to go in and teach Saturday school for four hours.

Yeah.

Every teacher reading this— or, at least, every teacher in Chicago reading this, since the ISAT is breathing down *all* of our necks right now— knows exactly what the hell I'm talking about. The tests are the week after next, and to call the environment at my school a pressure cooker is unjust to pressure cookers, which, after all, can at least be used to produce tasty stew once in a while.

There have been no special classes for my kids this week. Gym, music, library, technology, all cancelled. The principal and assistant principal have been coming in during my breaks and teaching. Wanna know why?

Well, turns out Mr. Irish hasn't done *a fucking thing all year.*

I'm surprised, and I'm not sure why. One constant in my teaching career is that every year there's been some jackass who I had to pick up the slack for at the last minute. Usually this has involved the state-mandated Constitution test in some way. In some cases it has involved things like *art*. This year, *I'm* the jackass who is responsible for the Constitution test (incidentally, if I am ever stupid enough to ever even *think about thinking about* putting this in the same semester as the ISAT again, anyone reading has my permission to skullfuck me,) so naturally somebody else had to drop the goddamn ball.

A couple of weeks ago I discovered that the computer teacher had been assigned to assist Mr. Irish for, at the time, a couple of hours a week. Since then, the extent of the dry rot in the room has become clearer and clearer with every passing day, and in addition to the computer teacher, they've now got *another* aide in there for two hours *every day*— an aide that, by the way, was a student teacher in our school just last semester— and the assistant principal is coming in on Tuesdays and Thursdays to teach earth science, which has gone almost completely uncovered and which is a substantial portion of the 7th grade ISAT. Which I was aware of, and Mr. Irish, nine-year CPS veteran, was not.

If you're reading all that and thinking "Wait, when is Mr. Irish teaching?", which would be reasonable, the answer is apparently "about as much as he ever was", which is to say *virtually never*.

Want to know how we found out? While Mr. Irish had been careful to make sure to teach whenever an administrator was nearby, he was apparently not as interested in covering his ass when a student teacher was in his room. We have one student teacher in the school right now, who went into his room to observe early in January, right after she started with the school. She went into the room at about 9:30, perhaps twenty minutes after instruction had started for the day, only to be informed that "the lesson" had already been taught, but that she was welcome to stay in the room as long as she wanted.

Turns out that the rest of the day— probably about two and a half hours, given our schedule— was taken up with *ten pages of seatwork* for the kids, while Mr. Irish literally put his feet up on his desk.

Put his feet up. On his desk.

Recall that it is exceptionally rare if I find the time to *sit down* if I have kids in my room. I am never, ever, *ever* at my desk. This motherfucker had his feet up on his desk for over an hour.

Well, the student teacher reported the situation to her mentor teacher, who went to the principal, who began asking a number of very pointed questions and discovering a number of very alarming things. Like entirely forged lesson plans. Like grades for assignments that had never been *given*, much less actually assessed— ie, entirely fabricated. Thus a fair amount of administrative ass-whupping behind the scenes, thus the computer teacher being speedily dispatched to cover whatever he could, thus eventually the aide and the assistant principal and, as it became clearer and clearer just how much trouble we're in, I've been told to cancel anything I had planned for next week except for the actual Constitution test and start teaching science and math as much as I possibly can. I've spent the whole week scrambling for materials and planning out what to do, and the Saturday school session this morning was almost exclusively earth science stuff.

Nobody's worried about language arts; apparently the kids are doing about as well as they ever have there. Which, okay, I'll take it. I get to be a science teacher for a while. The kids need it. I'll figure out how the fuck to do six months worth of science in a week if that's what I need to do.

Afterwards, though, I'm gonna come home and put my fucking fist through the wall a few times, because God damn it, I'm a first year fucking teacher, and *it would be nice if somebody had to clean up after me once in a while.* Fuck fuck fuck fuck fucking fuckity fucker *fuck.*

Wanna hear something else funny? I spent most of the first semester stressing out because Mr. Irish seemed to be having zero problems whatsoever with discipline. The kids were running roughshod over me every goddamned day, and I'd comment to him about how awful whatever class had been that day, only to be told he "hadn't had any problems" with them or that they were "just fine today" when they were in his room. If it ain't clear, by the way, this sort of thing is *demoralizing as hell*, and after a while it simply became easier to never, ever mention discipline issues to him unless I thought something might spill over into his room. Well, suddenly now all of this makes sense. Because you only worry about noise or discipline or fucking paper-throwing if *you give a damn what's going on in your room.* I need to teach, so I need quiet. He didn't, so ... well, he doesn't.

The worst thing about all this? The kids think it's *their* fault. They think I'm teaching them math because they're dumb. And they don't believe me when I tell them otherwise.

If we miss AYP because of 7th grade math scores— science doesn't count toward it, thank God— I can't promise that I won't burn the sonofoabitch's house down.

On Writing Rubrics and the ISAT

March 23, 2006

I caught myself a *lucky goddamn break* today. My kids are taking a total of eight standardized tests over this week and next— three math and three reading this week (two a day) and two science on Tuesday and Thursday of next week. The science tests don't count for anything in particular and so I'm refusing to stress out over them. The math and reading tests are a big goddamn deal, though, affecting promotion and AYP and my *job* and a whole host of other things, so those are the ones we (and when I say "we," I mean "the administration and I," not "the 7th grade teachers") have been spending all of our ("my") energy on.

Yesterday's test was four or five short reading selections with half-a-dozen or so comprehension questions after each of them. Today and tomorrow features a longer passage, a dozen or so questions, an extended response piece, and then a nonfiction, "practical" reading selection— like a menu or a map or something like that— and a few more multiple choice questions. The extended responses are what I've been spending the majority of my time and energy on, since the scoring rubric for the things in no way resembles what reasonable people *do* when they write.

I've said this already, and I'll say it again: No one reading this other than the teachers is capable of getting a 4, the highest score, on an ISAT extended response question. That is because the scoring rubric is so bizarre. You need to be *trained* to do these right, because if all that was needed was good reading and writing skills we wouldn't be able to make much money on study guides, presentations, and remediation. And not making *every last possible fucking dime* off of the backs of my 12-year-olds would be *wrong*.

59

Anyway. I'm off-topic. Here's the lucky break: The reading selection for the extended-response item today? *They'd read it before.* By some amazing stroke of good luck, the story that they read on the ISAT today is *also* in their literature books, and we'd read it as a class as part of a short unit on science fiction in the first grading period, and discussed it extensively. Now, it was several months ago, so they didn't all *remember* that they'd read it before, but I had several kids in both classes giving me quizzical looks when they saw the material. Some obviously thought we'd been *cheating* when we read it before, which I thought was funny, because if I was going to cheat on the ISAT, I'd have done it in February or March and not in November.

The thing is, though, even the kids who *didn't* directly remember that we'd read the story were in the room during the discussion. Hopefully a fact or two bubbled up in their brains as they were reading the passage and there will be some sort of exposure effect driving their scores up. I don't know how they actually did on the response— I was too scared to look, and it's not like I could really do anything about it at that point anyway— but I'm keeping my fingers crossed, and I have some reason to be cautiously optimistic. Woohoo!

My Week

April 6 2006

MONDAY: I get up fully an hour and a half before normal, expecting bad weather that will make it take me a year to get to work. I leave the house by 6:45 in the morning and somehow walk into my classroom approximately forty-five minutes later, much, much too early. I spend the entire school day suffering greatly from a lack of sleep and also getting sicker and sicker by the minute. I am tired of being sick; I have been sick a lot this year (although the last time was food poisoning, so I don't think it really counts) and I resolve to actually get a flu shot next year and to consider becoming slightly neurotic about germs. I already wash my hands more times a day than the dictates of masculinity strictly allow, though, so my self-concept might require some modification before I officially descend into OCDville. I prepare the kids for the trauma of a sub the next day. Luckily, they're in the kind of the mood where they're *nice* to their ailing, sick teacher rather than becoming more evil. At 2:30 I realize that I can't take the next day off due to non-negotiable union responsibilities. I fight off a wave of wanting to die.

I get home and get bad news that I'm not getting into in this space. I decide that Monday is done and am in bed by 7:30.

TUESDAY: I give myself twenty extra minutes of sleep in the morning, meaning that I slept for very nearly twelve hours. It does not help me feel better. I give a fairly major assessment in class, conduct the union business, and have an entertaining misadventure after school while trying to find the proper place to drop the returns off. I spend the entire evening fending off calls from students and parents panicking about test scores. In the process, I discover that one of my biggest discipline problems has what his mother describes

61

as "a big tumor" in his chest and will be having surgery over spring break to remove it. Based on her description, I mentally replace "tumor" with "cyst" and resolutely refuse to even entertain the possibility that I have a twelve-year-old with cancer in my classroom. I have a long, depressing evening.

Also, *The Amazing Race*, which I look forward to with some fervor, turns out to not be on Tuesdays any more. They've moved it to Wednesdays. Opposite *Lost*, which you might also know as the only other TV show I ever watch. I say bad words.

WEDNESDAY: I awaken at the same time as Tuesday and get to work early again. The special ed teacher walks into the office as I'm clocking in with an absolutely horrible look on her face. She asks me if I "heard about the shooting yesterday." I had not, and my heart falls into my shoes. Turns out that the older brother of one of my students was murdered Tuesday evening in what, as far as I or anyone else can tell, appears to be a completely random event. The student in question was a ball of social and emotional problems already; this is a kid who once literally *picked me up and threw me into the blackboard* during a psychotic episode, a fact that somehow I never got around to writing about, and I cannot even imagine what this will do to him. Upon requesting further details, I discover that I was actually on the phone with this young man's mother at the exact time her son was being killed, as she'd called me the night before to find out how my student had done on the test. The remainder of the school day does not improve at all on the morning's news. I attend a union delegates meeting that lasts hours and is horrifyingly boring, and have to do it without my usual Union Meeting Buddy, who is strangely absent. My favorite team loses on TAR and is eliminated from the race.

Also, my computer melts.

THURSDAY: I haven't mentioned this yet, but this was Spirit Week at school, meaning that everybody was out of uniform and dressed in various different themes every day. Wednesday was Classroom Color Day, and my homeroom had been assigned the color yellow via a random drawing that I was smart enough to assign to a student. The class that wore the most of their color won a pizza party that was to happen today. My afternoon class, which wore black, a *considerably* easier color to drape oneself in from head to foot, won the pizza party. I spend the entire morning putting up with pathetic whining from my students. I start off with supportive responses like "Well, let's beat them the next time we have a contest" and by the end of the morning have degenerated to things like "Look, shut up about the contest already, because I'm sick to death of this whiny crap." I find out in the morning that there is a faculty-student basketball game scheduled for the last part of the day, which is a bit of a problem because I'd scheduled a retake of Tuesday's major test during that hour. I have to cancel gym for my afternoon class so that I can give them the test and put up with *more* crap.

The game, luckily, is a lot of fun (I'm not playing, which helps) and not anything like the acrimonious affair that the game at my student teaching school last year was. I spend most of it making fun of Mr. Irish. The game runs late, though, and ends with all of two minutes left in the school day, which means there's a lot of vaguely-panicked hustling to get the kids out of the gym, upstairs, into their coats, and out of the building. As I'm shoving my class out the gym door I notice a couple of eighth grade girls have one of my boys by the throat and are slamming his head into a wall. I deal with the situation, one of the girls gets mouthy, informing me that she wasn't doing anything wrong and I don't get to tell her what to do anyway, and she's written up and given detention for her trouble. Good job, knucklehead, get written up by a random teacher in the *last two minutes before spring break*. On my way into the building after making all the students go home I mention to the principal that Shakita X (not her name, obviously) had decided to be an idiot for the last few minutes of the day— trying, for no real good reason, to find out if she's a regular discipline problem or if this is an aberration.

"Shakita X? Ms. X's daughter?"

Oh, *really*? Ms. X works in the building. I wasn't even aware that she was a parent, much less that she had a kid in our school. Well, this makes things easier. Rather than actually dropping the write-up in the office like I usually do, I bring it downstairs and hand it directly to Ms. X, who gets quite a bit angry and embarrassed about the situation and tells me that she'll take care of it and it won't happen again. I *know* it won't happen again— it's not often that I interact with the eighth graders at all, obviously— and throw the write-up sheet away and go upstairs to get my stuff together so I can leave.

On my way out of the building Ms. X and Shakita catch me on the stairs. Shakita already looks a little shaky. Ms. X says that her daughter has something to say to me.

"What do you have to say to him?"

"I'mma tell him that..."

SMACK! SMACK!

Two wide, looping slaps, one a backhand. Straight to the face.

"Him who? Who the hell is him? Who you gonna tell?"

Shakita raises up her hands to protect herself.

"PUT YOUR GODDAMN HANDS DOWN!"

Smack. Smack. Smack. Smack. *Smack.* Three forehands, two backhands. And we're talking full-arm affairs here, it's not like she's slapping from the *wrist* or anything like that. The girl is bawling. I'm horrified. I wouldn't exactly know how to deal with this situation if it were a random parent; this is a *co-worker*, making things considerably worse. I try to defuse everything as best I can. "Let the girl talk, I'm sure she's sorry." Shakita apologizes several times, punctuated by another slap from Mom— this time, in a display that is equally absolutely awful and unintentionally hilarious, delivered with the words "You *keep your hands off of other people!*" Shakita swears she'll never touch one of my kids again and she's really sorry she smarted off. I ask Mom if I can talk to her alone for a couple of minutes and ... God, I don't even remember what I said, but it was as close to "I wouldn't have said anything if I'd known your mom was psychotic, so let's both make sure this never happens again" as I thought I could get away with.

I'm going to bed now.

On My New Job Description

March 13 2006

I can come up with ways today could have been worse, but they aren't especially comforting for some reason. My afternoon class did a math extended response for me on Friday, and we went over it with them today. I also gave another one to my homeroom kids.

With barely a week to go until the tests, I am proud to announce that my kids have *no fucking idea what they're doing*.

I have trouble describing just how deep this goes or just how angry I am about it. I broke a pencil in my right hand this afternoon without realizing I was doing it. My kids seem to really, genuinely think that the way to get the right answer to a math question is to guess and guess and guess until the teacher tells you you have the right answer.

Picture this: There's a grid, right? It has a right triangle on it. The kids are trying to figure out the area of said triangle, in square units. Note that my 5th grade after-school group can handle this with no problem. I'm sitting with a table of kids, which, just for the record, includes one of the brightest kids in my room.

"How many squares high is the triangle?"

"Um ... five?" (Note: the answer is four.)

"Take another look and count again."

Student does not look at paper. "Six?"

"<Student's name>, *look at the paper*. Count how many squares high this triangle is."

Student looks. "Eleven?"

Other guesses from table. "Seven?" "Three?" "Five?" (Note, yes, "five" has been guessed again.)

65

At this point I started doubting my own goddamned sanity. Took my pencil and counted out the squares myself. "One ... two ... three ... four. See? There are four. *Four*. Where in the world did that *eleven* come from? You guys have *got* to get over this habit of just firing numbers at me. I'm not going to be there to say yes or no on this test."

"Oh. Mr. Irish told us to guess on those things."

Snap.

I looked down and my pencil was a ruined mess in my hand. The kids? Horrified. My hand? Bleeding a little.

I'm not going to pretend that guessing isn't a time-honored— and occasionally genuinely useful— strategy, particularly when you back it up by actually testing your guess. Hell, that's basically what *science* is. But the fact that they're guessing on something like *count how many squares this is*, when the number of squares is *four*, is ... God, I don't even know *what* it is. It's goddamned *criminal* is what it is, and as a union rep I would like to suggest that Mr. Irish be tossed in jail and scourged daily for the *destruction* he has visited upon these kids. They've got enough working against them already without their motherfucking teachers making it worse, and God help this guy if he makes the mistake of coming into my classroom tomorrow.

It went on like that all day. Completely ridiculous conversations about *very basic precepts* of math— like when you should multiply or divide or add or subtract something. And no evidence whatsoever that any of them have any strategies in reserve at all for dealing with mathematical frustration other than guessing until the teacher tells them the right answer. I don't expect perfection, mind you— but they *don't do this* in my room. They don't just guess when they don't know an answer until I give up and give it to them. They *think* in Language Arts and Social Studies. They aren't demonstrating any reasoning ability at all in math, and it's driving me crazy. I have a week until the tests. I could probably fix this if I had, say, a couple of hours a day for a month or two. I don't know what the hell I can do in a week.

Fuck this shit. I want cookies.

On "Faggot!"

May 10 2006

We did this half-assed little writing exercise today. I've grown tired of my students using impoverished, boring language in essays and written assignments when I *know*, beyond a shadow of a doubt, that they have non-sucky vocabularies. So we've been doing these little quizzes and games lately where they come up with lists of words to describe things and stuff like that. Today's activity was to choose an object from somewhere in the room and, together with your classmates, describe said object in every way you can possibly imagine. I mean *everything*— what it looks like, smells like, sounds like, *tastes* like if you're brave enough (I had never said the words "Mark, please stop licking the crate" before today,) everything.

My afternoon class is picking their objects. Students in two groups simultaneously request "the globe." Now, as it works out, I have two. As it turns out, they both wanted the same one, but one group requested it just a little faster, so I handed the electric light-up one to them.

A student in Group B, shocked at my transgression, shouts out "Aw, man, you a faggot!"

Dead. Fucking. Silence. In my room.

"Excuse me?" is the only thing I can think of to say.

A touch of context: This is a *good kid*. He's messed up maybe three times all year. His mom calls me regularly. I know both of his little brothers by name, and I know *very few* kids by name who are not either 7th graders or in my 5th grade tutoring group. If anything, he said that out of an overdeveloped sense of *familiarity*. This is not, in other words, the killing offense that it might originally seem to be.

67

Plus, within *milliseconds* of the words coming out of his mouth, he was clearly completely horrified at what he'd done. Apologies were instantaneous.

Further context: "Faggot" is well-known at my school as Mr. Siler's Least Favorite Word. I have succeeded in stigmatizing it to the point where it really doesn't get used in my presence any longer. When it does, the class reacts to it.

So, I wrote him up— I couldn't *not* write him up— but I sent him down to the office with the thought in the back of my head that I would talk to the AP on my break in a few minutes and make it clear that I preferred a "put the fear of God into him" solution over something more drastic. A suspension, frankly, would not have surprised me for something like that under normal circumstances, and I didn't think that the context warranted that punishment.

He took the write-up sheet and went down to the office. Already *crying*, mind you. And came back about five minutes later. I was a little surprised, but not completely— if there's something going on in the office or the AP is busy they often send kids back until they have time to deal with them, unless an issue of violence is involved. So, twenty minutes later, when I went on my break, I mentioned to the AP that I wanted to talk to him about what had happened with the kid before he called him back down.

"What situation?"

"You mean he didn't come down?"

"Nope. I haven't seen him."

This is the point where we both start laughing. See, they don't realize that I do *actually check up on people* once I write them up, and I get documentation that they've been to the office. If that documentation doesn't show up, I know that they just took their write-up and went for a little walk rather than actually going down to the office like they were supposed to. In other words, we aren't *completely fucking stupid.*

Approximately twenty seconds later, the student was summarily ordered to the office via the PA system. Approximately three minutes later, the AP called Mom. Approximately *fifteen* minutes later, Mom had *left work* and the office temporarily dispatched an aide into my room so that I could have an impromptu parent conference. I made the situation clear to Mom; it was obvious to me that this was a stupid slip, that there was clearly a fairly intense amount of remorse going on on her son's part, and that her son was in more trouble for not taking the write-up down than he would have been for the comment in the first place.

I'm not convinced she was comforted by that fact. After talking to me for a few minutes, apologizing profusely and repeatedly, we called her son back down again for a three-way conference. I have rarely seen a kid in such poor shape— by the time the conference was over, I was convinced that there was no need for the school to take any action on the matter at all, because believe me, *Mom's gonna take care of it.* Darius (not his name, obviously, but I'm tired of nonspecific pronouns) was *bawling*, and his admission that he hadn't taken down the write-up because he was "scared" was as close to heartbreaking as anything I plan to experience this week.

Oh, and after explaining precisely *how* "faggot" became a slur for gay men, and witnessing his reaction, I'm pretty sure I'm never going to hear the word out of his mouth again in any context whatsoever.

Tomorrow's going to be interesting. I'm halfway expecting a handwritten apology.

So what happened to you at work today?

Bad Teacher Moment, #1

MAY 23 2006

Today's Bad Teacher moment: *humiliated* one of my jerkier kids today. Today was one of those awful days where we were basically doing seatwork all day. Progress reports go out at the end of the week, and despite bringing it to their attention multiple times that Very Little Homework = Very Poor Grades, I still wasn't getting any assignments in. Since failing all my kids would reflect poorly on *me* for some reason, I decided that today was just going to be used to catch up on missed work. Yes, they *all* have enough missed work that that's not a wasted use of a class period.

Well, as you can guess, this led to some off-task behavior and some ... let's say *management issues.* At some point, I was attempting to restore (or create, take your pick) some sort of sense of order in the room and said something or another that one of my kids thought I ought not to have said. I phrase it that way not to be cute but because I honestly don't remember what the hell I said.

"I'm tellin' my momma," she says.

It pissed me off something fierce. I enjoy the suggestion that I'm *afraid* of their mothers.

"Go ahead. *Tell* your momma. In fact, why don't we bring her in for a conference? We can talk about your ... *(flamboyantly checks grade book)* SEVEN PERCENT that you're pulling in social studies right now. Then, when we're done talking about that, we can talk about your attitude problem, and when we're done talking about *that,* we can talk about how you've been in my class for over an hour by now and have managed to answer *(checks)* all of THREE questions on the six unfinished worksheets in front of you."

"Go 'head. *(Pulls cell phone off of belt, extends to student.)* Call y'momma. Tell her what I said. Go for it. I *dare* you."

I'm pretty sure I'm not supposed to say stuff like that.

Summer School and the ISAT

August 22 2006

I taught sixth grade summer school— kids rising to seventh grade, in other words— after my first year. I started off with a group of twelve. Two weeks into a six-week program, the district decided we didn't have enough kids and collapsed both groups into my class, firing the other teacher. That gave me around twenty kids from three different schools in areas controlled by two different gangs, on the days all of them bothered to show up.

I only lost one of them, out of around fifteen. I ought to feel better about that.

I went in to work for a few hours today to get some stuff done in my classroom and stuck my head into the office to find out how my summer school kids had done on the summer ISAT. As it turned out, only one of my kids had failed. Well, two, actually— the kid who only seemed to show up to make everyone else's life miserable and who didn't do a damn bit of work all semester but insisted on showing up anyway for some fucking reason scored a fucking 4 in reading and 5 in math (that's out of *100*) but is being passed anyway because the worthless little shit has already failed sixth grade once.

Strong language? Yeah, I know. It's extraordinarily rare that I genuinely dislike a kid. In fact, I can't actually come up with another example right now. But in a situation like summer school? If you *want* to waste a year of your life by failing *again,* go right the hell ahead. I had twelve other kids, and then twenty other kids, to worry about, all in similarly dire straits, and I don't have time for the kid who isn't bothering to try. Stay your ass at home and out of my way, I just don't care. I will, and did, bend over backwards for anybody

73

willing to *try*. If you're going to get in their way, God help you, because I'm not going to.

<cough>

Yeah. Anyway. He didn't count, because *fuck him*. One kid failed out of around fifteen who had to test.

But, dammit, that one shouldn't have failed. I had two that I was genuinely worried about. Both passed, one with surprisingly flying colors. This was a girl who, at the beginning of the six weeks, couldn't manage multiplying two-digit numbers, mind you. Pulled a 51 on the math test. Not a great score in absolute terms, but a tremendous improvement— like, *tripling her score*— and a pass nonetheless. I'll take it. The other kid I was worried about just took a hell of a long time to *take* the test, and I was worried he was going to end up failing because I'm sure he had to just guess at the last several questions on both tests. I didn't notice his exact score, but he passed, so he must have been doing pretty well on the questions he did manage to answer.

The only thing I can come up with to blame is test anxiety. The kid that failed— and her scores *dropped* in both reading and math, from scores that were *already* in the bottom quartile— was one of the best students in the room. She was one of those kids who you *stop calling on* after a while because she volunteers for every single question and always has the right answer. I never did figure out what she was doing in summer school; she was getting everything right, did all of her work, paid attention, did everything she was supposed to do. She was even the only kid who had some parental involvement. Her dad dropped in four or five times over the six-week summer school program to check on her, and I told him repeatedly that his daughter was doing just fine and that he didn't have anything to worry about.

Anything, that is, except for the fact that she was going to fail summer school and repeat sixth grade next year.

I should be happy about the ones who I got through the test. Two-digit number girl in particular should have me jumping up and down. But there's going to be an empty seat in my god damn classroom next year now, and that empty chair is the one I'm thinking about.

Stupid fucking standardized tests.

The Beginning of the Year

August 31 2006

I have officially gotten my way with respect to my failed summer school student. After conversations with her other teachers, the principal, and her parents, she's going to be eligible for promotion to seventh grade at the end of the first quarter provided that she keeps her grades up and stays out of trouble. The room is looking lovely and I'm still ahead of the game with a full day of work still available tomorrow. It'll still be a late Friday— I refuse to leave anything to be done on Tuesday, and that's going to take a while, but I'll be able to hit the ground running like I've wanted to do.

On the other hand, school supply costs are driving me bananas. I'm revamping my classroom library, because it (meaning the presentation, not the books themselves) sucks. This means lots of reorganization. Now, the good news is that I managed somehow to acquire (by which I mean steal) a wire spinner, a lockable six-foot cabinet, and an eight-foot-tall metal bookshelf for the room this year, so I have *tons* more space and the library isn't nearly as cramped as it was last year. The bad news is that I got everything at least a little bit set up the way I wanted it today and then I looked at it and realized that one of my students is like *three foot eight.*

I'd already abandoned the use of the top shelf of the bookshelves I was using due to height and vision issues, but ... *shit*, I hadn't even *thought* about the fact that I have a little person in the room. Due to the depth of the shelves I doubt he can even *see* most of the books. I'd buy a stepladder for him but I'm worried about liability issues. I'm going to have to think seriously about how to handle this tomorrow, because I want him to have access to all of the stuff, but putting everything so that it's accessible to him will only

75

mean that everybody else (including me) will have to bend over or sit on the floor to get to most of the books, and that's not acceptable either.

I'll talk to the principal about what happens if I buy him a stepladder and he falls off of it. Or is pushed. I suspect I get sued into oblivion, but you never know.

Also— take a wild guess. Library cards and the little paper envelopes they slide into are sold individually, in 50-packs, or in lots of 500. It is entirely possible that there are *more* than 500 books in my classroom library (I'll find out next week) so buying smaller denominations wasn't really an option. How much do you think such a thing might run you in a reasonable universe? Well, five hundred library cards cost fifteen bucks, and five hundred envelopes for those five hundred cards cost *thirty-eight fucking dollars*. Granted I bought the slightly more expensive self-adhering version but, Christ, it would take like *a million years* to tape all those goddamned things into place and then they'd just fall out anyway.

Teachers shouldn't have to pay income taxes, is what I'm saying here. It's insane how much money I put into this freaking classroom every year, and I'm going to *cry* when I find out that I have over 500 books next week. The taxpayers won't pay for any goddamn school supplies for me (there will be an *epic* rant about textbooks coming very soon. Short version? We're not getting any because the school can't afford them) and if I'm paying for shit like pencils and paper for other people's kids out of my pocket ($10-20 every week, easy, and that's ignoring the several hundred dollar hit I take at the beginning of every school year) I should be able to turn up my nose at paying for a bomb to kill some poor fucking Iraqi's kid.

Oh, and I have a rapist in my class. A student's uncle caught him anally raping his *mentally handicapped* younger brother two years ago.

Whee.

On the First Day of School

September 5 2006

Well, one down ... quite a few left to go.

I just looked, and somehow I *didn't write anything* on the first day of school last year, a fact that astounds me. I didn't say anything until the second day, where I was already complaining about the brutal heat wave that my school was enveloped in for the first two or three weeks. Today was lovely and temperate enough that I didn't notice the windows weren't open until the last hour of the day. Hopefully it'll hold; I know I won't get what I want if I say I never want another September like last September, but I can at least hope the next one doesn't come anytime soon.

So, what to say about the first day of school?

I had a good day today.

I'm fairly pleased, but in a much more guarded way than last year. The first week of school, despite the fact that it is *horrible*, is actually a honeymoon. The kids seem bright, behavior was uniformly good, the various and sundry new policies I'm using this year all went over without any griping, etc. Note that I'm saying this as if I actually did anything today. Any pretense to having performed any education today is somewhat misleading, because my prep schedule, which was damn near perfect last year, is *fucked* this year. Last year I had a prep period first thing Monday and Tuesday morning, which was *awesome*, because I'm never in the mood to deal with humans, much less teenagers, at 9:00 on Monday morning, and shoving them out the door for another teacher to deal with right away was awesome. On Wednesday and Thursday my preps were right after lunch, effectively giving me an hour instead of the customary twenty minutes for lunch. On Friday, my prep was the *last forty minutes* of the day, meaning that my week ended early. Awesome. Flawless.

Karma's a motherfucker.

I've still got the Monday and Tuesday first-thing preps. I've still got the Thursday prep right after lunch. That's the good news. My lovely Wednesday and Friday preps, on the other hand, have vanished to the winds, and have been replaced with *two extra preps on Tuesday*. Here's how my schedule went today (203 is my homeroom, 207 is the other 7th grade):

- •8:55-9:10 203 introductory activities
- •9:10-9:50 Prep; 203 in library
- •9:50-10:30 203 in classroom, fit in a bathroom break somewhere
- •10:30-11:10 Prep; 203 in technology
- •11:10-11:40 203 in classroom; switch classes at 11:40
- •11:40-12:10 207 introductory activities
- •12:10-12:30 Lunch
- •12:40-1:20 Prep; 207 in music
- •1:20-2:45 207 in classroom

All I did, all day, was walk kids up and down the hall. I'm not going to get a damn thing done on Tuesdays all year long, and man, Fridays without a prep (much less Wednesday) is going to *suck*. Furthermore the time periods where I *am* with my students are absurdly short; I recognize that 40-minute periods are what most middle school teachers have to work with, but *I think that's stupid*, and when you consider that my seventy or so minutes of social studies split into three distinct periods on one day are followed by two and a half damn hours of language arts *straight* the next day you get a better idea of what I'm used to.

I dunno. I'll figure it out; I thought my schedule last year was insane and I worked it out. Tuesdays aren't gonna get less weird, I don't think, but I'll figure out how to use them.

Have I mentioned the sad fate of Mr. Irish yet, by the way? I don't think I have, so forgive me if I'm repeating myself. Mr. Irish is no longer my partner teacher in the 7th grade. He's been replaced with a new teacher (she student-taught at my school during fall semester last year, and did a maternity fill-in at some other school during second semester, so she's newer to CPS than me but not a total babe in the woods,) a new teacher that I think I'll have a much better fit with as an instructor and who I haven't come up with a new nickname yet. I'd stick with ethnicity-based nicknaming but *Mrs. Black* sounds more than a little inappropriate so I'll have to come up with something else.

Mr. Irish hasn't been let go, mind you, just reassigned. To *first grade*.

I can't decide whether I feel more sorry for *him* or for his students, who have effectively no chance of learning to read or much of anything else before second grade without massive parental interference. I think I feel more sorry for them, because I find *his* predicament hilarious but not so much theirs. Since I spent the whole day wandering around the building ferrying my kids from one place to another I had several opportunities to watch him interacting with his kids. When I went down to pick my kids up from music in the afternoon, he was taking the tiny little buggers on a bathroom break and clearly having some trouble maintaining order, hissing "They just *don't stop talking,"* at me under his breath as I walked by, struggling not to laugh.

I shouldn't make fun of him at work. So I told the 8th graders (my ex-students, remember) to do it instead at every possible opportunity. Consider it my last official order as their teacher.

And now I'm off to take a nap. True to my first-day-of-school tradition, I got all of two hours of sleep last night, and I think I'm probably going to die soon. Tomorrow I get to teach all day with no break and then go to a union meeting. So, if I end up dead? That's why.

What up, Dog?

September 18 2006

So I get to work, and there's this dog.

The dog's a German Shepherd. A *big-assed* German Shepherd. It doesn't appear to be with anyone, and is running around making a nuisance of itself. In fact, when I first noticed it, our school crossing guard was *kicking* the poor damn thing, trying to get it either away from her or out of the street, it was hard to tell. The kids? Terrified. Now, the dog wasn't *barking* or anything, and didn't look either especially mean or angry, but still: big-ass German Shepherd. No owner. Potential trouble, right?

I went inside, dropped my stuff off in my classroom, and wrote off any chances of getting anything done before school started. This is hardly unusual; I've been working at the place for just over a year now and have yet to *ever* actually accomplish anything before school starts. There's always a different ~~excuse~~ reason, but the point is there's *always* one.

I went back outside and took a closer look at the situation. At second glance, the dog looked like a creampuff; he had a collar on and seemed rather old-ish and weak in the back legs. Still big, but more awww-lookit-the-puppy big than Cujo big, knaamean? The trouble is he's chasing the kids around, nipping at their heels, and running out into traffic whenever he damn well feels like it. This is somewhat of a predicament for (I assume) obvious reasons. I don't especially want to watch the dog get hit by a car and and am also not interested in seeing one of my kids get hurt.

The kids, while all this is going on? *Panicking.* You'd think the damn thing was foaming at the mouth or something, and the reaction seemed both universal and entirely out-of-proportion to the

81

actual situation. The dog's behavior is kinda weird, though. He's not trying to bite anybody. He's running behind groups of kids, picking the kid in the back, and doing this little nippy thing at his or her heels until he or she runs ahead of the group. I'm standing still, and he's running past me every now and again, but he's not trying to nip at me.

And then it hits me.

The dog, I'd already discovered, had been outside for about fifteen minutes, and animal control had already been called.

The dog was a German Shepherd.

Our kids are supposed to wait in the *fenced-in* playground before school starts.

The dog was nipping— not biting, not trying to hurt, not being mean, just trying to get the kids to move.

The goddamn dog had figured out that the kids were supposed to be in the playground, and it was *herding my students.*

Somehow I was able to keep from falling on the ground laughing.

Anyway, long story short, I grabbed the dog, which proved to be excessively friendly once I distracted it from work, and held onto it until the kids were inside. This made me a minor celebrity; you'd think I had wrestled a rabid demon to the ground with my bare hands instead of grabbing a widdle puppy dog by hims collar and holding onto him for a while. Once I had him the poor thing didn't fight me *at all*, even rolling onto his back for his belly to be scratched for a while. I had, seriously, parents and kids coming up to me and *thanking me* for preventing him from tearing out any young throats. Then, knowing that animal control had been called, I got the maintenance guys to bring me some twine and tied him by his (tagless) collar to the fence across the street so that he couldn't wander into traffic before the police came to get him. He's at the humane society right now. The moral of this story is *put tags on your goddamned dogs, people.*

The Author's Use of Humor

September 26 2006

Today was a half day. Half day plus Tuesday virtually guarantees that I wasn't going to get a single goddamned thing done. As I've mentioned before, I have *three* forty-minute prep periods on Tuesday, so (especially once you toss in a couple of bathroom breaks) my whole day is spent ferrying children from place to place and it's really, really hard to build up any sort of momentum in my teaching when I keep having to stop all the time. I had my homeroom for all of forty minutes today, and my afternoon class for about an hour.

During the afternoon the teachers were supposed to get together in grade-level subject matter teams (i.e., I meet with the 5th-8th grade reading teachers) and grade the extended response portions of the Learning First test that we took the second week of school. I had rather deliberately not even glanced at the responses in between taking the test and today; I knew we'd be grading them in a group at some point or another and didn't feel like stressing myself out beforehand.

Well, I should have, because now I have to re-administer the goddamn thing tomorrow.

The teachers were given a choice of two different extended response questions to administer. We were given the questions without actually being allowed to see the material the questions were over, mind you, but we got to choose. The first was something really simple and silly, something along the lines of "Why does this poem have this title?" and then it's a poem about an owl called *The Night Watchman*. C'mon. The second looked a little better. Again, I'm paraphrasing (this is what I get for not bringing shit home when I know I'm going to write about it), but something like "Humor can be useful in distasteful situations. How does the author's use of humor help the family in blah blah blah."

Now, read that for a second and think to yourself: *what kind of story is this question about?*

As I said, I'm paraphrasing, but I've got the critical part right: How does the author's humor *help the family*. They're, like, going camping or something. So the author's a funny guy, and the fact that he's funny helps the family, right? Okay.

Must be first person, then. Because the author is *clearly* in the story, and his humor helps the family. This sounds like a good idea. Let's roll with this question, then, instead of the childishly easy one that I could write the answer to without seeing the reading.

Can you brainless sons of bitches responsible for writing the tests that determine my kids' lives *please stop setting them up to fucking fail?*

Because today I sat down and read some responses. Read some bewildered, confused responses, responses from kids who didn't have any idea what they were being asked and didn't have any idea how to answer the question. And I thought back to test day and remembered how a few kids put their hands up and told me the story wasn't funny, and how since I hadn't been allowed to read it beforehand and wasn't actually allowed to help them anyway I couldn't do anything about it.

The story's in third person. Let that sink in for a moment.

The author isn't Dad, or Mom, or Grandpa, or Billy the Youngest Brother. It's a goddamn third-person narrative with no author viewpoint of any kind apparent to the reader. The question is *how does the author help the characters*, and the author *ISN'T IN THE MOTHERFUCKING STORY.* So, right away, the question is completely incoherent. The author can't help the characters, because the characters don't exist. It's like asking how JRR Tolkien "helped" Gandalf. It doesn't make any god damned sense right from the start. The "author's use of humor" doesn't help the characters *at all*. The question is unanswerable.

And *somebody* needs their ass kicked for writing it.

What's worse? I kinda passed over the kids who complained that the story wasn't funny during the test, because first of all there's nothing I can do about it, and second, kids complain about stupid bullshit all the time. (Randomly: "This doesn't make sense" is very close to my least favorite thing to hear my kids say. 95% of the time, yes, it makes sense. You just *don't get it*. That's not at all the same thing. You don't get to blame *mathematics* if you don't understand geometry.) Today I read the story in preparation for grading the responses. And the story well and truly is not *remotely* funny. The author is "using" humor much in the same way that I am "using" an abacus to type this, in that it is nowhere evident that the author ever even considered such a thing. There is one bit of what may be dry sarcasm. That's *it*.

This is standardized testing in Chicago, folks. The question asks how the author uses humor to help his characters, and the answer is that the author does *not* use humor and it is metaphysically fucking impossible for him to help his characters. And no, they *weren't* supposed to figure that out.

Once I realized what was going on, I stormed down to the office in a high rage and demanded the test be thrown out. Because if I, a grown goddamn man with two fucking Master's degrees, can't figure out how to answer a question meant for *seventh graders*, then they damn well shouldn't be expected to. And, wonder of wonders, I got what I wanted. So tomorrow I'm going to give them back their first responses, whip them into a fury over how these tests are trying to screw them over, then turn them loose on the ridiculously simple second question. Which they will *destroy*, and I will look like a genius.

God, I hate standardized tests.

On Rain

OCTOBER 2 2006

It poured today from 1:30 or so until a little bit after 3:00. This was also one of those afternoons where the PA system kept going off every two or three minutes all damn afternoon, which is *enormously fucking annoying* and a wonderful way to break momentum. Over, and over, and over, and over, and over again, leading to me fantasizing about a story Bill Ayers told me once about actually disconnecting his PA system in his room after such an afternoon and then reporting it broken, knowing that it would very likely never actually be fixed. The only thing preventing me from a similar stunt in my room is that our maintenance guys are *really* good and it would actually get fixed, likely within a day.

Anyway, between the PA system and general seventh-grader squirreliness (although my afternoon group is the smart, well-behaved one this year, and my homeroom has almost all the ~~boys~~ knuckleheads in it,) I was already having a frustrating afternoon. Then the rain started. You'd think the damn kids had grown up in the fucking Gobi Desert and had no idea that water was capable of falling from the sky.

I, always in possession of little patience in the afternoon, attempted to calm my room via the brute force method (something slightly south of "You motherfuckers grow up in Egypt or something? You've seen rain, goddammit. This ain't Noah's Flood. Calm the fuck down and pay attention before I whup somebody.") which managed to get them back in order. Okay, good. With something like twenty minutes left in the day, I've got my room back, let's see if I can't do some last minute educating before they go home, right?

87

Luther M. Siler

A *millisecond* later. Huge thunderclap outside. Massive gust of rain.

All five windows in my room, which had been closed, but foolishly left unlatched, *blew open*, letting roughly a ton and a half of rain into the room. Every kid within five feet of the windows, as well as every piece of paper and notebook within range, wet. One kid was *drenched* by the time I got the windows closed and latched, particularly since I had to do all five *myself*, since the kids kept closing them and not latching them right. Comedy of motherfucking errors, folks.

At least it wasn't a hundred and thirty degrees outside.

On Math and Math Assignments

October 23 2006

I know somebody who spent a couple of summers as a gas station attendant. I'm wondering if I could make a living doing that. I bet I could.

Today was a frustrating fucking day. I started off the morning with a staff meeting where they handed us— three weeks before the end of the quarter, mind you— a document explaining exactly how many grades in each subject we're expected to have per week. By the end of the meeting half of me wanted to scream and half of me wanted to collapse in a corner and sob, and the rest of the day has not improved my mood even a little tiny bit.

In a single week, I'm expected to give 45 minutes of homework every night, plus two reading assignments, one spelling assignment, one writing assignment, one "Language Arts" assignment (note: there is no "Language Arts" grade, and when you lift out reading, writing, and spelling, I'm not at all certain what's left) and one social studies assignment. That is five total assignments for the *three classes* that I have for Language Arts, plus the SS grade every week. Plus five homework assignments. This is *every* week, so if we have no school on Monday, apparently I'm still supposed to shoehorn *five graded assignments* into the two classes I have left. Plus five homework pages.

In perspective: I have 51 students. If everyone does their homework, and each "graded assignment" or homework sheet represents only a single sheet of paper, that's *five hundred and sixty-one pages of student work* that I'm expected to wade through, *each fucking week.* At one single minute to read, grade and record each assignment, that's damn near ten hours a week. Most of that is

89

Luther M. Siler

supposed to be LA— and, again, because of the way our schedule works I only teach Language Arts three days a goddamn week.

Oh, and apparently I was supposed to have been doing this since September. Might have been good to *tell me* in September, then.

It's bloody fucking insane and I won't do it.

And then, after that, I spent the whole day getting reminded in various and sundry subtle ways just what a bad reading teacher I am. I'm good at teaching History, and I'm a *great* Government/ Constitution teacher. But I know where my weaknesses are, and I suck at teaching reading. Just plain flat-out suck at it. The kids are learning, somehow— or at least their test scores last year indicated that they seemed to have been— but I couldn't tell you what the hell I was doing that might have caused that. I'm not doing anything the "right" way, either by Board fiat or my own coursework and reading, and much of what I am doing is stale and stupid. My repeated attempts at fixing things have all failed for one reason or another, and I'm tired of it. And now my workload has fucking tripled and I get to look forward to drowning in fucking paperwork for the rest of the year.

Want the kicker? The partner teachers to the LA/SS folks, who teach Math and Science? Three assignments a week, *total*. Two for math and one for science. Fuckin' bullshit. If I'm *mandated* to do over twice as much goddamn work I should bloody well be getting paid more.

The Walkthrough Team

January 11 2007

Ponder this, and try in your head to make it make sense: Chicago Public Schools places a filter on their Internet access, as one might well imagine they would. This, in and of itself, I do not have a problem with. In previous weeks, I have learned that the term "slavery," despite the many perfectly legitimate reasons one might search for such a term in a school context, will hit the filter. You can't do that.

I discovered today, to my somewhat greater surprise, that the phrase *Martin Luther King, Jr.* also hits the search filter.

Let me say that again. CPS' computers *won't let you do a search on Martin Luther King, Jr.* It hits the filter and sets off a fucking loud alarm, unless you're smart enough to have your volume turned off. Which I do, needless to say. Please, someone, give me a reason why that might be a good idea. There's *got* to be one.

Horrifyingly, I was told today that I have been put on the team for my school's AIO walkthrough tomorrow. This means that I get to spend the entire morning rubbing shoulders with (drumroll, please) *Mr. Johnson*, a man who has no known first name and has been described by people who weren't kidding as "scarier than Satan." I also have to evaluate my co-workers' classrooms, a prospect that fills me with dread, since virtually all of their classrooms look much, much better than mine. And yes, "look" is exactly what matters, if you don't already know that; the AIO team is basically there just to look at what is on the walls on the room, so if you're not much of a decorator, which I'm not, you're going to lose out. Plus, as I keep explaining to people who really don't care, the configuration of my room really does rob me of a lot of possible wall space.

The most annoying thing about this, I think, is the fetish for *labeling* things that always occurs right around a walkthrough, as if a thing does not exist if there is not a large printed sign near it giving it a name. To give a couple of specific examples, it was suggested that I label my writing center as the "Writing Center" and my student mailboxes as— get this— the *Message Center*, despite the fact that I do not, in fact, pass messages through it. Now, every kid in the damn room knows where the writing center is, and there aren't many things that I'd swear that all of my kids know. So it's silly to suggest that all this labeling is for them. It's to keep the *adults* on the walkthrough team from having to *think*. And yet it's my ass if it isn't done right.

Of course, the plus (the very, very small plus) side to this is that since I'm on the walkthrough it's highly unlikely that the team is going to visit my room. I suspect that this is, in fact, why I'm *on* the walkthrough team. Between my bad handwriting, my shoddy decorating skills, and my sweet, lovely, darling seventh-grade students, I don't think the principal wants the team anywhere near my room. I flat-out threatened to resign today. My frustration has reached the point where I start overextending metaphors to try and describe it to people: I've clawed through the bottom of the barrel, I can't reach the end of my rope anymore, shit like that.

2015 Luther update: I no longer remember what AIO stands for. He was in charge of a big chunk of schools, basically an intermediate level between the principals and the Lord High Muckety-Mucks of CPS.

The Walkthrough Team, Pt. 2

JANUARY 12 2007

Remind me to never, ever, *ever* be on a walkthrough team again. That may have been the worst thing ever.

I got to work a good hour and a half early, because when I left last night I left a couple of things that still remained to be done. Once I got there, I spent about an hour frantically finishing my room, whipping everything back into shape, all the while saying to myself *"They're not going in there, don't stress out about it too much."*

Yeah, right.

The day had already started off poorly, by the way, because of my wardrobe. I've lost a hell of a lot of weight since the last time I had to wear dress pants, and I literally don't own a single pair of non-jeans that fit me any more. I'd have just put my suit on, but the damn thing's filthy from the last time I wore it, and I didn't have time to get it cleaned, given that I got about eighteen hours' notice that I was going to be on the team. So I was wearing jeans. My *nicest* pair of jeans, but jeans nonetheless.

(Yes, I know I could have cleaned my suit already. Generally one gets enough warning that one will be needing to wear such a garment that one can get it done. This hasn't happened before.)

They arrived at 9:00, so thank God I'd gotten there early—because showing up at 9:00 was half an hour late, and if I'd shown up at regular time I'd have had no time to get anything at all done. The walkthrough, including the meetings before and after, went for nearly *four hours*, and it was easily among the most stressful contiguous four hour periods of my entire life. Basically, nothing went like I thought it was going to. On my way out of the building Thursday

93

night, I asked my boss if there was anything I could do to make certain I was prepared for the walkthrough while I was at home. Last year, we had a thick binder of test results, scores, and a number of other things we were supposed to be familiar with when the walkthrough people came in. This year we hadn't gotten any such documents and I was a little worried about it.

"No, they won't be asking you anything," she said.

Yeah, right.

Y'all remember high school, right? You remember that teacher who would ask the room a question, and not only did nobody know the answer to the question, because you hadn't studied, but nobody was even really sure what the *question meant* in the first place? You remember the awful fucking frozen silence that would descend upon the room, while everybody fidgeted and tried to avoid notice, and eventually some poor fucking soul ventured some sort of answer just to end the goddamn pain?

Two fucking hours of that, plus the actual walkthrough, which *also* sucked. And they went into my goddamn room. It got to the point where I was cracking jokes as often as I felt it possible just to break the tension in the damn room. It was *terrible*. My favorite bit, I think, was where we talked for a few minutes in the "breakdown" meeting, after the walkthrough, about how there was minimal evidence throughout the building of "explicit" vocabulary instruction and "interactive" word walls.

I don't know what an interactive word wall is. And I for damned sure don't know how to prove I'm doing "explicit" vocabulary instruction on a regular basis to somebody who is only in my room for *five minutes* when I'm *not there*. I finally snapped and asked about the latter point, because seriously, you're there for *five minutes*, how the hell can you judge us on that, and I discovered that my real problem was that I didn't know what the word "explicit" meant. It's one of those words that doesn't mean what it means if an education bureaucrat is saying it.

I can't actually tell you what it does mean. It was a mistake to ask— Mister Johnson *does not* like to be challenged— and the terror prevented me from really recalling anything he said.

My second favorite part? There were two walkthrough teams. I put myself on the primary grades one, so I didn't have to see anyone's reaction to my room. There was a team breakdown meeting before the group breakdown meeting, and it was explained to us that the team breakthrough meeting was to be held *while standing*. I cannot imagine why, other than pure sadism. They literally didn't let *anyone sit down* while we were talking about everything our school was doing wrong.

Remind me to never do any of this, ever again.

More on NCLB

January 26 2007

This was quite a long day. Ordinarily days where I don't see the kids don't really qualify as long days. Yesterday was the last day of the quarter, so today was Finish your Goddamn Report Cards day. (Yes, I know, my kids never actually come to school, blah blah blah. There are two three-day weekends and a half-day in February. I'll trade jobs with anyone out there who wants the time off. Any takers? Okay.)

Anyway, normally Grading Day isn't a long day. The principal decided to waste the whole day in meaningless meetings and copious emotional abuse, however, meaning that I got nothing done and I need to get impressive amounts of work done tonight and tomorrow so that I don't have to cancel some very important plans that I have on Sunday.

The meeting started off with my boss telling us, basically, that our lives were over, and then dumping a whole fuckton more federal mandates and paperwork on our heads. Exact, literal words: "Your lives are not your own any more so long as you do this job."

The new program is IMPACT, an online gradebook/report card/attendance book thing. Sounds good, right?

It can only be done from CPS computers on a CPS network. It keeps track of when we enter everything we put into it. It's a giant fucking Big Brother program and we effectively *can't work at home any more.* I'm really not sure how I feel about it. I intensely dislike the aspect of teaching that says that we must put in hours after hours of unpaid overtime at home every weekend doing grading, planning, and so on and so forth. The job literally *cannot be done* within the parameters of the hours that they pay us for.

97

Luther M. Siler

Now, on the other hand, the workload isn't any different (well, some of the end-of-the-month dickery with attendance is going away, but they're replacing it with even more annoying in-building entry procedures) but *it must all be done at school.* Which means that not only are they robbing me of my time and not paying me for it, they're forcing me to stay in the fucking building while they do it, thus moving back my leaving time back to where it's going to start taking me two hours to get home every night. It annoys greatly.

Sadly, I just burned six paragraphs and haven't even really gotten to what's bugging me; it's just that that was the bit you haven't heard me talking about a thousand times. I simply cannot take No Child Left Behind any fucking longer. I'm tired of pressure about standardized fucking tests. I'm tired of trying to raise test scores in a room full of kids who don't give a fuck. I'm tired of being told that making them give a fuck is my problem. No, making them give a fuck is *their parents'* problem. Frankly, I'd prefer the ones who don't care just stop showing up so that I can concentrate on the kids who have a chance.

There are two provisions to the No Child Left Behind act: It Gets Harder Until You Fail, and It Gets Worse Until You Quit. And I'm done. I'm quitting. I'll finish the year out, but I already knew that remaining at CPS next year was a highly unlikely proposition (ignore everything else: I can't afford the upcoming teacher's strike) and I don't think I'm going to seriously pursue getting another teaching position. Because it's not just my school— if you happen to think that your school's doing okay, that they're not obsessed with test scores yet, that it's just my neighborhood or my principal or my kids?

Wait two more years. Being white is only going to save your schools for so much longer. By 2012, every school in America— I am not exaggerating or being facetious— *every school in America* will be a failing school, because the demands of NCLB are literally impossible to fulfill. Literally. Fucking. Impossible.

Two more years. That's all it's going to take. But I won't be there to take the blame for it.

A Long Day, Pt. 1

JANUARY 30 2007

Let's talk about my day. If I've spoken to you today and didn't mention any of this, it's because I honestly suppressed the memories until having late dinner with my roommate tonight. Like, seriously.

My day started with twisting my ankle on my way into the building. I was carrying my laptop, three bags from Target, my satchel (completely stuffed with papers) and a cardboard box filled with additional papers, walking on ice and snow. Everything went flying. My ankle's okay now. It was tender for about an hour, but whatever. Point is, I started the day with twisting my ankle. I should have taken it as a sign and gone home.

As I walked to the office, I discovered Poke Boy (the reason for the name will become apparent in a few minutes) and his mother sitting outside the office. Now, a little detail on Poke Boy: He's new. He's been here about two weeks. He's also basically illiterate. Whole language was inflicted on him to such a degree as a kid that I'm not convinced he actually realizes that individual letters represent sounds. When spelling words he doesn't know, he can literally miss *every sound in the word*. Like, "spell cow," and he starts with an *F*. And his mother doesn't think he needs to be in special ed, because she doesn't believe in it. We had a rather tense meeting where the other 7th grade teacher (his actual homeroom teacher; Mom was trying an end run by meeting with me) and I basically explained that we can't really do things like algebra and 7th grade social studies to people who cannot read. It was ... stressful. And annoying, because she interpreted everything we said as "Your kid's fucking stupid," and got all self-righteous about it. Plus, I had work I was supposed to be doing. I don't know why I

99

continue to allow myself to believe that I can accomplish things before school or on preps. It's impossible. There is *always* something.

The rest of my morning didn't go *that* badly. I gave my class a Stern Talking To about the upcoming ISAT tests, for reasons that I'm sure are entirely obvious. We *aren't* making AYP this year and that's all there is to it; my kids simply aren't taking the test seriously at all. I also gave failure notices (basically pre-report-card report cards) to all but *two* of my homeroom students. At 11:40, we switch classes, and I get my afternoon group. I gave them basically the same talk I gave my morning class, and then started to get them lined up for lunch. One of my special ed kids, who is behavior disordered to the *gills*, actually *vaulted over a table* to get to another student and started hitting him. They disentangled instantly upon my (loud) command to do so, and as I was pointing backwards, over my shoulder, at the line, ordering them to quit acting like little assholes and get into it, I inadvertently poked Poke Boy in the eye.

Oops.

He was okay; I quickly found out that what I had initially thought to be *convulsions* were actually laughter, because he couldn't believe that a teacher had actually poked him in the fucking eye.

I still had to fill out an accident report. Ever seen one of these things? Just imagine what an ass-covering accident report from one of the largest educational bureaucracies in the country might look like. It's more annoying than that. I fucking hate accident reports. I also had to call Mom and explain to her that I had poked her precious not-stupid-but-still-not-literate baby boy in the eye and it was a terrible accident and I was very sorry.

It, uh, kinda sucked.

After lunch, I packed most of my kids off to Music, holding back, I don't know, maybe nine of them who wanted to continue with something we'd been discussing. I think they got something useful out of the conversation, which was good, and then I got them set up to go down to pick up the rest of the kids, because I can't leave them in the room to go do it myself.

As we were walking down the stairs, two of the kids hid in the room, apparently just to fuck around. As they were doing said fucking around (they were planning on catching up with us after a sec; I'd have noticed they were gone when we got to the bottom of the stairs) one of them— the same kid who had vaulted over the table earlier— stepped on the back of the other kid's ankle. She took a faceplant into a desk and took off running into the bathroom, bleeding all over various things.

I, at the bottom of the stairs, knew nothing of this.

I turned around, noticed Sally was missing, and asked where she was. Table-vaulter, slightly out of breath, and without being directly asked, claimed he didn't know.

(Sidenote: this is common behavior, and it drives me fucking batshit insane. If I ask "Who has this?" or "Who knows this?" or anything vaguely similar, three or four kids will *always* say that they don't. Shut the *fuck* up, that's not what I asked. If the answer is "no," keep your mouth shut.)

"Yes you do."

"Oh, she bleedin."

"*Bleeding?* Where is she?"

"She in the bathroom bleedin."

Just imagine the rest of the conversation.

Hiding in a stall, as it worked out, where I had to corral a female staff member to go find out what the hell was going on, because shithead had conveniently forgotten *tripping her* in order to cause the aforementioned bleeding. Meanwhile, the music teacher has *kicked my kids out of music*, because I hadn't come to pick them up yet what with all the *blood*, and they're spread out over the whole goddamn first floor making trouble, because they're *idiots,* and so is the goddamned music teacher, because who the *fuck* does that?

And then, since the kid claimed that table-vaulter hadn't tripped her on purpose, I had to fill out *another fucking accident report.*

At the end of the day, I had to pass out failure notices to the afternoon class. Two of the kids who failed social studies *immediately* began shrieking and whining about it. I'm not sure why; they were failing at midterms, too, and did nothing about it, so this shouldn't be surprising. One kid goes "How'd I fail social studies? We never do *anything* in Social Studies!"

Hmm. No, sweetie, *you* never do anything in social studies. Which just may be the reason for that 36% grade point average, there. Maybe. It's a crazy idea, but let's go with it. Anyway, there was much crying and weeping and gnashing of teeth. Maybe they'll both drop out. I can hope, right?

The bell rings, I get everybody outside, and another student, much calmer but still upset, comes up to me to talk about his grades. I talk to him for a few minutes (which does, in fact, include my pointing to his "F" in Spelling and saying "This is bullshit," because it was) and as I finish I notice maybe sixty or seventy students halfway down the street in a big group. On someone's lawn. Oh, *goody*. Fight!

I broke the mob up from two houses away. Sometimes it startles *me* how good my lungs have gotten after a year and a half of teaching seventh grade. Guess who was fighting?

Yep! Two of my homeroom girls. One of them took off running, and the second one was bleeding from her ear and looked like she was missing a fistful of hair. So I took her back to the office to call mom. And got to fill out *another goddamned fucking form*, since I was the adult on-site for the incident.

And then I told the secretary to get me a sub for tomorrow. I'm taking a fucking mental health day. Because, seriously, this shit is ridiculous.

(I'll give you a dollar of American money if you can read through this essay describing my job at a school in great detail and find the word that I did *not* use anywhere in it. Because I didn't do any of that today.)

Stabbings, Pt. 1

February 8 2007

So my boss walked up to me yesterday, as I was leaving the cafeteria after dropping off my kids for lunch, and kinda rubs my shoulders a bit and says "Don't give up on me yet, Mr. Siler." I'm not sure I realized that I'd been quite that transparent. We had *another* "things they've changed and not told anyone about since the last time you took the ISAT" meeting today, and there's less than a month to the damn test, including *two* four-day weeks, since Illinois recognizes Lincoln's birthday *and* Presidents' Day as holidays.

We're fuckin' doomed— which is, of course, the sole point of the tests. Insert the standard test-based whining here. I'm pretty sure ISAT actually stands for I Suck At Teaching.

This has been the week for *knife violence.*

I had one knife incident last year, which was relatively benign. I had a kid bring a switchblade to class, and caught him with it while he was casually cutting up paper at his desk as if having a knife wasn't anything particularly unusual. Nothing in particular happened, as CPS policy is that the blade has to be over a certain length to count and his wasn't. By, I believe, an eighth of an inch. Today I found out that one of my students from last year is getting *expelled*, because she chased another student off of her front lawn with a butcher knife when said student showed up to beat up her brother. This incident led to a rather heated joint parent conference the next day (this harassment has been going on for a while) where the *parents* got into a fistfight in the office, injuring the principal when she tried to break it up, leading to a wide variety of police charges being filed. The fight, by the way, was started by the

103

mother of the kid who showed up looking for trouble and got chased off.

My former student— one of my favorites, frankly— is going to be expelled. The other kid got a five-day vacation, despite a lengthy history of violent behavior (oh, yeah, she's one of mine too) because she's special ed and thus can't be expelled, despite being the *cause* of all the trouble.

And today, one of my kids stabbed another one in the hand with a pocket knife. So I got to fill out another goddamned accident report. Stabbing a classmate in the hand only gets you a two-day suspension, by the way.

I'm supposed to be worrying about motherfucking extended responses while all this is going on.

Sigh.

On Chemical Weapons

FEBRUARY 9 2007

Thankfully, this did not happen to me.

This morning, in my partner teacher's class, a student came up to the teacher's desk and asked for permission to use the bathroom, which was granted. The student is the same one that, a couple of weeks ago was suspended for calling her a bitch and me an asshole in the same day and is failing *every single one* of his classes. Apropos of nothing, his first name rhymes with the first names of each of his three brothers, differing only by the first letter— the rough equivalent of naming your kids Billy, Dilly, Filly, and Killy.

In fact, let's call him Killy.

Killy goes to the bathroom and returns, complaining of an upset stomach. Five minutes later, he's rolling on the floor moaning, and an *incredibly* powerful stench begins to fill the room. Powerful to the point where the windows have to be opened, in freezing weather, because freezing is better than putting up with it. Kids are complaining of headaches. Various trauma occurs, and the student is removed from the classroom to infect spaces less filled with other human beings. About twenty minutes later, the stench still lingering in the room, he returns (no parents being available to come get him; surprise surprise) and repeats his performance.

This time, however, he starts laughing as he's rolling on the floor, and as he leaves the room— *again*, mind you— the teacher smells a rat so to speak, and the other students, now heartily sick of the gut-churning stench, begin to remark that they'd heard Killy talking about how he had "a surprise" earlier in the day. A quick search of his desk reveals a broken, half-empty glass vial of some

105

sort of yellow fluid (not urine, some sort of chemical) with "CAUTION: CHEMICAL IRRITANT" printed on the side.

All hell broke loose, predictably.

Well, a few minutes later, Killy finds out about his upcoming ten-day suspension, virtually guaranteeing that he fails seventh grade, as if his grades and previous suspensions didn't already do that.

And begins *punching himself in the face*. See, sometimes stupid does hurt! Parents are called, again, to no avail. Counselors and the upper-grades special ed teacher (he's not special ed, but she's *good*) are dispatched. The counselor begins yammering on about how poor poor thing and traumatized and fucked up he is and how we need to be oh so very nice to him. The counselor's a yammerer. We're used to this, even when she's right. The special ed teacher, who has seen him in action, diagnoses him as, not kidding, "just being a damn idiot," an assessment endorsed by both of his current teachers.

Whee.

On Snow Days

February 14 2007

It was cold and snowy outside again today. Unlike, as far as I can tell, *everywhere* else, school wasn't canceled. They don't *do* that in Chicago. Official board policy basically boils down to They're Always Safer At School Than On The Streets, so unless you *die immediately* upon exiting your home, I'm always going to have to go to work. They did cancel the school *buses*, though, because Chicago seems to have forgotten how to plow streets and very little of it has been done. I am startled, frankly, that I've been able to get to work for the last two days, given how light my car is and the depth of the snow that's been blocking me in.

School bus cancellation triggers a curious aspect of CPS policy, one that I wasn't aware of until today. Apparently, if the buses are cancelled, kids have the right to just go to whatever damn school happens to be closest, even if they aren't enrolled there. So it was entirely possible that I was going to walk into my classroom this morning to be greeted by a passel of kids who a) I didn't know, b) didn't go to my school, c) were therefore *entirely* unaccountable to me, and d) I had to put up with anyway. Luckily, this nightmare scenario did not come to pass, but one of *my* students attended some other school (and she's obnoxious, too, so good for them) because I got a message from the school clerk around 10:30 telling me to mark her present in my book.

I have suspected on numerous occasions that teachers were considered to be little more than higher-paid babysitters. I did not think that the theory would ever be be confirmed quite so conclusively.

107

It gets worse, of course. It always does. The fact that school was not cancelled did not mean that my students were actually going to *attend*. I had only half of my homeroom class present and a touch under 2/3 of my afternoon class present. Attendance rates are an NCLB mandate. Because the law dictates that No Number May Go Down, Ever, Or the School is Failing, my school has to have over *ninety-five percent attendance* this year.

Consider that for a moment, just on its own. We *had* 95% attendance last year; an astounding statistic in and of itself.

We must *beat* that this year, however, despite the addition of (for example) a student in the first grade who has sickle-cell anemia and thus spends a substantial amount of time in the hospital. And despite days like today, where there is a blizzard outside, half the damn *country* is not in school, and half the kids don't show up. The school as a whole had something like 62% attendance today. It was in the mid-seventies yesterday. And it will hurt us on NCLB. It is entirely mathematically possible that we will end up a failing school at the end of the year solely because Chicago public schools weren't cancelled this week. Our attendance is *that close* to making us a "failing" school. "Failing," here, meaning 95.1% attendance instead of 95.2%. I'm *not kidding.*

Oh! I forgot, there's more. I had to have class in the music room today because my room had no heat. Again. On a day so cold and snowy that half the kids didn't show up, my room had no heat.

Again.

Happy fuckin' Valentine's Day.

To Aid and Inspire

February 23 2007

The "tutors" from Chicago State University came by again today. They have come to visit ... what, three times this year, I think. The first time, I wasn't actually at school, so I didn't have to deal with them. They left the kids with a ton of lengthy applications that needed to be filled out in order for the kids to "participate in their program." Naturally, none of the applications were turned in, and those that were were generally missing information, such as the kids' social security numbers, which neither they nor their parents generally know, and where they *do* know they generally want to know why they have to put them on silly applications, and parents' income levels, which they are *also* reluctant to divulge without a reason of some sort.

The second time they came was two weeks ago, with no notice. They were *supposed* to show up a month ago, and we were all prepared to lose an hour or so out of our mornings, and they didn't show up. They showed up two weeks ago, on a day when I had a ton of stuff planned, which I immediately had to carve an hour out of. And what essential tasks did my students perform during that hour? Misbehaved, mostly, as the entire seventh grade got shoved into the library to perform such essential tasks as "fill out this application," "sign up on this piece of paper if you want tutoring from this group of complete strangers," (no one did) "bring a pen with you," which is only useful if you tell the kids *before* they file into the library, as I do not keep 48 pens in my fucking pocket, and "look at this list of adjectives and circle the ones that apply to you."

I try to pretend these things are important, because I'm supposed to, but there was no earthly fucking way that it was worth losing an hour so close to ISATs, much less any *other* time in the year, and the awful behavior during the program led to a number of kids getting detentions they shouldn't have gotten and *continued* bad behavior in the room, since they'd spent an hour getting all fucking riled up. They were also warned *again* that if they applications weren't turned in they wouldn't be allowed to participate in "the next program," which was today, and which all of them got to participate in again. The new warning is that now they won't be able to participate *next year* if they don't turn in the applications, and I don't know why in the world anyone should care. I got dragged into a morning meeting last week where the principal railed at us about how so few applications had been turned in; I rather unsympathetically pointed out that they didn't feel like doing the work to waste their time and that perhaps if Chicago State thinks they should apply to be in the program they should do it somewhere other than on my fucking class time.

Anyway, they showed up again today. They walked in, divided the class into groups of four more or less at random, leading to a number of entirely predictable personality conflicts and kids declaring they weren't gonna do anything, then gave them *five minutes* to come up with a "news broadcast" on a topic that they gave them. The topics were, get this, Abortion, Sexually Transmitted Diseases, Drug Abuse, and Drunk Driving. Maybe something else, I don't know.

Do you know what happens when you give seventh graders to *improv* a skit on STDs? They get up to the front of the room and start pretending that everybody in the room has AIDS from fucking everybody else, and then start arguing about who fucked who. Wanna know what happens when you ask them to improv a skit on drug abuse? They roll up pieces of paper into rather convincing-looking joints and start acting high.

All of this is entirely predictable by anyone who is not an idiot.

It did not take long for me to simply give up on keeping shit under control and vaguely appropriate. *They* unleashed this nonsense, so let them deal with it. I just sat at my desk and tried to get work done. Every so often, someone would look at the back of the room and notice the look on my face. This always led to whispered conversations and other kids looking at me. Once the program was over, I left my room, shutting the door behind me— something I *never, ever do*, for what are probably obvious reasons—

and explained very carefully to the Chicago State people that there would be lesson plans emailed or mailed to me *one full week* before the next time they intended to enter my room or they would be denied admission. The phrase "nine and a half days until the most important test of their lives to date" was used, in addition to the words "it will take me the rest of the morning to get them back under control, which means that my entire day with them has been destroyed."

When I walked back into my room, I was greeted with *perfect silence*. All of the desks had already been returned to where they belonged— and without me noticing it in the hallway, which is pretty fucking impressive— and there were hands folded on desks and 24 rather mortified-looking kids carefully watching the front of the room, clearly expecting the tongue-lashing of their lives.

"I am not mad at you. I am, however, in an *extraordinarily* poor mood right now. I would like to suggest that we use the rest of our time together productively, since we have lost our morning."

And, unbelievably, they cooperated.

This will probably be the last time that happens this year.

More on Guest Speakers

MARCH | 2007

We had another guest speaker in the room today. It wasn't Chicago State this time, but a member of the Black Star motivational speaker group. We had a couple of these last year and while they're not the best imaginable use of a class period the speakers have generally been intelligent and engaging and not a complete waste of time. Today's speaker was a local poet and musician by the name of M'Reld (like the stone) who, I had been told, was "excellent" and would not have any problem maintaining the attention of the kids.

Hah.

Never underestimate the ability of my students to make embarrassing assholes of themselves under *any* circumstances. They had M'Reld— a guest in our building, remember, taking unpaid time out of her day to come talk to them— begging for their attention for more than five seconds at a time within about fifteen minutes of her entering the classroom. This was despite the best efforts of *both* of us to keep them paying attention, and it wasn't her material or her manner at fault here. I thought she was captivating, personally.

I hope I haven't said this in the past few days, but I had a revelation recently. These kids genuinely don't have the *slightest motherfucking idea* how to behave. It's not that they know, and they're not doing it. They *don't know*. They have no fucking idea that it's rude to run their goddamn mouths constantly while someone else is trying to *help them*, and it's too late for anyone to *teach* them that. Something that I hear constantly, when I berate a kid for talking, is "I wasn't talking. I was XXX," where XXX is "asking" or "telling" or "saying" followed by whatever they were asking for or telling someone or saying. None of these things are "talking" to

Luther M. Siler

them; I have no idea what they think the goddamn word actually means.

I have pointed out that all of those things are *still talking* about a million times. I have lost count of the number of times the words "if your mouth is moving, and sound is coming out of it, you're talking" have come out of my mouth. I'd always assumed that it was just simple obstinacy that kept them from getting it. I was wrong. They genuinely *don't understand* what "talking" *is*. It's the only explanation that still makes any sense. And I'll be damned if I have any idea how to teach them.

After work, I had my after-school group, which, remember, is composed *solely* of kids who *volunteered* to be there. Same shit. Even the kids who *come to school for extra time*, when they *don't have to be there*, run their fucking mouths ceaselessly and don't pay attention. I just don't know what the fuck to do anymore.

Stabbings, Pt. 2

March 15 2007

In the last two days I have threatened to resign in front of my employers, damn near broken into tears in front of my boss and my AP, and witnessed said AP pick a student off the ground by either her jacket or the scruff of her (yes, *her*) neck and lift her eight or nine feet off the ground, slamming her into a door, in order to prevent a stabbing. There were also two miscellaneous three-day suspensions of my students today.

But hey, ISATs are happening and at least I'm not leaving any fucking children behind.

Full explanation to follow when I have some energy. I'm taking Friday off.

(Note: By "when I have some energy," I mean "sometime Friday, probably.")

Man, I don't even know where to *start*. The kids were complete bastards all week (I'm writing this on Friday, obviously, after having taken the day off) and if I ever have another week like this one I'm resigning instantly, no questions asked, and I don't care what it does to me financially. I'll declare fucking bankruptcy; there's no way it's worse than this.

Here's what happened: Tuesday featured no preparatory periods whatsoever, a morning of incredible test-related stress, and an afternoon full of such intense bastardry that I told the class "You win, I quit," at the end of the day and ignored the little fucks at my desk until the bell rang. After work, I went downstairs and sat out in front of the office until the principal and AP came back, and explained, as calmly and carefully as I could, that unless some shit changed somehow I was going to leave. I believe the way I put it was "I cannot afford to quit, financially, and I cannot afford to stay, emotionally." I can't take this anymore. Period. Try and understand that I am not kidding when I say that all I do for six hours a fucking day is scream at people who don't give a wet shit what the hell I think to shut the fuck up and sit the fuck down. I do not understand why my kids come to school. My only assumption is that their parents don't want them at home either. (Here's another thing about the parents: I'm physically assaulting the next person to tell me that they "don't play" with their kids. *Fuck you.* Yes the fuck you do. Nothing's changed in the last four or five parent visits. Nothing's going to change this time either.)

Anyway. Tuesday night was utter misery. My one consolation was realizing that one of our 8th grade teachers is leaving at the end of this quarter for a job with the central office. The current plan is to put a sub in her position until the end of the year. I am considering asking for it myself. Now, this would hardly solve all of my problems— last year was hardly a walk in the park— but last year was never this bad, and 8th graders are always better behaved than 7th graders anyway. I may ask for it; I still haven't decided. We'll see.

On Wednesday, I got a different proctor (the dean of students) for the test, which helped with noise/distraction issues much more than the previous proctor did, who is of such inconsequence to the students that she may as well not be in the room. I also decided to just keep my own kids all afternoon, which meant that I didn't have to see my other class except for the hour or so when they were taking the reading test.

In addition, it was announced to my students that 7th grade misbehavior is now to be met with instant suspension, which, really, *fantastic*. By the end of the day, I had two of my boys on three-day vacations.

After lunch, one of my girls came into the room sobbing. I got the class started on something and went to talk to her to see what the problem was. She asked to go downstairs and make a phone call, a request I granted. About half an hour later, the assistant principal buzzed up to ask if a female student could be sent down with Shanice's belongings. I dispatched a student with her stuff and went about with what I was doing.

Ten minutes later, maybe, she came back upstairs, without her stuff, and sat down at her desk, still crying. I pulled her back to my desk to figure out what the deal was— usually when somebody's stuff gets called for, it's a sign that there's no way in hell I'm gonna see that kid again that day. She was still crying, and talking way too fast, so it took me a good five or six minutes of pretending to be patient and understanding before I realized *why* she was upstairs without her stuff— she wasn't supposed to be upstairs *at all*. She was supposed to be outside in front of the office. About a millisecond after this clicked, the assistant principal came into the room and said that Shanice was going to have to come back downstairs. She said no. He repeated the question, and she refused again. At this point, he buzzed the office to request that our security officer be sent upstairs as a "witness."

Uh-oh.

A few minutes later, after a couple more verbal refusals to move, the kid was being physically removed from the room, fighting all the way. Once they got outside the room, she got away from the AP and went and crouched down in the corner by the door to the library.

Lemme explain something about my assistant principal. The guy's probably five or six inches taller than me, and built like a football lineman. He's stronger than hell, too. He reached down, grabbed Shanice by (I assume; I didn't have a good look) the front of her hoodie, or maybe under her arms or something, hell, I don't know— and not only yanked her to her feet but lifted her up above his head, basically to the highest point his arms could reach. He's 6'3" or 6'4", easily. Do the math. The kid dangled there, probably nine feet off the ground, while he explained carefully and calmly that once he put her down they were going to go back to the office and there was to be no further nonsense from her of any kind whatsoever.

Meanwhile, my class is going nuts. And, honestly, I'm doing my best not to laugh, because I've spent most of the year wanting to slam this damn kid into a wall. (This is what this job has done to me, by the way.)

After school, I went downstairs to talk to the AP about what exactly had happened, because I was still highly fuzzy on what Shanice's problem was in the first place. Turns out that she'd gotten into a dispute with another student during lunch, and while on the phone with her parents describing the incident had said, within earshot of the AP, "You know I didn't want to come to this school in the first place. I'm just gonna go stab that boy so that they kick me out."

So you can imagine why the AP was so insistent that she leave the room. The weird thing? She was back the next day. I would think that announcements of impending stabbage would merit a suspension. She did get wanded with a metal detector before being allowed in the room, though, and ... well, lemme go on with the story.

Thursday, now. By the end of the day, I'd have nine kids, nearly a quarter of my students, on either two-day or three-day suspensions. I repeated the keep-my-own-kids trick again, which combined with Wednesday's suspensions made the afternoon marginally more bearable. At about 1:45, I got called down to an "emergency meeting" with the principal and they stuck an aide in my room.

Legal services called. An anonymous phone call has been made to CPS central offices accusing us of giving students answers on the ISAT. The principal had spent the afternoon methodically calling teachers down trying to figure out why anyone might think or suggest such a thing, to much confusion and consternation on the part of the staff. I sure as fuck know we're not cheating on the thing.

This could mean that we have to re-take the goddamned tests in a month or so. The *whole fucking school.* Because of one motherfucking anonymous phone call.

Do you see, now, why I took Friday off?

Learning First or Maybe Not At All

April 29 2007

The third Learning First test was this week. I've talked about these before; the quick recap is that they're CPS' three-times-a-year method of showing that the kids are making progress in school, as opposed to the ISAT, which is administered only once and goes to the state. The thing about the Learning First tests is that they're not norm-referenced, *at all*, so ... well, they're not really testing much of anything other than how difficult the test itself is. This week's administration was as pointless and cynical as anything I've ever seen or heard of while I've been involved with education, and it kinda makes me sick that I had to waste my time being involved with the damn thing at all.

Here's the deal: My kids' scores dropped precipitously from the fall LF test to the winter test. This annoyed me greatly at the time, as it seemed to indicate that all my effort (even that early, the character of my class was beginning to become apparent) had only made my students *dumber*. Since then, from asking around, it's become pretty clear that scores on the second test dropped across the city. What does this say? It says that the *test was harder*. That's it, really. Since the only thing we get is raw scores, if a given kid gets a 23/32 on one test and a 20/32 on the second, that kid's scores have gone down, even if the city average is 24 on the first one and 17 on the second. Now, *with that context*, we can see that this kid seems to have improved, or at least had a luckier day. We don't get that context. All we get are scores.

Teachers get to keep previous editions of the test, and are encouraged to use them heavily in preparing the kids for the next test. They *know* this. They know this because it's their policy. To

119

that end, on Monday, I gave the kids last spring's LF test and went over it carefully, paying attention to any vocab terms they might not know and stuff like that.

It's good that I did that, because this spring's test was *exactly the same*— word for word, letter for letter, question for question— as *last* spring's test.

You see what happened here, right? The board got all jumpy because scores weren't where they were supposed to be, and the schools therefore weren't Demonstrating Progress. Therefore, *knowing* that teachers use previous tests as practice material— and that therefore it was likely that the students of any language arts teacher with two functioning neurons were likely to have recently been exposed to the Right Answers on last spring's test— proceeded to give that exact same test to artificially inflate scores, so that they can go tell people who don't pay attention that we're doing something in our classrooms ... which they wouldn't have to do if the test were a functional metric of our progress in the first place.

God, I fucking hate No Child Left Behind.

Graduation Day

JUNE 13 2007

Went to graduation today, for last year's group. It was an interesting experience. I've grown used to being The Only White Guy In The Room— six hours a day for two years will do that for you— but I'm not sure that I've ever been the literal only white person in a room with *hundreds* of other adults and not just a bunch of kids. Graduation was incredibly well-attended; I wouldn't be surprised if there were 10 people for each graduate, and we graduated close to fifty kids. Do other places make huge deals out of 8th grade graduation the same way Chicago does? There are two or three people reading this who have known me since eighth grade. I don't remember my middle school doing *anything at all* to "graduate" us. There might have been a yearbook-signing thing in the gym, maybe, but certainly no caps-and-gowns fooferol. I'm pretty sure there was just a touch of high school orientation stuff and then we got kicked out the door.

That said, one thing occurred to me (not for the first time) while watching this graduation, and our graduation speaker (his name escapes me, but he was from the Rainbow-PUSH coalition) made it explicit: for many of these kids, at least statistically, this is the only graduation they're ever going to get to go to. Fully *seventy percent* of Chicago's black males do not graduate from high school.

Seventy fucking percent.

You can understand, given that, why an 8th grade graduation might be celebrated the way it is. 8th grade graduation simply wasn't an achievement for me. Entering high school was certainly a milestone, I'm not going to dispute that, but I grew up in an environment where graduation in all of its forms was simply not an optional thing. I, and everyone I knew, was *going* to graduate from high school unless *death itself* intervened. These kids simply don't have that luxury. I mean, if you *ask* them, they all plan on graduating and they all want to go to college. Sadly, many of them and most of them, respectively, aren't going to realize those goals. A substantial portion of the graduation speech was on the topic "please stay out of jail," which really wouldn't have come up at my school even if we had had a graduation ceremony.

On a slightly lighter note, I think Chicago's school structure probably makes a difference, too. Where I grew up, you went to the same school from K-6 and then "middle school" was only 7th and 8th graders. That's relaxed a bit now; I believe that "middle school" is now 5th-8th, but they *don't* do things the way Chicago does, where if a kid doesn't move she's going to spend nine years in the same building before heading to high school. Leaving a school after nine years certainly merits more of a celebration than leaving a school after *two*, particularly since those two years were essentially high school lite; we switched classes eight times a day, so there really wasn't a ton of time for any of the teachers to get to know any of the students all that well.

The other difference was that, also unlike the graduation ceremony that I didn't have, this graduation was basically *exactly* the same as being in church. I've commented on this before, but any notion of the separation of church and state basically flies completely out the window in an all-black school. Or, at least, it does in *this* one, and I don't have a good reason to assume my school is more religious than any of the many other similar buildings on the South Side. The school's former music teacher was on hand (this woman's reputation was one step short of God's in the building; the choir was fully 1/3 of the *entire school* while she was there) to perform a song— more on that in a sec— and she began her bit by spending a moment talking about just what an awesome God our God was. She then launched directly into a gospel tune. I'm not complaining— I could listen to gospel music all goddamn day, believe it or not, and this lady was *amazing*. There were tremendous sound problems throughout the entire (1 1/2 hour) graduation ceremony, and she could have filled the room entirely unaugmented if she'd wanted to. You know you're dealing with a powerful singer when she's holding the mic at arm's length from her mouth and still damn near blowing out speakers.

'Twas an interesting day.

Part Three: Indiana

2007-2014

After two years of unrelenting standardized test stress, I was happy to go back to computer teaching for a few years, and after returning to Indiana I landed a job teaching fifth grade Keyboarding (basically teaching typing) and sixth grade Computer Applications, which basically meant one unit on each of the Office programs and an extra one where we tore old computers to bits and learned how to put them back together again. The next several years featured a marriage and a house and a baby who is, as I'm writing this, now four years old. Licensing changes at the state level eventually forced a move to sixth grade math and science, and from there to seventh grade math and eighth grade Honors Algebra. The Algebra group, composed mostly of kids I'd had in sixth grade already, ended up easily being the best class I ever had.

Oh Shit It's Shit

September 5 2007

My kids (and I) have lunch during fourth hour, which is from 10:18 to 11:00. It's inhumanly early, but that's not what the story is about and it's the only part of my schedule that I have any reason to complain about. Toward the end of my *sixth* period class, which begins at approximately 11:45 and ends at 12:28, one of my students called me over, a horror-stricken look on her face. She points at something on the ground next to her chair and whispers a question at me.

"Is that poop?"

What? What the fuck? Did you just ask me if there was fucking poop on the *carpet* in my *classroom?* Hell no there's no poop on the floor in my classroom. That can't possibly be poop. There's no *poop on the floor* in *school*.

I look.

It's poop.

I blink, squeeze the bridge of my nose for a moment, and look again.

Goddammit.

Definitely poop.

No, really. It's poop. On the floor. In my classroom.

There's nothing in the teacher manual to describe what you ought to do when you discover *shit on the floor* in your room. Luckily, there didn't seem to be much of a smell. Okay, priority one, and I can't believe I'm having to *think this phrase*, much less actually do it: locate the source of the poop. A moment later, I notice that there's *also* poop all over the wheels of the chair next to

127

where the girl was sitting. And there's more ground into the carpet under said chair. There's a kid in the chair.

I nudge his shoulder.

"Hey. Dustin."

Dustin looks up.

"Look at your shoes, Dustin."

He looks down and says, I swear to God, "Oh, *shit.*" See, my kids get recess after lunch. Dustin— not his real name, obviously— had had shit on his shoes for *over an hour*— a *voluminous* amount of shit— and somehow hadn't noticed.

Very quietly, not angry, but using my Obey Immediately voice, I say "Get out of the classroom. Go directly to the bathroom, and clean your shoes and pants off with soap and paper towels. I am not taking the time to write you a pass. Go now." He gets up and does this comical side-of-his-shoes walk out of the room. Luckily, students haven't started noticing what's going on yet. I look at the other girl, and the girl next to her, and tell them to change their seats if the smell bothers them, but to do it *quietly.* They, being good kids, comply. I go to the phone in my room and call the office.

"You're gonna *love* this."

"I'm not gonna love this, am I?"

"Not even a little bit. Somebody stepped in something they weren't supposed to at recess and now it's all over my furniture. Care to send the janitor my way?"

"I love you too, Mr. Siler."

"Thanks! Bye."

Okay, so far, things are under control. Granted, there's *poop on the floor in my classroom*, but things are under control and no one has noticed what's going on except for a few mature kids who are dealing with it properly. No problem.

And then Warner, who sits on the other side of Dustin, notices what's going on. Jumps up. Knocks his chair over— and the chairs are *wheeled*, so this is harder to do than it sounds.

"Holy crap, there's dog crap on the floor!"

The pandemonium described in the bloody menstrual pad story from a couple of years ago had *nothing* on this. At least that was only the girls. All hell breaks loose, including one kid who keeps asking "Is that doody?" over and over again, not seeming entirely convinced that the presence of said doody in the room is possible, and about half the kids miss the word *dog* and think that Dustin has managed to shit himself. After a couple of minutes of attempting to restore order, the bell rang, and I booted the kids from the room after explaining to their teacher why they'd all *lost their minds* and why Dustin wasn't coming back to class just yet. Then I kept my next class out in the hallway until the doody was removed.

I have a silly job.

A Long Day, Pt. 2

September 14 2007

Sheezus, what a day. I went in to work this morning under the assumption, for some reason, that today was going to be a really simple, straightforward day. I'm not at all sure why I did something so foolish, and I should have known better, and I'll never do it again.

Before school starts: I break up not one but *two* fights-in-the-making in the hallway before I even get to my room and shoo the kids off to their homeroom classes. I figure whatever, it's early.

2nd period (note that I have a prep first period): My second period class has earned a fun Friday by collecting five Easy Button presses over the course of the last five weeks of school. These are very simple for me; I explain the rules, turn them loose, and basically ignore them for 42 minutes. They're all happily (and, it must be said, quietly) websurfing away when one of my more annoying kids (he's not special ed, he's just *dumb as hell*, which makes him far more annoying to me for some reason) yells "Why is that guy so fucking fast?" at the top of his lungs, apparently yelling at the game he's playing.

Off to in-school suspension, you silly son of a bitch, for the rest of the day, where he proceeds to immediately lie to the ISS teacher about why he's in the room despite knowing that I'll be over there with the ISS paperwork in minutes. The ISS room is *directly across the hall* from my classroom, so it ain't exactly hard for me to go over there if I need to. Note also that, until today, I had put exactly three kids out of my room in five weeks, none for more than a single class period. I call his mother, waking her up, which pleases me greatly.

3rd period: Has lost their damn minds. I have no other way to describe it; they were just nuts. South Side of Chicago Mr. Siler

131

makes his first appearance of the year as one of my students tries to
tell me that he's too tired to type with both hands. I am, by this point,
not in the mood for goddamned excuses, much less the attitude he
throws back at me when I challenge his stupid assertion. To his
credit, the kid snaps back into his usual form by the time I finish the
ISS paperwork and I end up leaving it next to him as a reminder,
keeping him focused for the rest of the class and in the room where
he belongs. Lunch starts at 10:11. My class is usually the first one
there because the computer lab is substantially closer to the cafeteria
than the other 5th grade classrooms. My kids are so noisy and
obnoxious that we do not arrive at lunch until 10:18, and it takes *four*
tries to get them out of their seats and lined up quietly. In Chicago, I
was used to this sort of nonsense. I haven't seen it from these kids
yet.

4th period is lunch.

5th period: Two kids aren't in the room because they're in the
office. About halfway through class the assistant principal shows up,
returns one, and pulls another kid, apparently trying to get multiple
versions of some sort of story. The returned kid immediately begins
making sure kids #3 and #4 have their stories straight, and is doing
so blatantly enough that I actually saunter over and start taking
notes. A few minutes later, apropos of virtually nothing, one of the
girls blows up at a third party across the room, calling him a "fat
faggot" loudly enough that the AP hears her, from the hallway, with
my door closed.

Bye. That's *two* in ISS for the rest of the day.

My second phone call home of the day. Mom is not remotely
amused.

6th period: As the kids are coming into the room, one of them
pulls me aside and tells me that Billy "had a seizure" during
lunch. Now, I have no paperwork on any epileptics in any of my
classes, and that's kinda something that I *really* ought to know
about. I get class started and pull Billy aside. Yep, he had a fucking
seizure at lunch, but he feels okay now, and it's not exactly his first
time so he's not out of sorts about it or anything. Okay, fine.

The kids discover that they can make their own drills in the
typing program they're using, something I immediately regret
allowing them to do when I discover the phrase "Holy Fuck Ass" in
one girl's self-created drill. I nearly boot her, too, then decide that
she hadn't tried to show any other kids or made a big deal about it

and issue a Stern I Am Not In The Mood For This Shit warning instead. She provides no further problems.

I grab Billy's teacher after class and ask him to send me photocopies of any documentation he has on the kid when he gets a minute.

Teacher *also* has no idea Billy's an epileptic. He didn't even know about the seizure; nobody mentioned it to him. I express surprise that the nurse didn't say anything when Billy got sent back to class. Wrong again; Billy came back with his class. I call the kid over and discover that *he had a seizure and didn't bother to go see the school nurse*. (Note: it was a petit mal, so he just went away for a couple of minutes, meaning that it's not like the lunch staff didn't notice a kid in convulsions on the floor or anything.) I stick an aide in my class for five minutes and escort him to the nurse myself. Christ.

7th period: Their homeroom teacher, thankfully waiting for me with her class, doesn't give me any guff when she finds out why I wasn't there, but mentions that her class is "acting poorly" today. Ah, lovely. I quickly discover why: Lena's back from her suspension. This kid deserves a whole damn essay of her own; needless to say, I spend *much time* wishing I could break my foot off in her ass. It's been very peaceful all week with her gone, and the kids are having trouble readjusting to having Satan's Neediest Little Bastard back in the room with them. She drives me batty, but for the most part this class goes okay.

8th period: Usually, my angels. Caesar calls me over to take a look at the story he's been working on for the last several days. Caesar's nuts, but most of the time he's nuts in a good, smart, entertaining sort of way. When we did one of our career days a couple of weeks ago, he calmly and straightforwardly announced that he planned to rule the world when he grew up. He phrased it *exactly like that*: "I plan to rule the world when I grow up. What must one do (*I swear, that's what he said*) to become a dictator?"

I told him to run as a Republican.

Anyway, I'm reading his story, and ... well, it's *super* special, and the only reason I'm not including it in this collection is that he wrote it and I'm not sure it's actually legal. I make Caesar get out of his chair so that I can sit down to read. He stands behind me. As I turn around, laughing, to talk to him about it, the kid *puts his arm around me and tries to sit in my lap*.

133

What the FUCK. DUDE. GET THE HELL OUT OF MY LAP.

He looks me in the eye and says, again, this is *absolutely fucking true*, "But you're my daddy!"

Uh, no. Not so much.

9th period: Prep. Last period of the day, no kids, no problem, right? Wrong. I'm in my room checking my email and waiting for the day to be over when I hear a ruckus in the hallway. I investigate the nature of the ruckus and discover one of our more hard-assed teachers escorting a kid to the office. The kid's swearing and hollering about what he's gonna do. He ain't gonna do *shit*; he pulled the same stunt last week— yelling and screaming and cussing about who he was gonna fuck up and who wasn't shit while he was getting his 4'10" ass taken to the office. All mouth, absolutely no action. Anyway, the teacher drops him off in the office, explains why he's there, and returns to his classroom, shaking his head at me as he walks past.

Two minutes later, as I'm still in the hallway talking to the ISS supervisor, the kid *leaves the office and starts going back to class*. Now, I know for *damn sure* that he didn't get released, so he left the office without permission. Ah, great, this'll be fun.

We look at each other.

"You wanna handle this or you want me to?"

She glances back in the ISS room. "You can do it."

I walk down the hallway toward him. "You have *one* chance to turn around and walk back."

"I ain't doing shit! Fuck y—"

I used to work on the South Side, bitch. Ain't no punk-ass 4'10" white kid gonna say fuck you to me. I had him spun around before he finished the sentence, hand locked on his elbow, and dragged him back toward the office. He started hollering again. "You can't touch me! I'm gonna—"

I cut him off again. "You ain't gonna do *nothing* except put your butt back into that office and cry. You don't get to swear at me, son, and your short little self doesn't scare me one little bit." And I drag him back to the office. Sure enough, the tears start flowing and he shut his damn stupid mouth. (And am I looking forward to having him in my class next semester? Yep, sure I am.) By the time I got him, there, the principal and AP had come out, and they took over from there. (And before you say anything: No, I'm not worried about repercussions from putting my hands on the kid. There are cameras *everywhere* in the building, and I know *exactly* where they are, and I made sure to intercept him in full view of a camera. I know how to do my job by now, thanks.)

Then I pulled my 6th period kid out of ISS and gave her the Faggot Talk. Whee!

I decided I wasn't doing my usual hall duty at the end of the day. Who the hell knows what would have happened.

This is what we get paid for, folks.

What the Fuck You Gon' Do?

September 20 2007

Note that, at the time this was written, Indiana administered their ISTEP test at the beginning of the school year, not the end of the year, making it even more useless than usual. This timing would change repeatedly over the course of my years teaching in this state.

A note to any future student, born or unborn, who might ever feel the urge to ask me the question "What the fuck you gon' do?": *Don't.*

Is it just me, or is *eleven* just a bit too many standardized tests for a fifth-grader to handle over the course of a week? I gave up entirely on trying to teach today, and threw my classes over to fun days to give the kids a chance to breathe after how brutal their testing schedule has been. They did two 45-minute to an hour tests a day from Monday through Thursday, then did *three* science tests today—two before lunch and one after lunch.

Folks, this is *not* the way to assess what our kids are learning in school. By the end of the week even the *motivated* kids just didn't give a damn anymore. Kids were closing their test booklets after *ten minutes* on tests that were supposed to take 50. And these are not my geniuses I'm talking about. I walked around the room while I was proctoring 2nd hour today, during the first of the three science tests, and I swear I didn't see a single correct answer. What I *did* see was some shockingly shoddy tests; the ISTEP appears to have somewhat lower quality control than the ISAT, because I saw at least two or three questions that were poorly-written enough that it took *me* a minute to figure out what they were talking about (there was something about what would have to happen to make the earth's day longer that I had to read three times to make comprehensible; the question had clearly been rewritten at some point but the editor had left a segment of the initial version still in there) and several typos to boot. When I get asked eight or nine times over the course of a test what *one question* means, I stop blaming my students. And the fact that I can't help them is frustrating as *hell*; I'm not about to get the school accused of cheating by walking a kid through what a question means.

Lovely Big Fun disciplinary events this week included the abovementioned "What the fuck you gon' do?", asked of me by some silly bastard in ISS who wasn't even one of my students and is now suspended, one of my kids stealing some money from one of my special (really, *really* special) ed students and then *helping her look for it*, and some minor bathroom vandalism. Oh, and I had the distinct pleasure of being told by one of the sixth grade teachers that his class is "terrified" of me because they seem to have decided that the blacklight-ink tattoo on my right arm is a self-inflicted burn mark. Which, okay, it's still not completely healed and I get it if you don't know what it is right away, but it doesn't look like a burn.

The terror I'll take, though. The sixth graders appear to be considerably more roughnecky across the board than the fifth graders, so anything that has a chance of making them behave is a good thing. I'm actually pretty glad the one kid in ISS decided to challenge me, because every kid in the room saw my reaction and I suspect they all take me a little more seriously now.

Not a bad week, educationally speaking.

Is That Weed?

November 27 2007

So I'm standing outside my room today, waiting for my 2nd period class, which is actually my *first* class of the day, since I have a prep first hour. They walk around the corner and stop at my door like they're supposed to, and quiet down like they're supposed to, and as they file into my room I get this *incredible* blast of weed stink in my face.

Why do my fifth graders smell like weed?

A couple of minutes of research located the smell squarely on one kid. Have I said around here that I firmly believe some of my students are actually vegetables? When I say that, Chevrolet is the kid I'm thinking of, and the reason I've given him that name entertains me greatly but I can't share it. Now, it's the first time at this school, granted, but this isn't the first time a kid has walked into my class stinking of weed, and I've sent kids to the office with notes that read "He's high as a kite; please deal with this" once or twice before. Chevrolet, on the other hand...

...well, he's never *not* looked high, is what I'm saying. There's not a whole lot behind this kid's eyes *at all*, so he's never gonna look like he's gone away any more than he usually does, y'know? So I told his teacher, mostly in a "walk behind dude and tell me I'm not crazy" kind of way, and *she* took it to the nurse, who pulled him in during third hour and asked him many probing-but-not-obvious questions that got her nowhere and now apparently if I ever notice him smelling of weed again we have to refer him to the social worker. So, fun.

I had a good laugh with the nurse, by the way, when she said that she'd tried to sorta phrase her questions in a subtle way so that

139

Chevrolet didn't realize that he smelled like weed and we'd noticed it. The idea that he'd *realize* something is kinda hilarious. "Dude, you fucking stink of weed, rat out your parents so that we can arrest them" might *still* not clue him in.

ISTEP scores

December 7 2007

Got the ISTEP results back yesterday, and ... *man*, were there some long faces at that faculty meeting. I don't know if the ISTEP is just a lot harder than the ISAT or if it's that Indiana generally takes their tests much earlier in the year or *what*, but *man*, were the test results brutal. I've only had the chance to carefully examine the fifth grade results specifically, mind you, but I believe my kids did the worst of all four grades. The pass rate on the science test was *twenty-five percent*.

Twenty. Five. Fucking. Percent.

By contrast, my kids at my previous school, who had Mr. Irish for science, and as a result had virtually *no science teaching whatsoever*, had pass rates in, I think, the high eighties or possibly the nineties my first year. I should look. (EDIT: A good 40 minutes later, they got a 91.) (EDIT 2: I just looked up my previous school's test results for *last year's* ISAT results, which I'd never actually looked up. They actually did *better* in Reading than the previous year, and jumped fourteen percent from the scores they'd had as sixth graders. I rule. Wonders never cease.)

A few observations should be made here, chief among which is that I can't in good conscience assign any real blame to any of the fifth grade teachers for the scores, since they're based on having the kids in our school for about a month, right after summer break. Granted, that makes the test a decent assessment of what they *remember*, but no assessment whatsoever of what they've *learned*. We're basically finding out what my district's various fourth grade classrooms are like, four months removed, and I'm not convinced that's useful data. Scores in other grades went up in, I

141

think, a linear progression— i.e., sixth graders did better, seventh graders did better than the sixth graders, and the eighth graders did the best at all. That tells me we're doing *something* right in the school.

We're still way below making AYP, though. Way, way below, and this confuses me, because I feel like I'm working with a *much* smarter class of kid this year than I saw at my last school. The vast majority of my kids failed at least one subsection— either English/Language Arts, Mathematics, or Science— and over 40%, I think, failed all three. 75% failed Science, 56% failed English, and 50% failed Math.

That ain't good. Not even a little tiny bit. It's *so* not good, and so out-of-step (pun intended) with what I've observed about my students that the only conclusion I can reasonably draw is that the ISTEP is a *hell of a lot harder* than the ISAT was. I'm not claiming that all of my kids are geniuses, not by a long shot, but hell, they're better than *that*. I have A students, kids who *deserve* to be A students, who still failed a section or two of the test.

And the fifth grade teachers are going to get blamed for the miserable results, despite only having had the kids for a handful of days before they took the tests, and despite the tests taking several hours a day for a *week*, a testing regimen that no adult would *ever, ever, ever put up with*. In a way, I'm *not* surprised by the results, because if you shovel two or three high-stakes tests at a ten-year-old every day for a *week* you shouldn't be surprised if by Friday they're not giving their best effort any longer. Which, guess what, makes it no longer an entirely reliable assessment.

What a surprise.

Bad Teacher Moment, #2

December || 2007

I found another entry for the Bad Teaching Practices file. If you tell a kid to type a word in a particular place, and he asks you, after sixteen weeks of a class that is called Keyboarding, for God's sake, *how* to make that word appear on the screen, do not succumb to the fact that it is eighth hour and you are tired and sort of irritable and not in the mood for what seems like a very dumb question and tell him to bang his head on the monitor until the words appear.

Because if you have *even one* student who is Just That Special, then it will be precisely *that* student who you are talking to, the *one student you have* who is genuinely unable to comprehend the, shall we say, *higher levels* of your wit, and that student will suddenly acquire a vague look of betrayal and horror on his face and then turn away and, very slowly, *actually bang his head on his monitor*. And he will do it *twice* before you stop him, because you will spend the first few moments of the head-banging not sure that you are actually seeing what you are seeing, and wondering what the hell has happened to the world that you thought you lived in, where you understood the basic rules, one of which was *banging your head on computer screens doesn't make words appear,* and so did everyone else. And it will not be sarcasm, he will be doing it because he actually thinks that the adult who he is accustomed to obeying has commanded him to do so, and he should do what adults say.

So, yeah. Don't do that. Ever. It's *really* mean, and it will make you feel bad about yourself for days.

Trust me.

143

Happy and Special

JANUARY 13 2008

It's been a hella busy week. I teach sixth grade now— still computer classes, but not the *same* class, and obviously I've entirely flipped the roster of students I have, with no kids in common at all. The sixth graders? They *scare me.* I know that I've said this at the beginning of semesters before, and occasionally been spectacularly wrong about it. Hell, I've probably been wrong about it *most* of the time. But these kids? By the end of the week, I wanted to put music on in the afternoons because it was so creepily quiet in the room. They're doing exactly what I tell them to do, when I tell them to do it, getting all their work done, all that other good stuff. I've identified a couple of knuckleheads, but I mean that literally— a *couple* of knuckleheads, which means I don't even have one in each class yet.

Have I talked about the Easy Button? I bought one of those Staples Easy Buttons last year, right? And the way I use it in my classes is that if they behave and make my day easy, I push it at the end of class and put a tally mark on the whiteboard. When they get five Easy Buttons, they get a fun day in class. Last semester, my classes got a fun day maybe every two or three weeks. *All six of my classes got fun days on Friday.* That's never happened. There will probably be classes that get them two Fridays in a row.

Have I talked about the trivia question? I put one on the board every Monday, and the answer is due on Thursday. It's optional, there's a little reward on Friday if they answer it. Last semester, I had maybe thirty or forty kids answer it on a heavy week. I probably had seventy correct answers this week. It's going to be a good semester. No, really. I mean it this time.

145

The other weird thing is the way my status as no-longer-a-current-teacher to the fifth graders seems to have magnified my popularity with them. I literally cannot walk down the hallway any longer without attracting *followers*. I'm like fuckin' Jesus in Galilee, kids, and the fact that all the sixth graders now want to talk to me as well makes half of the building into a place where ... well, where I feel very, very special.

The Day of Two Shoes

January 24 2008

I've been a little ... *off* for the last couple of days, and so have many of the people around me. During fifth hour yesterday, one of my students, whose name is not Baker Builder but might as well be, calls me over and points at ... *something* on the screen of his computer.

"What's that?" he asks.

"What do you mean?" I reply, genuinely not certain what he is pointing at.

"That right there. What's the backwards p?"

"That's the letter q, Baker."

To his credit, at least he had the sense to blush and cover his face with his hands for a moment afterwards. The kid— a sixth grader, mind you— can read, as far as I can tell, so I have no reason to believe this was anything other than a brainfart of epic proportions, but ... *damn*. I was feeling pretty good about my nomenclatural and mental superiority to Baker until sixth hour, the very next class, when Katya, one of my quieter students, put up her hand and asked me why I was wearing one brown shoe and one black shoe.

Take note, please, that sixth hour begins at approximately 11:45, and that I'd arrived in the building at 7:30. I had been wearing two completely mismatched shoes for probably slightly over five hours and not only had *I* not noticed, but neither had anyone else. If I worked with adults, I'd be willing to believe that someone had noticed and simply not informed me, but children are not capable of such a thing. In my defense, it's January and I had gotten dressed more or less in the dark, but ... *Jesus.* I really don't know how you

147

miss such a thing. If nothing else, I should have noticed that the *texture* of the shoes was completely different while I was putting them on.

Needless to say, I cracked up, and the entire class rushed the front of the room to take a look at my feet and cackle at me. Only one other student noticed for the rest of the day, and I'm pretty sure she'd been tipped off beforehand. The story had made the rounds among the sixth graders by this morning, naturally, and just about every kid I walked past at the beginning of the day made a noticeable glance down at my feet.

Anonymous Notes and Racism

April 3 2008

I have been sticking my hand in the crazy at work again lately. One would think that, at 31, I would know better than to stick my hand in the crazy. Hands aren't *supposed* to go in the crazy, and adults ought to know to leave the crazy alone. Sadly, giving me such benefit of the doubt would be wrong.

Monday (dear God, was that only *Monday*? Let's pretend it was last week.) I was doing a little bit of photocopying in the teacher work room when I discovered something rather odd sitting on top of the photocopier. A note! An anonymous note, not addressed to me!

DEAR MRS. J, *it read cryptically, except it had her name.* YOU HAVE BEEN SEEN PARKING IN THE VISITOR'S PARKING SPOT. YOU KNOW YOU'RE NOT SUPPOSED TO PARK THERE. THE RULES APPLY TO EVERYONE, MRS. J, WHY DONT THEY APPLY TO YOU?

That was the whole note. The apostrophe in "don't" really was missing, by the way, and I feel like there was one other spelling mistake somewhere, too.

Before I say more, let me state unequivocally that Mrs. J shouldn't be parking in the visitor's parking spot. Not that I *care* if she does, mind you, I just don't want to give the impression that I condone lawbreaking of such serious magnitude. But seriously, folks, an anonymous letter? The anonymous scold letter is probably not actually the lowest form of cowardice known to the human race, but you can *see it* from there, if you know what I mean. I fucking hate anonymous scold letters, and I also hate the people who leave them.

149

That said, I must have been in a bad mood already. So I stuck my hand in the crazy. I took the note and wrote the following on it:

DEAR PERSON,

ANONYMOUS LETTERS ARE FOR JERKS. PLEASE DON'T BE A JERK.

LOVE,

MR. SILER

PS: YOU LEFT THIS ON THE PHOTOCOPIER. DON'T DO THAT EITHER.

PPS: DON'T HAS AN APOSTROPHE IN IT; IN THIS CASE THE APOSTROPHE IS USED TO DENOTE MISSING LETTERS.

And then I taped the note above the photocopier where anyone who walked by would see it. Then I went to find Mrs. J, figuring I should give her the option to tell me not to escalate the crazy. She approved, having received her copy of the note the previous day (why would you photocopy such a thing, do you think?) so I left it. Over the course of the next few class periods, no less than half a dozen teachers walked into my room to either tell me the note was hilarious or to actually *thank me* for leaving it.

And then Mrs. M walked into the work room and saw the note. From what I heard, she immediately began loudly grousing about what a jerk I was to anyone who would listen, then— get this— went and *got the principal*. Who, and again, I wasn't in the room so this is secondhand, took one look at the note, chuckled, and took it off of the wall. It has been several days now and he's said nothing about it to me. Mrs. M, on the other hand, spent the rest of the day telling anyone who would listen that she hadn't written the original note— which is curious, since to the best of my knowledge no one ever accused her of it. She also never confronted me, apparently feeling that calling me a jerk to a third party would suffice.

Funny how that works, ain't it?

(Randomly: Mrs. M is also the teacher who, the Monday after my wedding, insisted to another teacher that I had a son named Glenn who had just graduated from our school two years before. The other teacher, assuming that she must have had me confused with someone else, pointed out that I was only barely old enough to be the father of a sixteen-year-old and that furthermore he'd just been at my wedding literally three days ago and had seen no such human there. Despite what I would think would be fairly ironclad evidence, she held to her story and continued to declare that she knew I had a son.)

On a somewhat more serious note, here's what happened today:

I had to cover another teacher's class for part of first hour because the sub had either been called late or was running late, I'm not sure which. When I got into the room, the principal was in there, giving the standard You Will Not Make the Sub Miserable speech, a speech I gave them my own version of half an hour or so later when I left the room. Now, take note of something: By and large, the fifth and sixth grade teachers in our building (I am specific here only because I barely know any of the upper-grade teachers, as they're nowhere near us in the building, not because I think they act differently) treat everybody's students as their students. I have good reason to either correct or aid any kid in the fifth or sixth grade, because by now they've literally all been in my classroom, but there aren't any 5/6 teachers who will overlook something, good or bad, because the kid in question "belongs" to someone else. Furthermore, our kids are, to put it mildly, somewhat hard on subs.

My point is, it's quite likely that at more than one point during any given day where there's a sub in a room, some of the other teachers are gonna poke their heads in and see what's going on.

Fast forward to lunchtime. I've already walked my own kids down to the cafeteria and am heading back to the staff lounge for my prep when I walk past the sub, Mrs. R, taking her kids to the cafeteria. I noted that they appeared to be in a reasonable approximation of a line and asked her how they were doing.

"The boys are doing fine," she said, and then launched into a somewhat incomprehensible rant about the girls. Apparently two girls had stolen something, and then three other girls had gotten involved in it somehow, and yaaaah yaaaah yaaaah everyone treats me like I'm incompetent. I couldn't really figure out the details, but she was really pissed at the three girls. Then, seemingly out of nowhere, she drops this line on me:

"I got called a racist at [local high school] the other day. I'm *not* a racist. It's just that all these black girls have attitudes."

Well, fuck *me* sideways. How could *that* possibly get misinterpreted?

At this point, something, I'm not sure what, happened that distracted me from responding, which was probably a good thing. I

151

completed my trip to the teacher's lounge, at which point I got the rest of the story— the three girls had a) witnessed the theft of items from the (absent) teacher's desk, b) informed the sub, c) been ignored by said sub, and then d) reported the incident via handing a note to another 6th-grade teacher when she came by to check on the class. At which point the expected righteous hell broke loose, and the thieves in question were put into in-school suspension for the day.

The sub was pissed at the three kids that did the right thing, is what I'm saying here, and furthermore was pissed at the teacher for "treating her like an incompetent" by *coming by to see if they could help her out*. If it were not for her actual, real-life incompetence at her position, there wouldn't have been anything to complain about.

At that point, I excused myself to the cafeteria, where I shanghaied the three girls in question and gave them my I'm Not Mad At You, but Don't You Dare Mess Up For the Rest of the Day speech, then went back to the teacher's lounge, where chattering had continued in my absence.

Not much later, the sub came into the lounge and started up a conversation with one of our permanent building subs (who is, himself, also an incompetent, but that's a whole other story, one I don't remember if I've told here or not) wherein I heard her declare that "the two blond white girls were getting all the blame" and in ISS, while the "three black girls" were getting away scot-free with ... well, with their *whistleblowing*, I guess.

And I stuck my hand in the crazy again.

I tapped her on the shoulder and asked her if I could speak to her for a moment. There was someone in the work room right next to the lounge, so I walked out into the (empty) hallway to have the conversation there. Knowing full well, incidentally, that there would be security cameras pointed at me while I was talking.

"Ma'am, I'm going to say this as respectfully as I possibly can. Do not, under any circumstances, ever refer to any of my children by their race like that in my building again."

She interrupted me. "I didn't do that."

"Yes, you did. Less than half an hour ago you told me that your problem was that my black girls had attitudes, and I just heard you complaining that the white girls were punished."

"No I didn't. It wasn't like that."

Not much later, I would discover that she'd complained to another teacher that I'd stuck my finger in her face— not true at all, and I have the security cameras to prove it. She would also complain that I'd spoken to her like she was one of the students, which ... well, frankly, that's true, because this is how I react when people lie to me about stupid shit no matter how old they are:

"Yes, ma'am, you did. I just heard you. 'The white blonde girls are in ISS.' Those were your exact words."

"No, I didn't say that."

"Yes, ma'am, you did. Do not do it again. Do not refer to my students in those terms again in this building."

And so on and so forth, with me saying variations of the above, until she stormed off, saying that she'd not continue subbing in this building because of the attitudes the sixth-grade teachers had. Note that this is fine with me.

Note also, just for the record, that I am aware that it is unlikely that she knew everyone's names, and that in certain circumstances saying "the black girl" is simply the easiest way to identify someone. I believe that she crossed a threshold in a number of ways, and I should point out that in a very fundamental fashion we *can't have* subs in our building who blithely identify a group of perceived troublemakers as "the black girls" under pretty much any circumstances whatsoever, particularly when it's been several hours since the offense and she's had plenty of time to pick up their names. One kid overhears that shit, it gets to the parents, and we're in a *world* of trouble. I can't, at the moment, decide if I was out of line for saying anything to her. (Although note, just for the record, that at no point did I raise my voice. I *lower* my voice when I'm *really* pissed.)

Anyway, later on, when the class was in my room, I discovered that she'd started crying during eighth hour and had told the class that she was upset because I'd called her a racist. Which, first of all, isn't true— I was careful to avoid that word, and furthermore I don't give a damn if she's a racist, I only give a damn if she's fucking with my kids— and second, even *if* it's true, you don't bring that shit up in front of the students. I told them flat-out that I wasn't going to discuss a conversation I'd had with another teacher with them.

I mean, seriously, does anybody doubt that I could start a public scene if I had the mind to? That ain't something you half-ass.

Luther M. Siler

On the way out of the building at the end of the day, I told the principal I wanted to have a word with him in the morning when he had the time, since I was too tired and pissed off to rehash the whole thing just then. We'll see what he knows when I come in and what he has to say.

(2015 note: The principal had not a thing to say.)

Cameras and Trivia

April 26 2008

The following are all things that actually happened to me on Friday, although one will require a diversion to Monday to fully explain:

1) I do a little trivia contest every week, right? There's a question on the board when they walk in, and they have until Thursday to answer it, pretty much by any means available, which generally means that one or two kids bother to research the answer and the rest copy it from those one or two. This tends to have hilarious consequences when those one or two are wrong; I'll get 20 answers with the wrong word spelled exactly the same wrong way, which leads directly to me making fun of them in class.

Anyway, the reward for getting the trivia question right is a little piece of candy on Friday. It's not a huge deal, but the kids seem to enjoy it. I usually have those little Hershey Mini bars— the ones with Krackels and Mr. Goodbars— and sometimes there's some mini Snickers or Three Musketeers in there.   This Friday, after I've passed out some candy to some of the kids in the class, one of my girls comes up to me and asks if she can exchange the piece of candy she picked out. I shoot her a quizzical look— I don't *care*, mind you, it's just unusual— and ask her why. She shows me that she's grabbed a Snickers and says "I just got spacers in my teeth," (insert wide, metallic grin here) "and I can't have these."

I do not think before I speak, and the thought in my mind comes out phrased in the worst imaginable way, especially considering I'm talking to a twelve-year-old girl.

"Ah, you can't have nuts in your mouth, right?"

155

A split-second later it hits me that I just said what I said, and I sorta freeze.

Pleasedon'tgetitpleasedon'tgetitpleasedon'tgetit.

Because I really don't want to deal with that.

She smiles and says "No, it's the sticky stuff. I can't have anything sticky in my mouth."

I goddamn near had a seizure.

2) As I'm ushering the last group of kids out of the building to their bus at the end of the day, one of my favorite kids from last semester comes running up to me, not quite in tears but close to it, a digital camera in her hand. She hands it to me— shoves it into my hands, more accurately— and explains that her camera's broken and she doesn't know how to fix it and (picture this being delivered at high speed as we walk to the bus) *my parents are gonna be really mad that I broke my camera and I really want the pictures on it Mr. Siler can you fix my camera over the weekend and give it to me pleeeeeeeeeeease?*

I glance at it, and it looks like the lens isn't closed all the way like it ought to be, but there's no visible indication of damage, so I make a poor decision and agree to look at the thing and try to pull the pictures out of it, for which there is much outpouring of gratefulness. I had to rush from job to job, but I found a few minutes to take a look at the thing, the highlight of which was my managing to completely *snap off* the formerly merely-not-closing lens cover while not actually doing anything to fix the camera. My diagnosis: It beeps three times when you turn it on and then it shuts back off. Why does it do that? Hell, I don't know.

I did manage to get the lens back on— closed, this time— so it looks like I've sort of fixed it, and I've been entirely unable to figure out what the beeping means other than *you're fucked.* There isn't anything useful on Panasonic's website, and searching through other technical assistance sites only finds me other people who have discovered that they are fucked when their camera beeps three times and then shuts back off. I also had a lovely moment while pulling the pictures off of the SD card in the camera, when I suddenly realized what year it was and what I was doing and began wondering if I was inadvertently committing some sort of felony by copying the pictures to my hard drive. I remember who I am, and what my luck is generally like. There's *totally* child porn on this fucking thing, isn't there?

No, as it works out, although there are a couple of obvious self-portraits in poses that ... well, *squick*, for lack of a better word. But I neither need to report anything to the authorities nor should I be reported myself.

This is a good thing.

Scabies, and the Consumption of Pussy

April 27 2008

There have been two cases of scabies among the sixth graders
in the past week. The first student got it, I assume, by living in a
hellhole and rarely bathing, and the second student, who generally
has proper hygiene but has shown herself to have amazingly poor
judgment, got it from the first student being her boyfriend. The
problem is that the second student is crazy popular. I'm expecting
half the sixth grade to be sporting mite infestations by
tomorrow. It'll be wonderful fun for everybody.

Something else that happened on Friday, although not to
me: There was a lovely little eruption of nastiness in Mr.
Rideswithmetoschool's class, when several of his students declared a
third party to be a Vicious, Horrible Slut because she had let an ex-
boyfriend of one of the girls eat her pussy. Out loud. In
class.(*) There are a number of issues here, obviously, not least of
which seems to be the fact that I would think getting your pussy
eaten would be a *good* thing.

So Mr. R and I are discussing this on the way home from
school, as well as the various fallouts from the arguments and their
effect on the rest of the day, when a thought occurs to me: I never
came anywhere near to eating pussy in the seventh grade. Neither, to
the best of my knowledge, did anybody I know. I'm at the point
where I assume that any and all of my students are sexually active. (I
used to believe that the nerdy, filthy, and/or socially inept kids were
probably still virgins. After Scabies Boy, I can't make that
assumption any longer.)

159

Here's the question: What are these kids' children going to do to horrify their parents when they are in seventh grade? Are we going to start hearing about scat parties in seventh-grade classrooms? Because, seriously, I can't come up with much other than eating each other's shit that would qualify as sufficiently parent-frightening considering the various degradations these kids are already perpetrating on each other. There's got to be *something*, right?

Maybe it'll be virginity. That would be hilarious, if the next generation after these kids decided to horrify their parents by *refusing* to have sex with each other. I think they should try that.

(*)The declaration of slutitude was out loud in class, not the pussy-eating. Ordinarily I'd fix the unclear syntax, but it entertains me, so I'm going to leave it in and see if I terrify anyone.

On Periods

MAY 5 2008

Speaking of female anatomy, here's what happened Thursday and Friday. On Thursday, I repeatedly noticed that one of my favorite kids from last semester appeared to be having a really bad day. She was pale, looked tired as hell, and several times looked like she'd been crying. When I saw her at the end of the day, still looking on the verge of tears, I pulled her aside as she was walking out to the bus and asked her what was wrong. Initially, she denied that anything was wrong, which as a teacher sets off my alarm bells. Kids are shitty liars about whether something's bothering them, and if they're clearly upset and denying it it rarely means something good.

So I pulled the "don't give me that" move, right? "You've been upset all day, kid. Don't tell me nothing's wrong."

She'd just started her period. Like, her *first* period.

Ah. Okay. Uh, good luck with that, then? I'll just piss off.

As if that wasn't bad enough, on Friday I had to alert not one, but *two* different girls of the presence of fairly substantial bloodstains in less than optimal locations. I'd expressed some surprise to my wife that such a thing was even possible; I would think that I would *notice* if there was fucking blood leaking into my underwear, but apparently the ability to not notice such a thing is among the feminine mysteries. Luckily, I'm apparently the only male teacher in the building able to alert a female to such a thing without causing a meltdown, and both the girls popped off to the nurse and returned later, wearing different pants and looking none the worse for wear.

I'm just that awesome. Unless, maybe, I'm *triggering* these things, in which case I'm not sure what to think.

161

...and here's what happened *today*: the web is heavily filtered at my school, right? As one would expect, I think, for a middle school. The filtering's not local to the school; it's corporation-wide. When you go to a website that hits the filter, it pops up a page that will allow you to put in a username and password to override the block. I was never told what the username or the password were despite *specifically requesting them* on more than one occasion.

I had a kid come up to me today and tell me that so-and-so in the class had figured out the username and password. I scoffed at the idea, but said I'd keep an eye on the kid anyway. Sure enough, he was somewhere that I *knew* was supposed to be blocked by the filters. He confessed readily enough; he'd heard the password from someone else and had tried it to see if it worked.

Are you ready for this? Imagine the *stupidest username and password combination you can* for a school computer. "School," right? Close. Both the username and the password are *computer*. That's literally the second stupidest combination that exists. (Third stupidest would be "password," just for the record.) And the entire damn building is going to know the password by tomorrow morning unless the muckety-mucks change it.

I sent the following email to Head Computer Muckety-Muck lady:

My students, who are not by and large especially clever kids, have figured out that the username "computer" and the password "computer" will allow you to override a blocked website. I literally laughed in the face of the first kid who told me about it, because I couldn't believe that the password would be something so easily guessed.

We may want to change that.

I followed that up with a similarly-toned message to the staff informing *them* of the situation, because now, any kid on a computer in a classroom could literally be viewing anything he damn well pleases at any time, and because of the way the filters work, once they're turned off, there's *no way to turn them back on on that computer for an hour.*

Just ... fuck ... stupid ... *hurts.*

Want the kicker? I just logged into my email to get that email to Muckety-Muck, and there's an email from my AP to me telling me to come see him in the morning about the emails sent to the staff and

Muckety. If this somehow gets turned around to *me* being in trouble I'm gonna kick somebody's ass.

The ISTEP Video

September 14 2008

ISTEP testing starts tomorrow. Last year I commented on how laid-back the approach to standardized testing is at my building compared to the obscene pressure placed on us in Chicago, and even though we've had a change of administration I don't really feel like much is different in that respect this year. I'm feeling some pressure personally, but it's all leftover and internal. Nobody's breathing over my shoulder.

The interesting thing— have I mentioned this?— is that the state of Indiana is switching from a fall-administered ISTEP to a spring-administered ISTEP this year, which means that we get to take the thing *twice*. I'll be honest here. I haven't done my very damn best to make sure the media tech kids are prepared for this test, and that's because I know how this game is played. My job this year— the thing that will decide if the media tech class gets a second year or not— is whether my students demonstrate *growth* over the course of the school year, primarily as viewed through the lens of their test scores. It is, therefore, not in my best interests or the best interests of the class for them to do spectacularly well on the fall edition of the test, because high fall scores mean that the bar to jump over in the spring is *that much higher*. I don't want them to do *poorly*, but I'd be perfectly happy with scores roughly around what they got last year. That way, when they blow the fucking thing away in the spring, I look that much better.

Stupid? Yes. Slightly unethical? Possibly, although I think there's an argument to be had there. But, as I said, after seven years of this shit I know how the game is played.

One neat thing did happen, though, that I should mention, and I'm amazed that I haven't found time to talk about this yet— the boss came up to me as I was ushering the 8th graders out of the gym at the end of the day on the Friday before last and says "Hey, do you think the media tech class could put together an ISTEP video?"

I thought about it for a second.

"Sure. Not during class, though, because we're doing our own ISTEP prep right now, but if I can do it as an after-school activity, that would work."

I sent home permission slips on Tuesday, wrote the script Wednesday afternoon, nine of my kids stayed after school for two hours to shoot the thing, and I spent Wednesday night and part of Thursday editing it all together into a concise little six-minute package. I burned the thing to eight or nine DVDs and on Friday every single kid in the building had a chance to view our little ISTEP video. They are apparently going to put it on a loop in the office this week, and the boss has made noises about sending it to the superintendent.

My media tech class is that awesome.

Trouble T-Roy

OCTOBER 29 2008

Today? Sucked. I had assigned lunch detentions to three-count-'em-*three* different kids for three different ridiculousnesses by *seven forty five* in the morning, which for those of you not keeping track is a full ten minutes before first hour actually begins. Granted, one of those was in my official role as Bus Guy and so it probably shouldn't count (bus driver does the write-ups; I'm just the prosecutor) but if you thought I was sick and tired of telling the damn kids to quit running in the hallway already, you probably didn't want to see me after watching one of them take a header when she got tangled up in somebody's damn feet.

I had amassed nine referrals to in-school suspension or the office by 1:15 in the afternoon. Nine referrals generally means I've had a bad *month*, and I don't think I've come close to that in a single day since leaving Chicago. Ordinarily, with two prep periods to close the day out, even if I've had a long day, I still get some time to cool down before I get home.

Hah.

Fire drill. As a member of the administrative team (Have I mentioned that? I'm on the administrative team.) I have a supervisory role during fire drills, which means that I monitor one of the exit doors and call back to the office when the building has been cleared. The fire drill was right after the beginning of eighth hour. I knew that one of the teachers who usually uses my door had taken her class to the computer lab, and that another was on a prep. Still, when only one class of kids (out of what was supposed to be five) walked out my door, I waited a good thirty seconds before sounding the all-clear, assuming after that much time had passed that whatever

167

other class hadn't come out must be somewhere else in the building as well— the library, perhaps.

Turns out, they were still in the classroom. The teacher— a *veteran teacher*, mind you— had decided that they weren't behaving, so he *hadn't taken them out of the building.* Which ... holy fucking *hell*, is that the wrong decision to make. As embarrassing as it is (and I've had to do this) to lead a bunch of obnoxious, shrieking banshee assholes out of a building during a fire drill, you still *do it*, because, fuck, it ain't like they give advance warnings on these things. Chances are if the fire alarm goes off, yeah, it's probably a drill. But that doesn't mean you *ignore* it.

And, for that matter, I kinda dropped the ball as well, because I'd sounded the all-clear when it wasn't clear yet. If there had actually been a fire, nobody would have known that that entire class wasn't out of the building, and I need to sit down with my boss and find out precisely what my responsibilities are in that type of situation in the future.

Already a bad day, right?

Pfah.

When I went outside to wave the single class that had exited my door back in, I let the door close behind me. Which promptly locked, which meant that I had to radio into the office to have somebody come let us in. The AP came by to let us in, and both of our radios squawked that he was needed in a classroom. Generally, when the AP is paged to a classroom, it's bad news. Because I am stupid, I tagged along. As it turned out, one of my special ed 5th graders, who I will call ... hmm ... Troy, because it entertains me to do so, was in the middle of a full-scale meltdown, throwing chairs and desks around, swearing and screaming, and, oh, incidentally, had also refused to leave the building during the fire drill, because he'd already been in Meltdown Mode when it happened.

Now, understand something: Troy's maybe four foot *two*, and closely resembles an ambulatory potato with a perfectly round head and no neck. He is in fifth grade and still wears underoos. I know this because he has not mastered the use of belts and his pants do not fit, and despite numerous attempts by staff members to *buy him* new pants, which would include things like buttons and working zippers, which his current pants lack, his mother "doesn't accept charity," which is redneck for "hates her kids." He is perhaps the least intimidating human being I have ever seen in my life, and hearing him scream "Fuck you you stupid fucker! I'll fuck-kill you!" at me, which he did, is less enraging than it is *comedy*.

Well, the AP managed to get Troy out of the classroom without actually touching him, but as soon as he got into the hallway, he bolted, and by "bolted," I mean that a grandmother with a walker could probably have caught him, since he's hugely out of shape and has very short legs. That said, he made it out of the building before the decision was made that tackling him or physically returning him to the building was authorized. I didn't bother running after him, because the field around our building that he was running through is very large, and I figured there was little to no chance that he'd make it across the whole thing without having to stop for breath. Sure enough, by the time I got to him, he'd run out of gas, but had still managed to wrap his hands and arms around an incongruously-placed wooden pole in the middle of the field.

Long story short: fireman's carry, dead thrashing weight, assault charges on the kid for punching and kicking the janitor, who was backing me up, and for taking a few swings at and spitting on me, handcuffs, absolute bugshit freakout in the back of the police car requiring further restraints, referral to our local youth mental health center, possible jail time, absolute certainty of immediate expulsion. Spending ten minutes holding an enraged, screaming, swearing, completely out-of-control eleven-year-old down in the mud and doing your best to avoid his teeth, because the alternative is to let him run into traffic and the cops aren't here yet? Isn't fun. At all. And I don't know how it is that I'm always the one stupid enough to get dragged into this shit.

I was also pissed on today, but at least that was by a *dog*.

Hopefully tomorrow will be better.

Wait, What?

NOVEMBER 18 2008

Two things that I do not understand: First, how it is possible that at 1:04 AM last night I was still tossing and turning, but that by 3:12 AM last night I had managed to have a full-blown nightmare complete with *multiple acts*, and second, how it is possible that one of my students managed to come to school yesterday with an ejaculating penis shaved into the side of his head without some adult in his home noticing and doing something about it.

The Day of Many Fights

December 11 2008

It has been another relatively shit week at work, where my classes themselves have actually been okay, but stuff from either the outside world or the rest of the building keeps intruding and messing my shit up. There were no less than three fights in the building today, and I was somehow involved in all three of the fucking things. The first involved one of my kids from my class, who apparently snapped and beat the hell out of another kid who had been harassing him for, according to him, weeks. He hadn't said a single word about it to me or anybody else beforehand, of course, because it's much better to let shit fester for weeks and then do something that gets you suspended until fucking January than it is to actually tell an adult when somebody's bothering you.

The second fight involved two girls who were actually fighting and another nine or ten assholes who knew about it, probably set it up in advance, and all made sure to be in the bathroom when it happened. I wasn't around for this one— it was on the other side of the building from my classroom— but I got called into the office in my capacity as Not Really An Administrator At All but What the Hell Let's Make This His Job Anyway to help review the security tapes and identify the various participants. I'm pretty sure that one of the girls in the fight didn't especially want to be there, since the hardest girl to identify was the one literally dragging her into the bathroom. The other one was the one who was letting her boyfriend pimp her out for lunch money last year, if that gives you any idea of the caliber of the individuals we're talking about here.

During seventh hour, the first of my preps, I pulled another of my kids out of one of her classes to talk to her one-on-one for a few minutes. She's not really been acting like herself for the last few weeks, and she's well-known enough in the building that there has been no small amount of speculation among the staff about what was going on. It was suggested to me early on that she was pregnant, a suggestion that I didn't believe but has been preying on my mind mercilessly ever since. I've got her first hour, so if she was getting sick in the morning, I'd know about it— but she does have, for lack of a better word, a bit of a pooch that makes the speculation understandable. However, she had the pooch last year. She's just built that way, apparently. Anyway, the conversation started with an open-ended question ("What's been bugging you lately?") which led into a tale of Divorce and Possible Unwelcome Parental Reconciliation and Moving Away and Moving Back Woe that I won't get into, along with a dose of My Best Friend's Been Fucked Up Lately. (No, the best friend's not her; she named names.) I didn't cop to the pregnancy rumors but I did ask her point-blank how things were going with her boyfriend, which led to her eyes lighting up and the first genuine smile of the entire conversation— not the reaction one might expect from a pregnant thirteen-year-old. If she's pregnant, she's also the best liar in the world, and I don't think she's either.

The last of the three fights was after school, while the 7th and 8th graders were waiting in the gym for the buses to show up. It was between the worst kid in the building and another 8th grader, a kid who a year or two ago would probably have been on that list but who has made pretty impressive strides in getting his rather formidable temper under control and his grades into at least a vague semblance of acceptable. She was the aggressor in every way; she attacked him, she took the two of them down onto the bleachers, she was the one who somehow managed to kick me in the fucking head on the way down, and she's the one getting expelled. Me and another teacher managed to pull the two of them apart, the gym teacher somehow succeeding in calming the kid who got attacked down, a feat that would have been flatly impossible last year, and probably would have required handcuffs.

And then there was half an hour of doing paperwork, with more to come tomorrow morning, since I made the mistake of mentioning the kick to the principal and now I have to file an accident report in addition to everything else. And once again the entire fucking student body has seen me put my hands on somebody. Fuck an administrative license; one of these days some fucker is going to have to give me a *badge*.

Remember, like, two weeks ago, when I said I was as relaxed as I'd ever been at that point in the year and I thought that I could go another month or two before winter break?

That was a fucking stupid thing to say.

ADDENDUM: I forgot to mention this yesterday, but my favorite part of the day actually happened well *after* the third fight, where I was in the office talking over what had happened with the principal and one of the office secretaries, when some other dude (Parent? Grandparent? No idea) began going on and on about how Oh God The Schools Are So Bad Nowadays, that We Must Put Up with Such Things. I wasn't particularly in the mood for glittering generalities and was even less in the mood for his particular brand of The Past is Always Better than Now, so I injected a bit of STFU into my voice and pointed out that we had more fights at my high school in an average week than we have at my current school in a month, and that my father *still* occasionally talks about what he calls "race riots" at his own high school.

He blew me off to go into a rant about how we shouldn't need security cameras in schools, at which point I noticed the confederate flag tattooed on his hand and decided it was probably best for me to get as far away from him as I could before I decided to introduce him to what *adult* violence looks like.

"Thank you for helping me."

December 17 2008

I've been meaning to tell this story for a few days, and I ought to do it now before it falls out of my head: last week I wrote about the Day of Many Fights, right?

The next day, that Friday, I went looking for the kid who had been attacked in the fight. I said this before, but let me repeat it: every time, and by "every time" I mean *every single time* I saw this kid last year he had a snarl on his face, and more often than not he was swearing at someone about something or another. It's probably not literally accurate to say that he was the angriest kid I've ever encountered, but top 10 (out of, remember, hundreds— I've been teaching for seven years, and for most of that time I've had all or most of the school among my students) wouldn't be stretching it too much. I can't count the number of fights I *remember* him being involved in last year; suffice it to say that the only reason he wasn't expelled was that he was special ed, at least partially for his anger issues, and it's extremely difficult to expel a special ed student.

I left out some detail when I said that "somehow, the gym teacher managed to calm him down" in that story. The way I pulled the two kids apart was by grabbing Premiere (not his name; close enough) by his elbows and then basically rolling away from the other girl, basically using my own weight to my advantage. The problem with this was that once I had the two of them separated, Premiere was *on top of me,* with me stuck in between two of the seats on the bleachers. I changed my grip on his elbows to a lock around his chest and held on for dear life, mostly because he was struggling like hell to get away from me.

177

Luther M. Siler

Then the gym teacher came over to talk to him, and something astounding happened: he stopped fighting, and said to me, in a *perfectly calm voice*, "I'm okay. Let me go." Not, like, Crazytown lemme-go-or-I'm-kicking-your-ass-too mode. Calm. So I let him go, and, lo and behold, he did not take advantage of his newfound freedom to go after the other kid again.

Long story short: I went to his room to congratulate the kid for managing to calm himself down and for, basically, doing the right thing at more or less every turn during the fight. I cannot emphasize enough how impossible this situation would have been last year.

I stuck my head into his classroom before homeroom started, made eye contact with him across the room, and waved him over to the door. Before I said a *single word* to him, the first words out of his mouth?

"Thank you for helping me yesterday."

Sometimes shit works out right in this job.

School Dances

December 18 2008

We had a school dance yesterday, sorta. The only way that the Student Council could get our principal to agree to the dance was if it was held during school hours and in uniform, which means that, because of the way our schedule works, the seventh and eighth graders got about forty minutes for their dance during seventh hour and the fifth and sixth graders got about forty minutes for *their* dance during eighth hour. Those two hours are normally my prep periods; however, since I am awesome, I girded my loins and added myself to Club Chaperone for both of the dances.

The seventh and eighth graders stood around, too busy being cool to have fun, and spent most of their time complaining about how lame everyone else but them was. The fifth and sixth graders had a *blast*.

In case you were wondering, the following is one of the greatest regrets/mysteries/wonders of my life: I am, for better or worse, *exceptionally popular* with females between the ages of ten and fourteen. Popularity is generally a good thing, of course, but I am left with two problems: First, that if I had figured out whatever the fuck it is that's making me so awesome when I actually *was* between ten and fourteen, my life would have gone very, very differently than it has, and second, that whatever magic I can work on the preteen set utterly evaporates once they turn eighteen, and by the time they're 21 it's gone *negative*.

Well, with two exceptions. Maybe my wife, too, although I'm not completely convinced that she likes me. But those are the *only* ones.

179

Anyway. I had the following conversation, with a four foot nothing fifth grader I refer to as Pixiestick most of the time, about halfway through the dance.

"Mr. Siler! You're not dancing!"

"I don't dance. Ever."

"You need to dance. Now."

"I'm not going to dance."

"I said you were going to dance! Start dancing!"

At this point, she grabbed my wrists and began pumping them up and down in a vague approximation of someone doing, hell, I don't know, the Walking Run or the Cabbage Soup or whatever damn thing the kids are doing nowadays.

"Your feet aren't moving."

"They don't do that. I'm lucky I can walk right. I don't dance."

At this point, all hell broke loose. She spotted a group of about nine or ten of her classmates and decided to enlist them in making me dance. Seconds later, I was surrounded by a swarm of gyrating females— a feat I would have been proud of were it not for the fact that they were all *eleven* and that none of them were much taller than Pixiestick.

Fuck, I thought. I'm going to jail.

I'm not exactly sure how I escaped.

First hour today, the last day of school before winter break, and I'm going over the pictures taken at the dance with my SuperAwesome class so that we can pick good ones to use in the yearbook. This was a bit of an impromptu activity; what was actually going on was that all of them were crowded around my desk looking at my laptop. We're talking about maybe fifteen kids here, and the space behind my desk is *not* large, so when I say "crowded around" I mean it literally, with everybody sort of leaning on everybody else and at least two heads draped over my shoulders in a way that would ordinarily make me somewhat uncomfortable. There were about 250 pictures taken at the dances by the kids in my class, so it took several minutes to go through them all. Once I was done, I commanded everyone to get away from me so that I could breathe. One of my sixth graders looks at me and says the following:

"Mr. Siler, can I have a kiss?"

A brief moment of absolute frozen terrifying silence. Then I realize what she's talking about.

"Christ, <student name,> can you make sure to use the word *Hershey's* the next time you ask me that?"

She'd given me a Hulk mug full of cherry Hershey's Kisses for Christmas, see. And she wanted one. She just hadn't thought it through. Naturally, all hell broke loose, as the kids found the situation *completely the greatest thing ever*, and I spent the rest of first hour with 12- and 13-year-olds, female *and* male, asking me for kisses.

(The Hulk thing? Is hilarious. I had a Hulk bank on my desk at the beginning of the year, just for the hell of it, a sort of "You wouldn't like me when I'm angry" sort of thing. Then I got a foot-high action figure to go with it. I now have *seven* Hulk-related items on my desk, the other five all being gifts from either students or other teachers. Very soon I'm going to have to invest in a shelf.)

I have a silly job.

I Break Up Another Fight

March 4 2009

Broke up another fight today. This is the third time in the last week or, more precisely, the third fight out of the last two Wednesdays, which I don't quite get. This one was especially fun; the instigator took a flying leap off of the bleachers to punch the kid he was attacking in the eye, knocking him down, then jumped on top of him and started choking him. There were thirty or forty kids in between me and them and they were all trying to get out of the gym, so I had to wade through them in order to pull them apart. In the process of trying to separate them, I tripped over another kid behind me, falling *on top of him*—luckily not particularly hurting him in the process— and then had to pry Kid A's hands off Kid B's throat.

Let me make something clear: we were dealing with attempted fucking murder here, not a fight. Once I got the two of them apart I basically *carried* the first little shit into the office, where I planted him in a chair and warned him— charmingly, right in front of a couple of parents— that if he dared to even *think* of moving out of the chair I was going to put my hands on him again.

I don't know exactly what I meant by that, and that frightens me. Luckily, it frightened *him*, too. I was ready for basically any level of resistance, but according to the staff in the office the boy literally didn't move a muscle until the principal came and got him.

This was a fifth grader, by the way; they both were. Ten, maybe eleven years old. His brother, a sixth grader (although he should be in eighth) was expelled earlier last semester for bringing bullets to school. Feel free to imagine what their home life is like.

I think I have PTSD.

I've joked about it before, and I swear I'm not trying to compare whatever's going on in my head to what soldiers experience except by borrowing the term for convenience's sake, but I really, *really* don't like the place I go to whenever I have to break these damn fights up. Two years of stress and bullshit from Chicago hit me *all at once* whenever they happen, and the adrenaline has literally left me shaking. If I manage to shake off the bad mood, it generally takes at least a couple of hours. This has been a good job for me, and I don't like the stress and anger level that I've been experiencing lately at all. I thought I left that behind in Chicago, and I *definitely* thought I left it behind once our administration changed last winter. For the last couple of weeks, it's all been back. Except, like, worse, because all at once.

One of the kids last week punched me in the chest; I still have the bruise, although it's faded enough that it'll be invisible in another day or two. I think if someone's dumb enough to hit me in the face, it's going to be adults pulling me off of him instead of me pulling him off someone. And then there will be jail. I'm making an appointment with a union lawyer in the very near future, because I need to know exactly what my rights/responsibilities/liabilities are in these situations. I'm having nightmares about some lawyer listing the number of times I've put my hands on kids at work in front of a jury (Bare minimum this year? Six times.) and I really don't want to think about what could have happened if, say, I'd landed on that third kid's head and not his legs or whatever part it was. I'd like to be able to simply say that I'm not going to intervene in these things any longer, but I know the truth— I don't have that in me— and if I hadn't intervened today, the second kid would have been unconscious *at best* by the time another adult got over to them.

I need a fucking vacation, people.

In Which They Cannot Count

March 9 2009

The following is true, if completely ridiculous:

The activity I did with my fifth graders today takes precisely half an hour. However, my classes are longer than that. I start a few minutes late (I need to take attendance, explain what's going on, whatever) and then end a few minutes early. I have a set of flash cards that I use in situations where I need to kill a few minutes. They're numbered cards, bound at the bottom, with six questions on one side and the answers on the other, right? So I start by asking the kids to pick a number for one batch of the cards then pick a question to ask. It goes like this, ideally:

"Blabbity, pick a number between 95 and 135."

"130."

I look at the questions and pick something that is either already limited-choice or I can limit, since they're only fifth graders and I don't want this to be terribly difficult.

"Is the First Lady's office in the West Wing or the East Wing of the White House?"

"Ummm ... the East Wing?"

"That's right. Go get a piece of candy."

Or, alternately, I tell them they're wrong and pick another kid for another question.

Today, this is what happened:

"Kid, pick a number between 95 and 135."

"90."

(I assume kid hasn't heard me.)

"Between 95 and 135, Kid Who Probably Didn't Hear Me."

(Kid's forehead wrinkles and lips purse.)

"80?"

(At this point, I'm getting annoyed.)

"This is not the hard part, Kid Who's Running Out of Chances. Pick a number between 95 and 135."

"92."

"You're kidding me, right?"

Kid gets visibly upset. There are tears. I don't care. They do not get to pretend this is hard, and I am *desperately tired of guessing* right now.

"I don't know! Pick somebody else!" Pandemonium in the room.

I point at another kid, still not entirely sure what the hell is going on.

"140!"

"JESUS CHRIST, PEOPLE. THEY COVER COUNTING IN PRESCHOOL. BETWEEN 95 AND 135."

And then, finally, on the *fifth* try, one of my kids successfully pulls this difficult trick of "pick a number between this number and this other number" off correctly.

I do not know what this nonsense is, but I cannot fix it.

Body Fluids

MARCH 11 2009

Let's begin by talking about my dogs. Both of them refuse to go outside when it's raining, a fact which is annoying nearly all the time, but can be especially problematic when it rains all day long like it did yesterday. Just before we went to bed, my wife actually had to go so far as to drag the dog out into the front yard so that she would pee.

"She" being the dog, not my wife, obviously.

A few minutes after we went to bed, we heard some whining from the kitchen. Both dogs had just been outside, so there was bellowing for silence from the bedroom, which they eventually complied with.

This morning, literally less than a minute after I woke up, I had to clean *dog shit* from the floor in my kitchen. Now, as picking up dog shit inside my house goes, it actually wasn't bad; mind you, I don't want to do it again. But the fact remains that I had to pick up dog shit within two minutes of waking up.

We had an extremely rare out of uniform day at school today. One of the first things I had to do after letting the kids in was chase an enormous horde of girls out of the bathroom, where they were all busily doing whatever the hell they think they have to do to their hair and faces and whatever other body parts to get through the day. I didn't figure there were any *boys* in the adjoining bathroom, but after clearing the girls out (no, I didn't actually enter; bellowing from the hallway works just as well) I figured I might as well make sure the boys' bathroom was empty too.

There was blood all over the goddamned place. One of my sixth graders had a hell of a gusher going on, and after making sure

187

that he hadn't actually been punched in the face I helped him clean himself up a little bit and then sent him to the nurse and radioed for custodial attention to the bathroom.

Fast forward to waiting in the gym, maybe fifteen minutes later. It's Wednesday. There have been before-school fights in the gym for two Wednesdays in a row, so I was glaring at anyone around me (I'll be honest, I woke up in a *bad mood* this morning) and wishing various motherfuckers *would* do something stupid. I positioned myself by the particular group of girls that have been responsible for at least two fights this year, figuring that if shit was going to happen I might as well be there already.

Suddenly there's a *ridiculous* amount of commotion from the other side of the seventh-grade girls' section— the part where the *honors* girls usually congregate. What the hell? I dash over there, wondering where the fight is, to discover one of my Media Tech girls covering her mouth with an absolutely horrified look on her face. I look where she's looking, to see her twin sister looking back at her with a similarly horrified look.

"What? What's going on?"

The non hand-on-mouth twin just *points*. And I realize that Hand Sister is just about goddamn *drenched* in vomit. Clear, phlegmy vomit, which was why I missed it the first time. It's all over the ground, all over her hands, and all over her front. I am, in fact, standing in some, and there's been some splashing on a couple of other girls. I bundle her off to the nurse as quickly as humanly possible and, sort of chuckling about it, radio the custodians. Later investigation revealed that she hadn't even been feeling *sick*; just, wham, vomit time!

And then it hits me. It is 7:38 in the morning, and I have already had to deal with shit, blood, *and* vomit.

Anybody else want my life? Please?

Bad Teacher Moment, #3

March 28, 2009

This week was a bitch and a half at work, which didn't help with my desire to write when I got home any. My last two classes have been absolute fucking bastards all week, and my ability to put up with their bullshit has been severely goddamned compromised. I haven't had to break up a fight in a while— knock on wood— so we haven't had *that* bullshit to put up with, but everybody who has the ability in them to be a dickhead has been letting their flag fly all week. Spring Break's in a week, and *man*, I can taste it from here. Things always calm down once that week is up, so hopefully this year will hold true to the pattern every other year in my career has followed.

Not that the kids are the only ones being bastards, mind you. I made one of my favorite kids cry on Wednesday, and I didn't even mean to. On Tuesday afternoon, as I was dismissing the 7th and 8th graders to their buses at the end of the day, I noticed one of my kids from last year was having a complete breakdown right in front of everybody. The kid was sobbing, huge tears rolling down his cheeks, chest heaving, back hitching every now and again, that sort of thing, and he had a ring of other kids around him who were all doing their best to console him. He's one of the smaller kids in his grade, too, which didn't help the picture any. There was already a teacher sitting next to him asking questions, so I didn't intrude, but I did corral one of my Media Tech kids a minute or two later to see what was going on. Apparently Twin B (Remember her? She puked on herself a week or so ago) had just broken up with him amid accusations that he had been unfaithful, but he claimed he hadn't, and furthermore the accusations came from his ex-girlfriend, who apparently wanted him *back*, and this is when I tuned things out and told MT kid thank you but go away before you hurt my brain.

He shrugs at me, all like, *What are you gonna do?* and says "Nerd love." This cracks me right the hell up.

From a kid's perspective, of course, I can see how this is The End Of The World, but as an adult I found it vaguely amusing in a sort of "Awww, isn't that cute" sort of way.

So, next day, Twin B is in my room along with Twin A and Best Friend O, and they're all sitting there giggling and having their usual Teenage Girl Fun Time nonsense together before class starts. Now, understand something about me, in case it isn't already obvious: I live to blow my students shit, right? Half of them only respond to the word "knucklehead" by now, which is trouble if I want one *specific* knucklehead. So, with that in mind, I look at Twin B and say the following:

"Dude. Why you gotta make <other kid> cry?"

The tears started *immediately*. And they weren't much lower in caliber than Other Kid's from the day before. This bewildered me— she broke up with him! She's not supposed to be all busted up about it! It's not fair! Under my breath, immediately and *obviously* regretting the entire thing, I mutter "Oh, *hell*," which Twin A overhears, and Twin A, recognizing exactly what's going through my head and not at all concerned about her sister, starts *cracking up*.

I managed to bustle Twin B into the hallway fast enough that no more than 75% of the students in the room realized that she was crying, and no more than 50% or so realized that it was *completely and totally my fault* that it was happening. Luckily, both Twin A and Twin B are *very easy* to make laugh, so I was able to get her back into shape pretty quickly once I was done with all the apologizing. So it's not like the day was destroyed.

Nonetheless: I am a bastard.

More on Underwear

February 12 2011

And here, we jump ahead a couple of years, as I spend some time not writing very much. I am teaching at the same school, but I have changed positions, and now teach sixth grade Math and Science. My homeroom, incidentally, is all girls.

Long week. Long couple of weeks, actually. On the plus side, I've spent a fair amount of time recently digging deep into data from my classes, and have concluded that the numbers indicate I'm finally doing something right. There's been a pronounced upward turn on grade-level assessments for my homeroom over the past nine weeks, one that I'm not seeing replicated in the numbers for the other sixth grade math classes. This is important; if we're all rising and falling together, then what the data is measuring isn't teacher effectiveness— it's *the difficulty of the assessment*, which is useful information but not at all what I'm looking for. My kids, in *both* of my classes, have been trending upward for months now. Frankly, they've been trending upward to such an extent that it looks like I'm cheating. I brought the data to my boss right after I'd put all the graphs together, and told him that I wasn't terribly looking forward to the first staff meeting where I got accused of manipulating my numbers.

(Note: this upward trend is going to end in about two weeks. Memo to the curriculum people: dropping circumference and area of circles, surface area and volume of cubic and rectangular solids, and surface area and area of *cylinders* into the same goddamned three-week window is less an act of incompetence than it is *brutality*. Any of those three pairs of things would take your

191

average sixth-grade class a few weeks to internalize. Putting them all together— especially trying to do cylinders *a week and a half after encountering pi for the first time*— is just fuckin' unnecessary. Their scores are *going* to go down, a lot, from the last couple of windows. I just need to make sure my scores go down *less* than those of the other teachers.)

Anyway, without meaning to, I'd chosen a day to go talk to the boss when he'd just observed in my math class that morning. He laughed at me and showed me an email he was drafting to the office secretary to figure out a way to get the other math teachers classroom coverage so that they could come observe in my room.

Heh.

I, uh, think I might not have to worry too much about losing the math job next year.

Had to have a conversation with a kid this week about how while, yes, I can understand why you might be angry at a boy if he makes fun of you when he discovers your ruined, bloody underwear is sitting on a shelf in your locker, and yes, I can even understand why you might choose to *hit* a boy when he makes fun of you for such a thing, you should perhaps have thought through your "place my ruined panties on a shelf in my locker" policy in favor of something perhaps involving some sort of *bag*. I did not ask whether the ruined underwear was replaced with clean underwear after being removed; certain things I don't want to have to think about.

And here's a question: What do you do when you're letting your kids have a few minutes of free time in the computer lab, because they've finished what you wanted them to do and you don't feel like taking them back to the classroom for the few minutes remaining in the class period, and one of your kids performs the normally innocuous task of Googling his own name and then discovers that the reason his grandmother is in jail is because she murdered his grandfather?

What if this kid is a noted attention hog and doesn't display the *slightest bit* of sadness or emotional disturbance about the news, but reacts as if perhaps grandma's in jail because she won the lottery? What then? What if he immediately broadcasts that grandma shot grandpa and *oh that's why she's in jail man I need to go home and yell at my mom* to the entire room with a big shit-eating grin on his face?

Because I dumped the whole thing in the principal's lap. I'm not having that conversation with a parent. I don't get paid enough. You go do it.

There was more this morning, but I've been meaning to dump those two anecdotes on y'all for a while now and now I've done it so I can go play videogames in peace without the internet bothering my conscience.

On Bullying

November 3 2011

I have had a good two days at school and after a few days of
self-doubt I'm starting to feel like maybe I'm an educator again, so
I'm not ruining that by writing an essay about bullying.

You get that, brain? You hear me? I'm not doing it. Shut up!

No, I'm *not* talking about the time when there was an actual
article in the goddamn paper that specifically singled me personally
out for refusing to deal with accusations of bullying that took up a
full week of my time even though the "bullied student" was a seventh
grader, the bully was a fifth grader *a third her size*, and the kid being
"picked on" was a well-known drama queen who went on to have the
exact same issues at the private school her parents transferred her to
after pulling her out of my school. Even though the *entire article
was bullshit from start to finish* and only contained the lunatic
parents' side of the story because the school— ooh, surprise!— won't
comment to the goddamn news about discipline issues involving
their students.

I *will not write an essay about bullying.* Because it will
ultimately be counterproductive and stupid and make people think
that I don't take it seriously when I do. It's *because* I take bullying
issues so seriously that it makes me fucking crazy having to deal
with it. My life would be *much much easier* if I ignored bullying
accusations. Or if, say, my kids actually *knew what the word
meant.* Or, like, weren't constantly accusing their best friends of
bullying them, then admitting that they're doing the *exact same thing
to those friends*, and then two days later once you've wasted a bunch
of time on it everything's fine because that's what middle school girls
do.

Also? I don't know how many of you have ever tried to get a coherent story out of a sixth grader before? It's tough. You'll get lost in the pronouns about two sentences in. My wife went on a week-long field trip to Washington DC with me and a bunch of seventh and eighth graders two years ago. Two of the girls had a personal problem and tried to have her deal with it instead of coming to me. She was completely lost in like *three sentences.* It's hard! They aren't good at constructing coherent narratives at that age, even if they're telling the truth, and frequently figuring out What Exactly Happened is an *incredibly complicated act.*

More later about something else. Dinner's ready! I like dinner.

Okay. I'm filled with food and tasty so let's tell a story. I'm my school's bus supervisor, which puts about an extra $70 in my pocket every two weeks and is rarely worth it. What it means is that I have some kid-supervision duties that other teachers don't have before and after school and that I'm the school's first line of defense against any issue that takes place on the bus. Last year, during the first or second week of school, I got a note in my box that the parent of a fifth grader had called to complain that her son was being bullied on the bus. Fifth graders are as young as my building gets, so this is a kid who had been in my school all of eight or nine days. Furthermore, I didn't recognize the last name, meaning that this was likely to be a family that was new to the building.

So I call Mom back. Her son got pushed and possibly punched by an older kid on the bus. She's not clear about whether the punching actually happened or not but there was definitely some shoving. I get the kid's name and bus number and tell her I'll look into it the next day. Important detail: it is Wednesday, and the alleged pushing happened on Tuesday.

The next day I find the kid and ask him what happened. He says that the "big kid" (to a fifth grader, everyone is a "big kid") pushed him into his seat, told him to sit down, and called him a name, but he doesn't remember the name. He was not punched. This may or may not be true; frequently kids won't repeat things that they were called even if directly asked to. I ask him where the kid was sitting (he's not sure, the kid sat behind him), what he looked like (he gives me a description matching roughly two-thirds of the males in our building) and if he has any idea what his name is. He tells me he thinks the kid's name is, oh, let's go with Charlie; it doesn't really matter.

(SIDENOTE: This isn't bullying. Bullying requires a pattern of behavior. This may be a kid being an asshole. I'm still going to deal with it, mind you.)

I think through my options and decide to basically put the kid through a line-up. I ask him to look around in the gym in the morning and see if he can find the kid. And, amazingly, he does. Interestingly, the kid he fingers isn't named Charlie. Also, he's not a kid who I've ever known to pick on smaller kids or, really, anybody at all. He's one of the better ones.

At that exact moment, the bell rings. I have to dismiss the kids and I resolve to go talk to New Kid (let's call him Billy, which also isn't his name) during my prep. Before I do, though, I take a look at the bus roster. While Billy's name isn't Charlie, he's somehow the only kid on the bus who even vaguely matches the description the kid gave me. The kid's picked the right older student.

So I go find him and I ask him why he's bothering my fifth graders. He completely denies everything. He didn't push anybody, he didn't yell at anybody to sit down, and he didn't call anybody any names.

This is, right now, effectively a meaningless conversation. He could be completely lying to me or he could be telling the truth. But something about the look on his face tells me he's telling me the truth, and this is a kid who's always been respectful and honest with me. I put on my best scary face (and my best scary face is *terrifying)* and remind him that lying to me about something like this will lead to dire consequences. Like me telling his football coach.

His eyes get wide. He insists he didn't do anything. He *promises* he didn't do anything. I tell him I'll get back to him.

Okay. I gotta pull the security tape off the bus. This is gonna be a pain in the ass. I discover at the end of the day that Mom has called back already for a status update. I call her back. I tell her that her son has identified his bully, that his bully has denied everything, and that I'm still investigating. I say that generally the kid's a good kid, and that I'm not sure what's happening at the moment, but that I'm pulling the tape from that day and that will, one way or another, resolve what happens. I also say that the kid has good reason to make damn sure he stays on the straight and narrow because he doesn't want his football coach to murder him.

This, in retrospect, was a mistake. Here's what Mom just heard: I like this kid, and I'm protecting one of my favorites. Also, he plays football, and it's in my best interests to keep him on our football team because middle school football is important for some unclear reason even though we don't make any money off it or anything.

And honestly I don't blame her.

Fast forward to the next day: I grab the driver in the morning and get the tape. Before I have a chance to watch it, Billy grabs me in the hallway.

"I think I remember what you were talking about," he says. "I bumped a little kid on the bus while we were going to our seats the other day. I was behind him when it happened. I didn't push him on purpose but I can see how he might think I did."

Okay, I think, now we're getting somewhere. I ask him if he'd be willing to apologize to the kid. He says he would. I grab both of them in the gym, and Billy says, genuine-sounding, "I'm sorry I bumped into you on the bus. I didn't mean to push you and I'm sorry if you thought I did." This is, mind you, more or less a word-perfect apology, something I rarely get from eighth graders. I make them shake hands and then go about my day— which gets incredibly busy, so I'm not able to get to the tape until after school and after *another* conversation with Mom, who I tell that if the tape matches what Billy told me, there will be no disciplinary consequences for him. If it's a hard bump that the kid thought was a shove, I'm not writing someone up for that, particularly when they volunteered to apologize and did so sincerely.

Mom's not terribly happy with this. She demands the kid's full name. I won't give it to her. I tell her she's welcome to talk to the principal if she needs to, but that I'm doing everything I can to protect her son and that I think this is, unfortunately, One of Those Things that Happen.

I get off the phone, rather dissatisfied with the world, and watch the tape. Which is dated 2006. July of 2006, in fact. I watch her son get on the bus. I watch him neither stumble nor get bumped by anyone. I watch him walk to a seat near the front of the bus and sit down with no one touching him. Then, *three minutes* later, I see Billy get on the bus, bump *no one,* and sit his ass down, nowhere near the kid. I watch the tape until her son gets off the bus.

Absolutely no one touches him at any time.

WHAT THE FUCK.

I call Mom back and tell her that this kid, who *admitted to pushing her son,* did no such thing. She doesn't believe me. Claims I'm protecting our football players. I tell her that I have the tape right in front of me, that absolutely nothing has happened to her son at all, and that there will absolutely be no disciplinary measures applied to Billy. I am firm about this to the point where I'm worried about being rude. If she wants to come in and view the tape, that's fine, but at the moment I'm declaring this situation over.

I hang up, dash off an email to my boss filling him in, and go home.

Later that night it hits me.

The tape was obviously dated wrong, right? The driver said it was Tuesday's tape and I took his word on it. It wasn't Tuesday's tape. It had to be Monday's tape.

Billy was *at football practice after school on Tuesday.* He wasn't even on the goddamned *bus* on the day he admitted to pushing a kid he never touched because he's a good kid and if a grown-up says he pushed somebody he must have done something wrong.

And this is why I'm a bit neurotic about bullying issues.

199

On Snow

November 10 2011

I've got a kid who is basically an exchange student in my room this year. It's "basically" because middle schools don't actually have an exchange program, but when a kid comes to my school from Colombia for a year with clear plans to return to her home country at the end of said year, I don't know what else to call it. She's living with her aunt and uncle and not a bunch of strangers, but that's the only big difference.

She's a bright kid— the school she was attending in Colombia was obviously a good school, and she's visibly ahead of my own kids in a number of ways. The school also teaches most of their classes in English, so other than some occasional specialized vocabulary and her accent, she's not having the usual communication issues that I associate with exchange students. She's also frequently a pain in the ass. I've heard a couple of other teachers comment on how quickly she got "Americanized;" I think she was probably a pain in the ass in Colombia too.

(Also? She's the touchiest person I've ever met. She absolutely cannot have a conversation with me without touching me or standing *right the hell next to me*, so close it's occasionally creepy. We went through this hilarious thing earlier this year where she was trying to talk to me in the middle of a mob of kids, I kept removing her hand from my arm, and then she'd immediately get all sheepish and embarrassed about it, apologize, and *put her hand back on my arm* while she was apologizing. And then I'd remove it. And then the cycle would repeat. It happened, seriously, four or five times in a row before one of my other girls literally grabbed both her arms in a bearhug and told her to finish what she was saying.)

It snowed today. For the first time this year. She got to America two days before school started. She'd never been here before.

And she's never seen snow.

I ran out of stuff to teach with about twelve minutes left in seventh hour. Normally this is a pain in the ass, because ten minutes isn't really enough time to cover something new and if they don't have questions I either need to come up with a quick assignment or find a way to filibuster until the bell rings.

I looked outside and it was snowing like hell. It wasn't sticking yet, but it was coming down really heavy.

I looked at her. *Hypnotized.* I don't know if she heard a single word I said during the last five or ten minutes of class.

And so we had a field trip. I took my class outside in the snow for ten minutes and watched a twelve-year-old who had never seen snow before play with it for the first time. There wasn't enough to throw snowballs, sadly, but we had everything else. Two or three of my girls were really excited about the snow and were pirouetting and letting it fall into their mouths and everything else. The rest were just watching the Colombian girl. I really don't remember the last time I saw a kid that happy.

It was a good day.

On Pants

NOVEMBER ‖ 2011

Two things fascinate me. Well, way more than two things
fascinate me, but I'm going to talk about two *specific* things in this
piece. The first— and this will be a theme that I return to over and
over again— is the endless novelty and eternally recombinant nature
of language; i.e., despite having been a constant speaker and hearer
of the English language for the last thirty-five years, a not
inconsiderable amount of time, I still very frequently hear and say
things that I'm absolutely certain I've never heard or said before. The
second is related: the frequency with, despite a full decade of
teaching experience, my job hits me with situations I've never
encountered before.

And, that said, let us discuss Kelsey.

I love Kelsey to death, right? I'm not exaggerating when I say
that. But Kelsey is the type of kid for whom the phrase "bless your
heart," in all its Southern passive-aggressive derogatory glory, was
invented for. (I've heard it said that "bless your heart" is Southern
for "you fucking moron," and that's the sense I'm getting at
here.) Kelsey turns being scatterbrained into a goddamned art
form. She's reasonably bright when I can get her to focus, but she
doesn't even *need* anything shiny to knock her off-task. Dull boring
things are enough to be distracting.

My school begins the day with a homeroom, fifteen minutes of
time that is basically earmarked for administrative tasks: taking
attendance, passing out and collecting various important things,
uniform checks, and dealing with whatever the current day's batch of
insane nonsense twenty-two eleven and twelve-year-old girls can
bring to school with them. I think some teachers in the building try

to use the time for something academic— a quick bell-ringer or something like that; I do not. There's no time. I'm too busy dealing with nonsense.

It's cold outside right now, right? It snowed yesterday, I talked about that. When I got up this morning it was about thirty degrees outside and the wind was blowing like hell. It wasn't actually snowing anymore, but last night's little crust of accumulation that built up hadn't gotten around to melting yet.

Which meant I was a trifle surprised to notice that Kelsey was wearing her standard uniform shirt, a uniform-approved heather-grey sweater over her shirt, and ... shorts. Really tight shorts, not in the traditional teenage-girl *I painted these on; please look at my butt* sort of way, but in a "these fit me in third grade" sort of way. And they were cut really weird, too— maybe two or three inches above her knees, but they didn't look like they were *supposed* to be above the knees. I wave her over.

"Kels? It's cold outside. You're wearing shorts."

"Can we talk outside?" Oh, goody. Often this is the prelude to something menstrual. Sometimes to something more serious. *Frequently* to something ridiculous. And I suspect I know which way this is heading. We step outside the door— not so far that I can't hear my kids, but far enough that you'd have to deliberately eavesdrop to hear what we're saying.

"Explain your pants, luv," I say.

"They're not mine. They're Arizona's," she says. Now, context: Arizona is in my honors class, not my homeroom. She's all of three foot six. She's not people-sized. She's got enough personality for any *twelve* normal-sized humans, but she is not shaped like one. I'd adopt her if I could, and I'm being reasonably serious when I say that. I've thought about it.

"Why are you wearing Arizona's pants?" I ask.

"She wanted to wear mine," she says.

Oh.

"Arizona is wearing your pants?"

"Yeah, and I put on her pants because I didn't have any other ones to put on."

It hits me that that's why the shorts look like they're cut weird— Kelsey is normal sixth-grade-girl sized; she's at least a foot taller than Arizona is. They're *not shorts*. They're really pants. They're just wildly inappropriate for someone Kelsey's size.

"Why did Arizona want to wear your pants?" (Sidenote the first: This is what I mean. She's the kind of kid who can make *hey, take off your normal pants and wear these teeny pants that I have so that you look completely ridiculous* seem perfectly normal and like something that a person would do.)

"I don't know," she says.

I notice that my headache has already started. I briefly consider insisting that Kelsey recover her own pants so that she can wear them. It occurs to me that, if I do that, I will be required to insist that another preteen girl take her pants *off*. This seems somehow slightly dodgy. It occurs to me that there may well be some other reason why Kelsey and Arizona have switched pants, one that might actually *make sense*, and that investigating further does stand a chance to increase the headache. It also occurs to me that it is not yet eight o'clock in the morning and jesus god please let this be the most ridiculous conversation I have to have today.

I say a sentence I've never said before.

"Kelsey, would you like to be wearing your own pants?"

She thinks about it for a moment.

"No, I'm okay."

"Would you like to call home and request supplementary pants?" (I phrase it exactly like this. She takes a moment again, this time to parse my vocabulary before she answers.)

"No. I think they'll be mad if I call home."

"Are you sure?"

"Yeah."

"You understand that this will be the last time that I will be saying the word *pants* until at least after lunch? New rule 9: no using the word *pants* before lunch." (Sidenote the second: I have eight official class rules and ten thousand rule nines.)

"Okay."

"You sure?"

"Yes."

"Go away, please."

She goes away.

Seventh hour, she comes back into the room wearing her own pants. She immediately begins complaining that, while wearing her pants, Arizona and another (male) student wrote on them. I do not ask if the male student was *also* wearing her pants. I tell her the location of the nearest dry cleaner and refuse to discuss the situation any further.

I have a silly job.

This Is a Unicorn

November 15 2011

This? Is, believe it or not, a unicorn. You'll have to imagine a coordinate plane LCD-projected on top of it for it to be clear; I was doing a simple exercise with my honors class and they decided after about two kids put points up that they needed to make the points join into a picture somehow, and after another half-dozen had put stuff up Arizona decided that it had to be a unicorn. Every kid did one point without consulting anyone else or taking any advice on where the points should be; Arizona connected everything up afterwards.

I, naturally, being the caring and supportive educator that I am, mocked them mercilessly for it, and then brought another teacher from across the hall to evaluate their work ("I told them that if you can figure out what they drew they get fifteen minutes of free time") and of course she got it in one guess, leading to much rejoicing from the little bastards and no small amount of pointing and laughing at their chastened math teacher.

The good news is that both classes appear to understand how coordinate planes work— and, miraculously, even how equations of a line on a coordinate plane work, which has got to be some sort of goddamned miracle, considering that three weeks ago they were having trouble wrapping their heads around the idea that a letter could represent a number. Then again, I was reasonably confident before the last window test we took, too, and I got the worst damn scores in the sixth grade. They'd better do better this time; my tutoring group has met a couple of times and the material, hopefully, is a little less likely to fall out of their ears. We'll find out on Thursday. Hopefully I won't have to go into parent-teacher conferences Thursday night annoyed at my class again.

Mitch Daniels Can <Go On A Lovely Picnic With His Friends and Family>

November 16 2011

Note that, believe it or not, I removed roughly two-thirds of the profanity in the original, online draft of this piece before allowing it to go to print. No, really. It was that bad. I have also replaced several of the insults with compliments inside triangle brackets.

It's eight nineteen PM. I just finished doing an hour of spreadsheet and data entry work for school. This is after not getting home until after five, which was ten hours after I arrived at work. And when I left school there were at least half a dozen teachers still in the building— and those are just the ones I saw on my way out to the parking lot.

My <charming success> of a governor has spent most of the last year of his life doing his level best to <make sweet love to> public education, and because most of Indiana's voters are <genteel, classy gentlefolk> who would happily live in the gutter under a goddamned cardboard box provided that there was someone nearby who didn't have a *box*, he's had a fairly easy go at it. Turns out the little <elected public official> was in town today, visiting a Catholic school and spouting off about his voucher program.

I made the terrible mistake of accidentally having local news on for a few minutes after I got home (I should *never ever ever watch local news*) and they interviewed Governor Daniels about his education program. The Governor, who did not deign to set foot in any of our public schools today (he has insisted, incidentally, that this voucher program isn't a church-state violation but apparently

209

couldn't find a non-Catholic private school to tour; whodathunkit?), got all of thirty seconds of talking out before my tired, overworked ass screamed "<GIGGLING BABY!>" loud enough that I woke my son up in the other room and damn near put the goddamn remote through the screen.

Basically, here's how it works: you apply for a voucher to put towards tuition at a private school. Governor <Role Model> writes you a check for the exact amount that the State of Indiana would usually fund a local public school district. You take that money and give it to the private school, who promptly spends half of it on Jesus. The local public school district loses out on that funding.

It's *almost* fair, at this point, except for the Jesus part. The fun part is the bit where the second the private school has that check and officially has their attendance numbers in for the year they can *expel your kid* and send him back to the public schools where we have to educate him anyway, only they get to keep the money for him. It happens every. Single. Year. As soon as their numbers are locked for state funding, they expel a few dozen of their kids— the poorly behaved ones, or the special ed students, or the ones who just aren't going to pass ISTEP— and those kids come right the fuck back to us. And they keep the funding. This way the process is even more streamlined and they can screw us even harder.

In this particular case, this precise school, the school our governor is visiting, has taken sixty-six kids from us. My school corporation has to make up something like four or five million dollars in lost funding. I guarantee we get a third of those kids back at *minimum* by the end of the year.

Somebody asked the <visiting dignitary> if he didn't think that the loss of funding was a problem for public schools. Here's his response:

In response to a reporter's question, Daniels said he rejects the notion that public schools "lose" when families choose to use vouchers at private schools. "Losing in education isn't about the money for adults. Losing is when children don't do well," he said.

Money for adults.

Money for fucking adults.

Like I get to keep that fucking shit.

I ... Christ, I gave myself goddamn near three fucking hours to calm the fuck down after hearing this shit and it still makes me so angry I can't see straight. *MONEY FOR FUCKING*

ADULTS? <Hug> you, you <cultured and erudite member of our governing elite>, those fucking adults are the motherfuckers that *make the fucking building run, you <esteemed resident of the Hoosier state>.* We've got fucking eighth grade English classes in my building with 34 goddamned kids in them.

You happen to have any idea how much goddamn teaching gets done in a classroom with 34 fucking kids in it? None at goddamned all unless you're a fucking *miracle worker* and then very little *at best.* But the school corporation won't pay for another teacher in the building because— get this— since the governor *also* gutted our union's ability to negotiate our contract, the school board got rid of class size caps and they say we don't have enough eighth graders to pay for another teacher.

There have been four fights *that I'm aware of* in the girls locker room during gym class this year. Wanna know why? Our gym teacher is male and we had to fire the paraprofessional who used to cover the locker room during gym. Since we don't have the staff to put anyone in there they're just unsupervised. And that's gonna be our ass if something serious happens to someone. We've got probably a dozen kids who aren't receiving the special education services that we are *mandated to provide by fucking federal law* because the school corporation won't fund the staffers necessary to do it.

Money for fucking adults. Maybe some of that money for fucking adults could fund the fucking paper and pencils that I have to buy every fucking week because the school can barely afford fucking photocopies and my kids' parents aren't buying them school supplies because they don't care and OH THEY DON'T HAVE FUCKING JOBS BECAUSE THE ECONOMY SUCKS. And seeing as how Daniels' relevant fucking experience to become Governor was being George <Charming> Bush's fucking *budget director,* I'm pretty fucking sure I can lay that at his feet too.

What do you think is gonna happen to the ISTEP scores of the 34 hormone-addled <sweethearts> in those eighth grade English classes? They're gonna drop sure as the sun shines. And that's gonna be used as more fucking evidence that public schools are shit and that we're not doing our jobs— as opposed to, say, the OBVIOUS AND FUCKING PREDICTABLE RESULT OF the repeated <back rub> that we have to put up with every single fucking time somebody lets a Republican near education policy in this country.

211

Luther M. Siler

<Wonderful, inspirational people>.

On Substitute Teachers

January 13 2012

I have a hard job, right? Educating's tough enough under the best of circumstances, and educating in an urban school in 2012, when half of society and one entire political party actively hates teachers and wants to make our job more difficult is certainly not the best of circumstances.

It's a hard job. But don't pretend— or let me pretend— that I don't do it on purpose. Because as tough as my job is, I love what I do and there are jobs that are harder than mine. Much harder.

For example, under no circumstances *ever* would I be willing to be a substitute teacher. Never. Period. The first day on any job sucks, right? You don't know anybody, you don't really know how things work in your new place of business, you don't necessarily know the best way to even get there; it's a mess. Substitute teaching is a job where *every day* is your first day on the job, and while I try to always leave ridiculously comprehensive lesson plans frequently you're tossed into a room full of kids you don't know with little if any actual indication of what you're actually expected to be doing with them. And the pay is generally ass.

It sucks. I don't ever want to do it.

Sadly, what this generally means is that the people who we are able to find to substitute teach are frequently ... *uninspiring.* And, sadly, just because a job is goddamned miserable doesn't mean that it's okay to do it poorly.

Especially in my fuckin' classroom.

I was out Wednesday morning for a meeting/conference/thing. There were, admittedly, probably a ton more subs needed by the corporation than usual, because the thing

213

pulled anywhere from ten to a dozen teachers (and, usually, more than one administrator) from every middle school and high school in town. That's a lot of people, plus the usual expected complement of people who were sick or out for some other reason. When we're out for something like this, generally our subs get scheduled for us. Which means that we don't get any input on who they are. Ordinarily, when I call in for a sub, I can request a specific person if I have a sub number for them. Not so much if I don't make the call.

My girls are a little rough, right? I can handle them— they're *my* freaking kids— but they're noisy as hell under the best of circumstances and I have to make sure to pay attention to what *kind* of noise it is. I can tell my girls being productive and chatty from my girls raising hell. They're rarely, if ever, completely quiet, and I've got a few who have serious attitude problems if they decide they don't like someone. I'm never sure whether I should let them know or not on days when I know I'm not going to be in. On one hand, it gives me a chance for the You Will Not Annoy the Sub speech, but on the other hand it *lets them know there's a sub coming*, so they do things like come in out of uniform because the sub's not going to notice or just generally plan to raise hell at school that day.

Well, this time I told them I was going to be out— mostly so that I could warn them I'd be *back* later in the same day and that the stuff I'd told them was going to happen in the afternoon was absolutely still going to happen. And I went off to my little meeting.

I heard from *four* different adults *before getting back to my room* that my kids had given the sub a hard time. Four. I have to walk through two hallways to get to my room. It's not actually that long of a walk. Maybe three or four minutes from the door.

That's a lot of people to walk past, much less to say "Man, your kids worked the sub over today."

So I walked into my room ready to be apologetic to whatever person had been stuck with my room and then to *flense* my students when they came back to me at the end of the day.

Within about thirty seconds of walking into my room I knew I had a different problem.

Namely, that the sub was a fucking lunatic.

Here's how my half-day interactions with a sub are supposed to go: I enter my room. You sigh with relief that your day is over and you don't have to be a substitute teacher any longer. I say "how did it go?" and thank you for taking care of my kids for me. You, hopefully, tell me you had a good day. If you had a bad day, I want to hear names of children who prevented you from having a good day and, preferably, I want to hear that those students spent some time either in another teacher's room, in ISS, or in the principal's office. I will frequently follow up with detentions for those students as well, although I don't let subs assign them. (Note: my sub notes are *always clear about this.* If a student is bothering you, send them away, and here are three different ways you can make them go away. You are an adult and your job is not to put up with my kids if they're being assholes. Send them to someone else who will.)

And then, after that conversation, which shouldn't take more than a couple of minutes, you *leave.* Because I, the adult and trained professional for whom you are subbing for, have *returned,* and I'd like to get back to doing my job now and you presumably want to go home.

You do not refuse to leave my room.

No, really. That happened.

This crazy bitch *made me wait* while she organized the papers that were on *my desk,* carefully labeling everything on Post-It notes by a) period, b) subject (Subject!! I teach math, people!) c) date (what the hell? I was gone three hours!) and, most inexplicably, by the *number of students who had completed each assignment,* as if that was remotely important to me, as if I couldn't figure it out perfectly easily on my own, and as if I didn't need my damn desk. She made me wait. In my own classroom. While she *counted* six piles of paper.

"Ma'am, it's okay. I've got this. You can go."

"Not yet."

What the fuck? No, there's no "*not yet*" here.

Then she shows me the summary sheet that we want all the subs to fill out at the end of a shift. She's gotten a bunch of details wrong— for example, she's claimed that I didn't include any emergency information when it's not only in my lesson plans but clearly posted in multiple places in the room. But whatever, right? I thank her and she tries to take the paper out of my hands. Like, literally snatches it from me.

"That's just going to get thrown back in my mailbox, ma'am. It's *for me.* The office doesn't need it. I can keep it."

"No, I need to give it to the office. They'll get mad if I don't do it."

"Tell them that you did it and that I've got it. It's okay. It's just going straight into my box. Really."

"No. You can't keep it."

Then she subjected me to a five-minute harangue about her mother-in-law. Seriously. I literally walked away from her at one point while she was bitching because *I have a goddamned job to do* and I don't care about your mother-in-law's goddamn health problems or why you're substitute teaching because you can't stand having to take care of her (!!!) and you need to get out of the house. It's not my problem. I tried to be polite for a minute or two but Jesus, lady, we don't know each other and— again— I have *shit to do*. The ISTEP ain't gonna pass itself and in case you haven't noticed the governor's decided it's my fault if my kids don't know anything.

I was a minute or two away from calling security by the time she actually left, after she told me that I really should have left answer keys for my sixth-grade math assignments because she "doesn't do math" and didn't know how to do anything.

I don't even fucking *have* answer keys. See, I'm a grown-up, so I can handle goddamned sixth grade math. Why are you a substitute teacher if you can't do sixth-grade math?

So, here's the thing: by the end of the day I'd talked to both of the paraprofessionals who were in my room with the sub. And they both gave me basically the same story: that my kids were more or less abominable until they themselves put their feet down, but that the sub was also obviously a crazy person who spent most of her time alternately bellowing for my kids to shut up and do their math, refusing to give anyone any help, and obliviously texting on her phone.

I don't want my kids to misbehave when there's a sub in the room. Ever. Because the goddamn job is hard as hell under the best of circumstances and I will *not* have someone complaining to their friends about the zoo they had to work in that day when that zoo was in my building, much less in *my classroom.*

But you know what? My kids are fuckin' *eleven,* dammit. Eleven-year-olds screw up. Part of the reason I have to teach them how to become adults is because *they don't know*. Hell, half the time their *parents* don't know. They're going to react poorly to authority figures if those authority figures clearly don't have the slightest clue what they're doing or what they're supposed to be doing. I told my kids when they came in during last period that they were to sit silently at their desks and write a one-page essay on everything that happened during first and second hour. And then we discussed what had happened, what my expectations were, and what to do in the future if anyone like that sub ended up in my room again. And some of the shit they told me had happened— much of which I'd already verified by talking to the other adults— was goddamned horrifying.

And then I did a long write-up for the office explaining in clear and precise terms why that sub should under no circumstances be allowed to pass through the doors of our building ever again.

I don't like it when my kids fuck with people.

But don't you *dare* fuck with my kids.

A Note to Parents

February 14 2012

Note to parents: If I gave your kid detention, they deserved it. If your twelve-year-old daughter tells you that She Was the Only One who Got In Trouble and Everyone Was Talking, the proper response from you is to 1) point out that maybe she shouldn't have been fucking talking and 2) ask additional questions that will reveal that she was specifically warned multiple times and was substantially less able than the rest of the students to shut the fuck up when the pile of detentions came out.

I don't do fucking paperwork unless I have to, people. I don't give a fuck if you think a fucking lunch detention was unfair. Maybe your precious daughter (who, for the record, is one of my favorite kids, but when I say "the next person to do this is getting a detention," I'm giving my *mother* a detention if she's the next person to do that. Middle school teachers don't bluff.) might *just possibly* have represented the situation in a fashion more favorable to herself than strict adhesion to accuracy might have demanded. Just *maybe*.

Or, alternatively, just remind your kid that it's only a goddamn lunch detention and not the end of the fuckin' world and she should stop whining. That works too.

(Note: I don't call you back when you send me notes like this. Everything from you goes into the "ignore" bin, forever.)

Thankyouthatisall.

Ass and Tits

MAY 29 2012

It is the end of the school year, which means that functionally and physically my sixth graders may as well be seventh graders by now. Anyone who works with this age group is already either chuckling at me or is going through the exact same bullshit and so has some sympathy. Here's what happens at the end of sixth grade: everyone's hormones kick in, *all at once.* Kids who have been entirely uninterested in the opposite sex all year suddenly wake up. Kids who have already been interested in the opposite sex suddenly kick everything into overdrive. And we have to start working a lot harder to prevent PDAs.

Oh, and this year we need to have a conversation with them about *same-sex* inappropriate touching. Because the two things going on at my school right now? Are the boys grabbing each others' asses and the girls ...

... wait for it.

... slapping each other on the tits. Yeah. That's a thing.

The completely crazy shit? They're mostly leaving *each other* alone. As I'm writing this I'm wondering if this is because we're mostly doing single-gender instruction in the sixth grade this year, but I'm seeing it happen in my mixed class, too, and in the hallways. So it's more of a building culture thing. The boys can't keep their hands off of each other's butts and the girls can't stop slapping each other on the tits. So sometime in the next couple of days, we're going to have to take a few minutes, separate them, and lay down the law on Keep Your Hands Off Each Other's Asses and Stop Slapping Each Other on the Tits.

Luther M. Siler

I'm pretty sure I'm getting the Each Other's Asses talk. It will be about *three seconds long.* The girls' talk may be a touch longer, because they're gonna dance around shit. "Keep your goddamned hands to yourselves or I will make the rest of your year miserable" does not take that long to say.

On Being Vietnamese, or Not

June 4 2012

Odd anecdote: there's an ethnically Vietnamese kid in one of my classes. He's first-generation American; i.e., born here, but both of his parents immigrated. I've met the father, who barely speaks English at all and has the lean, prematurely-old look of somebody who spent most of their lives struggling to make sure they had a next meal. His son does not share this look. I have not met the mom.

We had to take a survey the other day that the guidance counselor wanted us to do. No big deal, but one of the first questions was demographic: pick your race. Among the options were white, Asian, and mixed race.

The kid calls me over and says "I'm Asian, since my parents were born in Vietnam. But I was born here, so that means I'm part white, right? And I should choose mixed race?"

I ...

Huh.

A few clarifying questions later elicited that yes, Mom is just as ethnically Vietnamese as Dad, so ... no, you're not white or mixed. Mark Asian, thanks.

Damn, that was a weird conversation.

Am I Good at my Job?

June 4 2012

So. Let's play Am I Good At My Job? It's fun!

Short version for background: The corporation has set it up so that all of our middle schools are, at least theoretically, teaching the same thing at the same time throughout the year. This is primarily meant to compensate for our high student mobility; a kid who moves from Middle School A to Middle School B ought to be studying the same stuff and have already studied the same things as everyone else, so there's no missing, say, fractions because they already covered it in the class you moved to but hadn't gotten to them yet in the one you left. Instructional units are divided into three week windows; there are 12 throughout the year. At the end of every window is a pregenerated standardized test for that window; every student takes one for math and one for reading every three weeks.

(Note: I consider all of this a good thing.)

There are three sixth grade math teachers, with five different math classes, since one of us is self-contained and teaches her own kids all day.

•One of my two classes is the honors class, which had the highest number of green kids and green + yellow kids on the test all but two out of the 12 times, and most of the time were the best class by a pretty substantial margin; usually 15-20%. (Note: kids are scored green-yellow-red. Red is bad. Green is good. Yellow is OK.) We don't care about the honors class for the purpose of this conversation.

•My girls started off the year regularly at or near the bottom, with the worst results in the sixth grade twice. By the end of the year they were consistently the second-best group, behind the honors kids.

225

Luther M. Siler

•Teacher A, who is self-contained, posted the worst results ten out of twelve times, and most of the time was the worst by a substantial margin.

•Teacher B has two classes, one of girls, the other of boys. His girls beat my girls two or three times. His boys came in second behind the honors kids pretty regularly at the beginning of the year until my girls started beating them second semester. The two times the honors kids weren't the high group, his boys were. My girls never beat the honors group.

I walked into the ISTEP test feeling pretty good. While my class hadn't started off well, they'd been holding their own by the end of the year; I could show a positive trajectory to their scores that most of the other teachers couldn't.

Here's how ISTEP worked out:

•All the honors kids passed. Damn right they did; any kid in that class who didn't pass would be decorating my front lawn as a head on a pike right now. About a third of them were high pass. We don't care about the honors kids right now, though.

•Teacher A, who had absolutely miserable results throughout the year, had *68%* of her kids pass the test— which is pretty goddamned good. Her average gain (comparing individual students year-to-year) was eighteen points.

•Teacher B had about 53% of his kids pass. That's across both classes; I don't remember the individual breakdowns. His average gain was miserable— three points in one class and six in the other.

•56.9% of my girls passed the test— barely edging Teacher B and coming nowhere near Teacher A's numbers. But my average gain for my girls was thirty points. Average gain for the honors kids was 28. I moved one kid into high pass, kept one there who was already a high pass, had one pass this year who hadn't passed last year, and two fall from pass to fail. Note that one of those two still posted a score gain, but the passing cutscore also went up.

•Seven of the top 10 individual gains were in my classes.

So: based on that, and nothing else (since the state cares about nothing but test scores; honestly, even the window scores don't matter much outside the corporation, if the corporation even cares— they may only really matter to my boss), am I good at my job?

Go.

Teacher of the Year (again)

November 24 2012

So I won Teacher of the Year for my building. Again. I last won this in 2010, when I did not compete for corporation Teacher of the Year due to a horrifying confluence of multiple personal tragedies during the two weeks before the portfolio was due. I have determined that I am not going to allow this to happen again. I'm going to compete for this sonofabitch, and I'm going to do my best to actually win the damned thing. Because I am a badass, goddammit, and I want to be recognized for it.

Portfolio's not due until February. I'm starting, like, today. Right now. Only I have to be in a certain kind of head space to be able to write this stuff (there are 22 pages of it, plus a mess of "supplemental material" that I'm not quite certain how I'm going to handle) and I need to clear out some bad ideas first. So I'm taking the essay that's causing me the most trouble and I'm writing the first draft of it right here. Oh, and I'm going to be honest, which means that I'm not going to even come close to producing something that is actually going to be printable in my portfolio, but at least I'll clear the "honest" essay out of my head so that I can write something more appropriate later.

Yeah. Here's the question:

ONE PAGE OF DOUBLE-SPACED NARRATIVE WHICH INCLUDES YOUR COMMITMENT TO YOUR COMMUNITY THROUGH SERVICE-ORIENTED ACTIVITIES, VOLUNTEER WORK, CIVIC AND CHURCH ACTIVITIES, AND MEMBERSHIPS IN COMMUNITY ORGANIZATIONS. INFORMATION INCLUDED HERE MAY BE SCHOOL-RELATED BUT NOT EXCLUSIVELY SCHOOL BASED.

227

Okay, committee, first of all: fuck you. I believe the award that I'm competing for here is called Teacher of the Year, not Humanitarian of the Year or Community Member of the Year. I don't do any of those things. Do you know why I don't do any of those things? It's because I'm in my classroom fifty hours a week and frankly I think spending most of my waking hours trying to make sure that other people's twelve year olds understand mathematics and science is enough of a contribution to society all by itself. I do not get home from work and think "Damn, I haven't been useful enough to society today; I should spend all weekend at a food pantry." I *could* do that, yes, but once in a while I like to see my son. I don't go to church. Community organizations? I got named a Young Rotarian in high school; I went to one Rotary Club meeting, found it the most odious collection of status-seeking, self-congratulatory wankers I'd ever been exposed to and marched into the counselor's office and refused any further participation in the "honor" the very next day.

Service-oriented activities? I teach; maybe you're familiar with that. My entire goddamned CAREER is service-oriented. I'm sure as hell not doing this for the pay or the high social status that it affords me. You may have noticed society hates teachers; I put up with it anyway, mostly because I hate society *right back* most of the time and I want it replaced with something better. Trying to ensure that we have a populace that is at least marginally able to fend for themselves intellectually is kinda part of that.

I've done some volunteer work, mostly involving voter drives and some door-to-door and donation stuff to get my preferred candidates elected. But you might not like my preferred candidates, and I'd prefer not to get my portfolio rated down because you prefer to vote for somebody else, so I'm not going to say who they are. I took a bunch of kids to Washington DC three times, all for free. Is that volunteer work, or does that count as "school-related"? I dunno.

So, yeah, there's my commitment to my community: I put up with your kids and do my goddamned best with them on a daily basis so that you can call me a fucking union thug who is only in my job for the copious benefits, none of which you are interested in actually reaping for some reason or you'd be a teacher already. I stay late to teach them math so that they can go home to a house where there's not a single fucking book or a quiet place to do homework so that you can blame me the next day for everything they don't know how to do. I do this because I want your kids to be better than you. You don't want this, incidentally; one whiff of your kid being smarter than you or more into school than you were and you'll beat the shit out of them until they learn their place. You were an F student and you're doing just fine, right? Goddamn kids and their *airs*.

I want to improve my community because, as it currently exists, I kinda hate it. I don't want to hate my community. So I spend most of my time trying to fix it. But I don't do it through going to church and asking someone else to do it, so I'm probably not picking up any points on this section.

Hopefully that's less than one page of double-spaced narrative.

(I would eventually come in in the top ten in the district. The winner that year was my teacher in fourth grade. The award was well deserved.)

The End of the Year Assignment

June 4 2013

An experiment: I'm actually writing this at school and in class, with my students in the room, on the mobile app. Ordinarily (and, I hope, obviously) this is something I wouldn't be willing or able to do, but we've moved into the last three days of the school year and thus into my classic end-of-the-year assignment: Open your math workbook, and do something you haven't done yet. The main goal: keep them quiet and more or less working without making me insane. However, since my grades are done and I have no real other work to be doing, I'm experimenting with mobile blogging.

Literal transcript of a conversation I just had with a student:

HIM: "Do we have to do all the pages?"

ME: "Yes. All pages. Every mathings. You have one hour. Go 'way."

HIM: "I don't believe you."

ME: "Would I lie to you?"

HIM: "Yes."

They know me so well by now.

In Which I Provide Solutions

July 5-8, 2013

Recently the state of Alabama released the following information regarding the percentages of third-graders expected to pass their standardized Math test for 2013. This is *before* they take the test, mind you, as in "this many had better pass or you're in trouble," not "they took the test and this is how the scores are looking."

The Internet's all mad about it.

- *93.6 percent of Asian/Pacific Islander students.*
- *91.5 percent of white students.*
- *90.3 percent of American Indian students.*
- *89.4 percent of multiracial students.*
- *85.5 percent of Hispanic students.*
- *82.6 percent of students in poverty.*
- *79.6 percent of English language-learner students.*
- *79 percent of black students.*
- *61.7 percent of special needs students.*

I can hear your brain, you know. "What?" you're thinking. "That's terrible! How dare they set lower standards for everybody other than Asians and whites! That's racist!"

Diane Ravitch is hollering and yelling about it and so is everybody in her comments (most of 'em, anyway) and I barely had the strength to wade through a third of the comments on the original article.

Let that idea simmer a little bit; I'm sympathetic, believe me. I'm gonna change the subject for a bit but I'll get back around to this.

Let's assume that, as American educational officials pretend to at the moment, you believe that standardized tests of some kind are a good way to assess student learning. For the moment, I'm not going to debate whether that's actually true or not; let's just mutually decide that we *think* they do. It's good enough. If you care about standardized test scores, there's a couple of different ways to pay attention to how schools/classrooms/teachers/kids/whatever do on them. The first, which is the method No Child Left Behind followed for a decade or so, is the raw pass rate, and I think the pass rate is the number that most people are accustomed to wanting to look at. You just calculate how many kids passed out of how many kids took the test, and you're done. One number, easy to compare to other numbers. It's great!

If you tell a school, or a district, or whatever, that they're going to be judged solely on how many kids manage to pass Test X, here is what's going to happen: the "bubble kids" suddenly become the most important students in the building. Billy, over there, has parents who made sure he was reading before he entered preschool. His house has thousands of books in it, his parents both have graduate degrees, and he had the highest test score in your school last year.

You are not going to pay any attention to Billy. Billy's going to pass unless you blind him before he takes the test.

Shirley, on the other hand, is the product of a single-parent home and has an array of learning disabilities. The only book in her house is the Bible, and no one in the house can read it. Her mother has been unemployed for eight months and did not graduate high school. Shirley currently lives with her mother, her aunt, and the six other children they have between them and their home situation is at best wildly unstable. She struggles mightily with material four or five grade levels below her age.

Screw Shirley, too. It doesn't matter how much effort you put into her; she's *not* gonna pass no matter what you do unless you take the test for her.

The kid you're looking at is William. William's pretty bright, usually, but how well he does depends on his mood. If he's paying attention, and if he's taken his meds, he can be a good student. He struggles, and needs additional help, but he generally isn't the type to just give up on you; he's a hard worker if he thinks you like him. He didn't pass last year, but he was close.

Your Williams are now *the most important kids in your classroom.* Those kids– and they can be a large chunk of your room depending on what kind of school you teach at– are going to determine whether you pass or fail, or whether your school stays afloat or goes on probation. You're going to spend the lion's share of your energy on the kids who *have a chance* to pass the test but *aren't guaranteed* to pass the test. The rest of them are what they are; one way or another, it's a waste of energy.

Sad but true fact: Billy is more likely (but not guaranteed) to be white or Asian, and Shirley is more likely (but again, not guaranteed) to be black or Hispanic. William is a little more blended but he's a bit more likely to be some shade of brown than otherwise. The so-called "achievement gap" is so pervasive in American schools that I'm not going to waste the breath on talking about it beyond this sentence. It exists. It sucks that it's real, but it is.

If you focus on pass-only as your measurement method, you're going to get schools and teachers who focus solely on the *middle* rather than the top or the bottom. Kids who can't be moved from fail to pass, or who *won't* move from pass to fail, are a poor use of effort. You've got to get *each and every one* of those bubble kids because we have to show "improvement" on our grade's numbers from last year, even though these aren't the same kids we were measuring last year, they just happen to be the same age as those kids were.

This, obviously (I hope) makes no goddamn sense at all.

Here's a better way: pay little or no attention to pass rates, and instead focus on *improvement.* Okay, it's nice that Billy passed. Did he do better this year than he did last year? By how much? If the answer is "yes," you're doing a good job. If the answer is "no," there's a problem. If you have a bunch of Billys and they *all* did worse than they did last year, you have a *real* problem.

Shirley? We're not so worried about whether Shirley passes right now. Shirley entered sixth grade reading at a first-grade level. If you moved Shirley up to third grade in a single school year, you did a good job. Same as William– his score was 40 points higher than he did last year, but the pass cutscore moved up by 45 points. He still didn't pass, but he did better than he did last year. He showed improvement. This is a good thing.

It is also *hideously complicated*, and that hideous complication is why we tend to focus on pass rates instead, even though focusing on pass rates is stupid. Pass rates aren't complicated and they aren't hard to explain. Indiana, in particular, uses the improvement method, technically called a "growth model." Every kid that takes the ISTEP is compared to *every other kid who got the same score they got last year*, and then they're ranked as either a High Growth, Average Growth, or Low Growth kid. The problem is that sometimes you'll get some random-ass score that not many people got and a "high growth" score is a point. Or– and I saw this happen– some kids will *lose* points and still be High Growth, and other kids will gain immense amounts of points but because everyone who got a 512 last year ate their Wheaties before the test this year, that will somehow count as Low or Average growth.

It's still better. Indiana's model has stupidities embedded in it– those kids I talk about in the last paragraph are not hypothetical– but it's still better than relying on pass rates, because *every kid's scores count*. I don't want to just focus on my bubble kids. I want to focus on *everybody,* because Shirley having a bad year hurts me just as much as William or Billy. When we get down to the nitty-gritty details of who's High Growth and who's Low Growth I might find some places to quibble, but as an educator I can't afford to prioritize one group of students over another.

And that's a *good thing*. We want that.

Back to NCLB for a minute. One of the bigger pains in the ass of NCLB was the way it disaggregated groups of kids into subgroups. Not only did your school have to pass a certain percentage of its kids to stay in good standing, but a certain percentage of your black kids and a certain percentage of your ELL kids and a certain percentage of your special ed kids and a certain percentage of your girls and a certain percentage of your blah blah blah blah blah *all* had to meet Adequate Yearly Progress goals. If just *one* of your subgroups– and these damn things could be on the level of a *single family* in a smaller school– was out of compliance, the *whole school was*. God help you if you had a diverse student body. *Somebody* was bound to mess up; you were screwed. It made being in a basically segregated school a *good* thing. If everybody was black (and my school in Chicago was) then you didn't have to worry about eight different racial subpopulations screwing your numbers up because the Garcias or the Nguyens just got here last year and their kids don't speak English well enough to pass the test yet. Or because your school has a reputation for having a great special ed department, so you have *lots* of special ed students because parents fight to get their kids in your school– which means when that large group of special ed students don't make AYP, your whole building is labeled "failing" because of the *very thing that made your building successful.*

It sucked, mightily. And, again, this is *not* hypothetical.

What we're seeing, up there, in that looks-really-racist chart, is a combination of a growth method and NCLB's disaggregated student populations. They're acknowledging that the achievement gap exists. We cannot simply state that we want 80% of everybody to pass (to pick a number at random) because it's unrealistic for all of our groups of kids. Instead, what we want to see is for everyone to make *improvement.* Well, to improve, our Asian kids have to hit a 93.6% pass rate. Our black kids aren't passing at the rates that the Asian kids are. We *still want improvement from them,* but for that group, a 79% pass rate represents improvement. We're still trying to bring up *all* of our kids; we're just realistic about how much we might be able to bring them up from year to year.

Of course, when you present it that way, without– at the moment– nearly 2000 words that no one will read of *explanation* first, you look racist as hell. And it was a terrible mistake for the state of Alabama to release these numbers like this. But it was a *political* mistake, not a pedagogical one.

One of the ideas that always comes up when we talk about this is that we should have "high standards" and "high expectations" for our students, and that when we acknowledge that some people aren't starting the race at the same place as others we're somehow not properly Standarding and Expecting things of them.

Sounds good, right? High is better than low! Standards and Expecting Things are good, too! So we should definitely have High Standards and High Expectations.

Well, great. Sure.

What's that mean?

No, really. I'll wait.

And there's the problem, see. You aren't really saying much of anything useful when you say you have High Expectations and High

Standards, and you run the risk of saying something incoherent if you're not careful.

Let's address high standards first. "Standard" has a pretty specific meaning in the education world. The Common Core is a set of standards; most states still have their own, as the Core isn't completely phased in yet across much of the country (and is a subject of no small amount of controversy on its own, I should point out). To say that we should have High Standards is basically just saying that we should be teaching kids material that challenges them to some extent or another and (usually) what the speaker actually means is that kids nowadays should be learning either the exact same stuff they learned when they were in that grade or something more complicated.

You can argue the merits of individual sets of standards; I happen to believe that, at least in sixth grade math, which is what I'm most familiar with, Indiana's standards are pretty solid. While I have a quibble or two with how the Common Core handles things I don't have much of an argument with it. Just tell me what to teach; I'll get the job done. What we *don't* have, in any state or jurisdiction or locality that I'm aware of, is any situation where the *standards* are different for black students or white students or girls or ELL kids or anybody else. Standards are standards; they're out there and they're not disaggregated at all.

So what we're really talking about here is what we expect from our kids.

And for expectations to be meaningful, they *have to be specific*. You can say that you expect everyone to do well. Great! Also pointless. Heck, you can expect anything you want. I can expect that my students will bring me cookies and milk every day and hurl a virgin sacrifice into the smoking maw of a nearby volcano for me once a month, but that doesn't mean it's going to happen.

Lemme say it again: expectations must be specific to specific students in order to be meaningful.

A few examples, all based on real kids I had last year: Velma had the highest math score in the fifth grade before landing in my room. Velma, frankly, doesn't have a lot of *room* for growth. She was already pretty close to getting as high a score as scores can get.

I told her she'd gotten the highest score in the fifth grade. She was excited and proud.

"I expect the highest score in the *school* this year, y'know," I said. Which, honestly, was asking her for maybe a ten-point bump in her score. In all seriousness, my challenge with Velma last year was to keep her realistic. I haven't seen her ISTEP score for sixth grade yet, but when you start off with a score as high as hers is and there's an upward limit to how well she can do, the simple fact of the matter is no matter how good a teacher I am her score is likely to *drop*. Demanding perfection from her would have been stupid. It would have stressed her out and stressing her out would not have helped her performance. I used the "best score in the school" line once or twice over the course of the year, mostly to hassle her, but short of a nosedive there's not much she could have done to *disappoint* me with her score. She's a great kid and I know she did her best.

"Do your best!" sounds like weasel language, doesn't it? That's not high expectations! Should I have ridden the kid like a donkey all year about driving her enemies before her and hearing the lamentations of their women to avoid the "lacks high expectations" canard? No, of course not; screw that. Expecting a kid to do his or her best is really all you need to do if you have a kid who actually *will* do their best, and there was never any risk of Velma giving me less than 100%.

Fred, on the other hand, had the *lowest* math score in the fifth grade. His math score was seriously a hundred points lower than the second-lowest kid I had. It was so low that I was seriously wondering whether he got off by a number or something and had managed to answer every question on the wrong line.

Early on in the year, Fred's mother requested a parent/teacher conference with me and asked me flat-out if I thought he was going to pass ISTEP with me as his teacher. And I told her that there was basically no chance whatsoever of that happening. I more or less guaranteed her that her son was going to fail again. He was just too damn far behind; too far to catch him up to grade level in a single year barring a miracle or him moving into my damn house.

And then I told her that I wanted to see a higher point gain from Fred than any other kid I taught this year, and spent about fifteen minutes explaining exactly how we were going to do it, and then worked my ass off all year keeping him as close to on-track as I possibly could. And now, eight or nine months later, there's maybe *one* kid out of the fifty-some I had last year whose score I want to see more than I want to see Fred's. I bet I got a 200 point gain out of the kid– not remotely enough to get him to *pass*, mind you, but about 166% of the score he got last year.

And now there's Daphne. Daphne missed passing the ISTEP in fifth grade by something like *five points,* basically a single question. I looked her mother in the eye on Open House night, which is before school even starts, and guaranteed her that her kid was going to pass ISTEP this year. Dumb? Yeah, probably, but I was in a grand mood. Daphne spent the year ricocheting from one emotional crisis to another; I caught her cutting herself on two separate occasions (note that *I'm* the one doing this, not her parents,) rarely turning any work in, etcetera. Daphne had a terrible year– but a terrible year that had basically *nothing* to do with her math class or her math teacher. Do I expect Daphne to have made strides in my math class when Daphne probably did well by keeping herself out of a mental hospital over the course of the year? Of course not. I'd like to see that she made some improvement and, honestly, I suspect she did– she didn't turn in any work, which meant she spent most of the year failing all of my classes (and that's a discussion for another time) but she seemed pretty on the ball whenever I was assessing her on anything *other than* turned-in assignments. But her ISTEP score? I really don't care anymore. Staying the same is *just fine.*

You tell me: which kid do I have higher expectations for? Which kid is going to make me look better when and if our test scores get reported solely on pass rates? And, again, notice: for Fred and Velma, the answer is *neither*. One kid failed and will fail again; one kid passed and will pass again. Neither of them is going to move my numbers *at all* if we're using a pass-rate-only evaluation of our test scores. Daphne is a *perfect example* of a bubble kid (and, I can't make this clearer: all three of these kids are *real*, even if their names aren't) and so my skills as a teacher and my building's probation status are going to depend on whether one kid who takes one test on one day spent the night before using erasers to scar her own arms or not.

This is unacceptable.

The pass model fails because it *does not* encourage high expectations. It encourages a narrow focus on a narrow band of kids who can be motivated, bribed, pushed or dragged across that line. And if the state doesn't particularly like their pass numbers from a test, all they have to do is manipulate the cutscore and–

voila!– we had more kids pass than we did last year! We're Doing Things over here! I am certain that Illinois did this while I was teaching there; I had kids pass the ISAT my second year in Chicago who had absolutely no business "passing" anything at all, and the state and CPS crowed and crowed about our pass numbers.

They manipulated the test scores. Period.

While I'm not going to go so far as to claim that I didn't teach my own kids anything, what they *did* learn from me had precious little to do with their test scores at the end of the year.

And this year? I hoped that one of my kids didn't fall by too much, that one kid failed, and that a third kid just didn't crater. And I maintain that all three of those things represent "high expectations."

Any chance of me convincing anyone of that without 3000 words of explanation?

And now I'll present an outline of how a growth model for standardized testing ought to work.

•First, and most importantly: *remove any notion of "passing" and "failing" completely* from the testing process. The two most well-known standardized tests in America right now are the SAT and the ACT, the two tests for college readiness, taken by nearly every high school student at some point or another. Even kids who don't necessarily plan on going to college take at least one of those two tests, and many take both. Have you ever heard of someone "failing" the SAT? No. Because it can't be done. You can get a terrible score on it, yes, but you can't fail. Your score is your score. As it stands right now, creating a cutscore for "pass" and "fail" does the following: 1) It makes the test scores easier to manipulate (just change the cutscore and it looks like more kids passed– or that you've demonstrated "higher expectations") 2) it puts an artificial, pointless barrier between kids who barely passed and kids who barely failed. There is *no difference* between a kid who got a 450 or a 460; that's a question or two. It's I-had-breakfast-and-eight-hours-of-sleep versus I-sorta-have-a-cold-today. But if you put the pass cutscore at 455, it *looks* like a huge difference. 3) It embeds a shaming mechanism into the test that has no good reason for being there; 4) It creates an incentive for teachers to focus solely on the "bubble kids;" 5) It provides no useful information to anyone that the actual scores did not already provide. There's *no reason* for these tests to have a passing score. It is an entirely useless piece of information. I can think of only one exception, which is when districts use test scores as part (PART!!!) of a decision on whether to pass a student from one grade to another. Most districts don't do that, though, since frequently scores aren't available until very late in the year– it's the second week of July already and I don't know my kids' scores yet.

•Removing the notion of pass/fail from the equation makes it easier to focus on *growth* as the metric. As I've demonstrated already, this means that you can't exclude any of your kids as "unimportant" to your school's or your classroom's end-of-year scores. How a student's score changes from year to year becomes vastly more important than what their score actually is, which is as it should be. There's a bunch of ways to do this; Indiana's model has some good points but is unnecessarily complicated. Here's my suggestion:

•Pick a start year; any start year. Divide those kids into groups based on percentile scores on the test. I like using decile groups (in other words, ten) but you can use quintiles or quartiles or whatever. In Year Two, determine how much those kids moved in their test scores from year one to year two. There are a bunch of ways to quantify this depending on how mathy and technical you want to be about it; the simplest way is to determine movement by thirds. In other words, let's say the lower third of decile A went from a drop of 140 points to a gain of 10 points, the middle third went from a gain of 11 points to a gain of 90 points, and the top third went from a gain of 91 points to a gain of a million points. You could use standardized deviations from the average or something else if you wanted, but the point is there's a different standard based on your decile. This means that the kids in the top decile (who don't have a lot of movement up left for them) can only gain a few points or possibly even lose a handful and still be "high growth," and kids who start in the low decile and drop anyway would probably be "low growth" kids. This allows some recognition of where the kids started from without looking as random as Indiana's model does, where a kid who got a 525's growth model looks wildly different from a kid who got a 526; it should be a bit more predictable as well.

•In Year Three, you determine how much they moved from Year Two, and so on.

•Kids who transfer into a district aren't a problem because they should have *some sort* of score from their previous district, and even if they were taking a different test in their previous district a percentile score on that test should be trivial to determine. They then join whatever decile their percentile score belongs to. If they literally took no standardized tests in their previous district because of their age or their district's policy on standardized tests, well, the world doesn't end.

•Teachers and schools are evaluated by how many kids they have in the "average growth" and "high growth" categories. Those kids should have been enrolled in the district for a certain minimum number of days (I'd say no fewer than 75% of the school days up to the test week) and– and this may be controversial– should have been *present* for a certain minimum number of days as well, and I'd say the absence number should be more stringent than the residence number. I can't teach a kid who isn't in school, and I also can't *control* whether a kid's in my classroom or not. Individual districts or states can determine on their own what their requirements for average growth and high growth numbers should be.

One disadvantage of this is that it does make it more difficult to present school data to the public in an easy-to-understand, useful format. One big advantage of the pass rate is that parents understand it; moving from 50% pass to 52% pass has a clear meaning, while we'd have to present averages and medians and all sorts of other data to make the new model understandable when we're comparing schools. That said, if you want a "one number" comparison, providing the sum of the "high growth" and the "average growth" kids would do nicely; giving all three, combined with averages and medians of actual scores, would provide sufficient information, and anybody who wants to dig deeper (provide numbers per decile, too, maybe) is welcome to.

It's not great– we're still paying too much attention to standardized test scores– but it's certainly better than what we're doing now.

In Which I am a Bad Student

August 1-4 2013

Lemme put the tl;dr right at the beginning: I had a ukulele lesson yesterday, it didn't go well, and I've turned it into an exemplar for everything that's wrong with teacher training and evaluation nowadays.

I am not musically talented. I am an at-least passable singer; I believe this is true because I have been complimented on my singing by people who had no reason to lie to me about it. But that's *it*. I have, in my life, attempted to play the violin, the French horn, the trombone, the recorder, the harmonica, and the ukulele, with scattered examples of sitting in front of a piano and tapping at keys until I figure out how to play whatever song is in my head. I can play *none* of those instruments.

Important secondary fact: I am an autodidact. The way I learn best is by trying to figure out shit by myself, and I never learn *anything* unless I am interested enough in it to work on it on my own. My ideal circumstance for learning (and this, incidentally, is precisely how I have "learned to cook" over the course of 2013) is to muddle through on my own but to have a clear set of guidelines for what to do and– and this part's important– to have access to an expert (generally, my wife) nearby who can either answer my questions ("does this look done to you?") or occasionally check on me and note terrible mistakes in progress or provide advice for things I have missed. Everything, and I mean *everything*, that I am good at doing or know a lot about, I taught *myself* to do. It's how I learn. I know this about myself.

But back to the lack of musical talent thing: I know nothing about music theory; talks of diminished chords and As and flats and sharps and such goes right the hell over my head. I also, and this turns out to be super important for learning a stringed instrument, have *very little dexterity* in my left hand. My fingers, even when I'm at my thinnest, tend toward the short, chubby, and clumsy. I am also the most right-handed person I have ever known; my left hand is basically useless for most tasks. How the hell I'm such a good typist I'll never understand. My point is that being able to fluidly and quickly move the fingers on your left hand to precise spots along the neck and the frets of a stringed instrument is, obviously, *critical* to being able to play. I can't do that. I used to be really into Guitar Hero and Rock Band, right? I topped out at Medium difficulty. I could 100% basically any song I wanted on Medium, because I *didn't have to move my left hand*– but as soon as I moved into Hard and that blue fret came into play, meaning that I'd have to *move my hand* and *remember where it was* if I wanted to keep playing, I failed completely. The jump was too big. And I tried really, *really* hard to master that difficulty level, or at least get decent enough at it that it was *playable*. Never happened.

For these and other reasons, I am a *poor student* for anyone trying to teach me the ukulele. This is a fact. It is undeniable. I am also busy and, at least lately, not terribly prone to use free minutes to pull out my uke and practice. This is also an undeniable fact.

Now let's talk about my teacher, and I'm going to try very hard to be fair, because despite everything, I actually quite like the guy. I'm gonna call him Dale. That's not his name, but it'll do.

Dale is clearly impressively musically talented. He plays five or six different instruments and appears to have working knowledge of many more. He has perfect pitch; he's had me retune my uke a few times based on something that he heard and has then pronounced satisfactory a change in tone that I couldn't even *hear*.

He's also, at *best*, incredibly socially awkward. He's a giant of a man, probably a few inches over six feet tall, and bulky even at that height; he's got a lazy eye, and it's clear within a moment or two of talking to him that this is a guy who has always felt like he's stuck out. He doesn't like to touch people; he was clearly uncomfortable when I tried to shake hands with him when we first met, and did not have a confident man's handshake. I did not repeat the experiment for our second meeting. I wouldn't be surprised– no, let me rephrase that; I would be surprised if he were *not* on the autism spectrum.

Now, again, I want to make absolutely sure I'm being clear here: *none of these things make Dale a bad person.* Okay? Is that obvious? On top of everything else, he's nineteen at *most*, and heading off for college this fall, and I am willing to cut alllll sorts of slack to high school students for being gawky and awkward. It's entirely possible that I'm completely off on the autism thing and the kid's just been the oversized music nerd his entire life and is socially withdrawn as a result, and a few years in the music school he's headed toward will turn him around. I wasn't exactly a fuckin' butterfly at nineteen either, y'know?

Unfortunately, this combination of high amounts of technical and practical knowledge combined with little to no skill at communicating them mean that Dale is a bad *teacher*. He can *show* me how to play the ukulele and the mandolin and the guitar and hell probably the aquaggaswack all day long; he cannot *teach* me. It may be that if he had a student who had similar levels of musical talent to his, who knew how to play other instruments but didn't know the uke specifically, that he could teach *that* student. He cannot teach me how to do it. His method is to sit there with his uke– which, complicating things, is about 2/3 the size of mine, constantly out of tune (so he claims) and lacking many of the frets that mine has, which makes it impossible for me to follow what he's doing– play something in some way, then say "or you could do this," and play it another way, then spend a minute talking about what he just did, using vocabulary that loses me so instantly and completely that I can't actually give you an *example,* then do it again, then do another thing. It hit me about halfway through my lesson yesterday that I couldn't come up with a way that Dale might do things differently if I *hadn't brought my ukulele with me at all*. He never actually *asks me to do anything*. He'll show me something, I'll try to replicate it (poorly) on my own, he'll tell me what I did was right, most of the time, even if it's wildly apparent to me that it wasn't, then he's off to some other thing.

It is a sign of my own utter confusion and his lack of teaching skill that I don't even feel like I can *complain adequately* about how this lesson went. I don't have the vocabulary; I can't even tell you what he was *trying* to show me. I can't tell you what he was *doing*. He would play, look at me for a second, I would strum something, then he would go right back to what he was doing. Both of us checked our watches a lot. I think both of us felt like we were wasting each other's time. It was awful. I literally can't tell you the last time I was in a situation where I was supposed to be learning something and been so completely in the dark as to what the hell was going on around me or what I was supposed to be doing. Complete, total failure.

(That's as critical of Dale as I'm going to get, by the way. Again, I like the guy. He's very very talented. But he's not a *teacher*.)

Current "reformer" theory in teacher training states that so long as we get people who are trained in subject matter and good at said subject matter, it's not actually very necessary to actually have any training in *teaching*. Teaching's just something you can pick up– after all, anybody who knows a lot about something should be able to pass that knowledge on, right?

Well… obviously not. There is a *hell of a lot more to my job* than mere subject matter. Now, I'm both smart and arrogant, so I'm not going to pretend that the wealth of knowledge that I bring into my classroom doesn't *help*– but it simply is not sufficient to make me a good teacher. Dale's a perfect example here; someone with an immense amount of practical and technical and theoretical knowledge of his field who is, nonetheless, entirely incapable of passing that knowledge on to someone who lacks it. This is what we lose when we, as Indiana does, start suggesting that all you need to be a math teacher is to major in math, or that a competent engineer ought to be able to teach science. It's truthy: it *sounds* right, but it's bullshit. Teaching doesn't work that way.

Conversely, you get people with comparatively little subject knowledge who are nonetheless great teachers provided that they're in the right position. I couldn't teach kindergarten or nursery school to save my life; does anyone really feel that you need to be an especially book-smart person to do either of those jobs successfully? Hell no. You need a firm knowledge of child development, a hell of a lot of patience, and more compassion and empathy than any two normal people should have. Many of the band and orchestra teachers I've met haven't necessarily struck me as musical prodigies but they don't *need to be* to make kids love music. They need to be able to *teach*.

In my career I've taught computer classes to preschoolers through eighth graders, language arts and social studies to seventh graders, math, science and social studies to sixth graders, and now

I'm about to start teaching math to seventh and eighth graders. I did not take *a single math or computer class in college.* And I am better at my job than you are at yours. (Also more of an asshole, but that's neither here nor there.) I'm not a good computer teacher or a good math teacher because I have exceptional skills in either area. I'm good at communicating my knowledge. *That's* the important part. And that's what we need to focus our teacher training efforts on– not on acquiring knowledge, but at developing the skill to pass that knowledge on. It ain't the same thing.

And, for a rough segue into evaluation: let's pretend that Dale isn't just teaching uke classes on the side at a little community music center. Let's assume he's trying to make a career of this. Does he, regardless of whether I actually think he's skilled at teaching, deserve to be evaluated by how well I play the ukulele after I'm done with his class? I've already been clear, I hope, on both my own initial lack of skill and– importantly– the fact that I really haven't done much of anything to make myself better in between our sessions. Is me being bad his fault? Is my lack of trying, my lack of practice, my fuckin' ridiculous schedule what with my jobs and my two-year-old and (let's own it) my laziness toward improving at his craft *Dale's* fault?

Should I count toward his evaluations, if they give me a uke test at the end of his class and I fail it? How much? A little? A lot?

And now let's talk about Tony Bennett.

Tony Bennett is Indiana's former superintendent of education. "Former" because he got tossed out on his ass last year, after all of Indiana's teachers rioted against his lying, crooked ass. Turns out we have enough friends and relatives that the new Superintendent got three hundred thousand more votes than the new *governor* did. He then went to Florida. And less than a year later he's had to resign *that* job because his corporatist ass got caught cheating.

I'll nutshell: one of the (Indiana) schools that Tony *just knew* should have been an A school ended up with a C under his new, bullshit school grading system. That school just happened to be run by an influential Republican donor, who just happened to have donated several hundred thousand dollars to the reelection fund that wasn't enough to keep Tony from getting tossed out on his ass. The entire grade system therefore got revised until Tony's buddy's school got the A that he'd already predetermined it deserved. Meanwhile, several Indianapolis public schools in basically the exact same situation got taken over by the state for *their* poor grades. Coincidentally, I'm sure, the new system managed to lift the grades of several other ~~charter~~ for-profit schools. Amazing, innit?

Here's the thing: honestly? I ain't mad. This entire "school accountability"/charter school thing has *nothing to do* with educating children. It is solely and singularly concerned with shoveling taxpayer money into the pockets of corporations and people who are already rich. The system is already so corrupt and evil to begin with that it's hard to imagine anything that would make me see it as *worse*. *I already knew* these people were lying scum who were out to get me and enrich their friends. Additional proof of same isn't gonna make much of a difference.

Wanna hear a secret, though?

All grades are arbitrary bullshit.

Lemme say that again: All. Grades. Are. Arbitrary. Bullshit.

(Also, prepare for a segue. I'll throw in a line here to make it easier.)

We all know this, but we don't like to talk about it much, because everybody likes to pretend that that grades actually mean something. But *every teacher on Earth* has at some point or another adjusted something because somebody who *should have* gotten some grade got some other grade instead. And if they haven't done *that*, they've set their grade system up to prioritize some sort of behavior over some other sort of behavior. It's all gamed, one way or another; the only thing is how honest and how transparent you are about it.

Lemme give some examples. The easiest way to grade is just to make everything worth the same number of points as the number of questions in the assignment. So if I give you fifteen questions tonight, that's worth fifteen points, and the 50-question test is worth fifty points. At the end you divide the total number of points earned by the total number of points possible and then you have a score. Problems with this: one, it's a *lot* of grading, and two, it leads to weird inequalities like Monday's homework being worth a lot more than Thursday's just because Monday's worksheet had a lot more questions on it. It also leads to difficulties in quantifying anything that *isn't* a worksheet or a textbook assignment, and makes grading things like essays a huge pain in the ass.

So, okay, use rubrics, or something? And make every paper worth X points, where some percentage of that is grammar, some is "style," some is awarded for some nebulous idea of how well the essay adheres to whatever the essay was supposed to be about. You're still making arbitrary determinations here about how much you prioritize papers over other things. You're still gonna give the kid who turns in every single assignment but can't write to save his life a "C" because his papers weren't good enough, where Billy who is a decent writer but misses assignments and half-asses everything gets a "B" because papers are worth more than the assignments he skipped.

And you're gonna make some sort of decision about how to change your grading based on your *feeling* that Kyle *deserves* a better grade than Billy because he works harder.

Let's throw some special ed kids in the mix. What if Jenny's got an IQ of 60 and doesn't have a chance in hell of being able to do the same assignments that Monica can handle? Should she just automatically *fail?* Or do you alter your grading policies somehow to account for the fact that *she's doing the best she can do* and that ought to be worth something? Maybe she on her best day on Earth can't do better than Billy-the-halfasser can do. Should Billy get better grades? Is the sanctity of your precious grading system worth more than convincing Jenny that trying at school is worth something and tossing her a little bit of success once in a while? What if Jenny has an IQ of 60 but is *also* enormously lazy? Because, *I promise you*, special ed kids can be lazy just like everyone else!

What kind of person are you if you determine that not breaking the Rules of Your System is more important than keeping a kid from tuning out school altogether?

What happens if you give an assignment that you plan to grade a certain way and then all your kids bomb it? What if some of the kids who bomb it are kids who habitually get *everything done right?* Is that your fault? Can you change your grading system to give some kids better grades? Or just throw the whole thing out?

How do you tell the difference between Amber-the-A-student getting a C on something because your grading system was BS and Amber getting a C because she's slipping? And, again, do you care about the difference?

How do you handle missing work? Do you accept it? Because you'd better be prepared, in some schools (mine's one of them) to fail 2/3 of your kids if you don't take late work and if you record it as a zero. Or do you have a "floor" beneath which no assignment can fall? Where do you set that?

For the record, here's my grading system, for whatever it's worth:

•I accept late work up until a formal progress report goes out; this basically divides a quarter in half, so you can turn in late work from the first half of a quarter until halfway through it and then those grades are locked. I send informal PRs home every couple of weeks. Late work gets docked two points from a turned-in assignment.

•Missing work is a 0. No turned in assignment receives less than 50% as a score unless it's clearly halfassed or not finished. It's incredibly rare for ANY turned-in assignment to receive less than 30%.

•Assignments from the textbook are worth five points, period, and are graded on completion. I *do not* grade them item-by-item and do not correct them. If they're turned in and done roughly according to instructions (ie, work is shown, stuff like that) it's going to get full credit unless I can tell you just wrote some shit down and hoped I didn't notice it.

•Assignments from the workbook are worth ten points and are graded on partial correctness: in other words, I arbitrarily choose ten problems from the two pages and grade those. Not every problem will count. I grade the same ten problems for everyone, though.

•Tests are usually worth fifteen or twenty points and are graded completely. Occasionally I will give bonus points for spelling your name right if a test happens to have twelve questions or something like that. Tests are the only exception to the grade-floor rule; if you turn in a test with no correct answers you are going to get a zero for it.

•Occasionally I will collect morning bell-ringer work and grade that on completion; it's usually worth a point or two and cannot be made up.

•Extra credit is crazy-rare and is only given if it's available to everyone. I won't make up an assignment for you specifically.

Here's what I'm prioritizing: I put a heavy emphasis on effort, which is why those textbook assignments are pretty much automatic As if you turn them in. Similarly, the grade floor: if you *try,* you're going to get some points for your effort. I accept late work because I feel like kids should be able to make up for their mistakes; I don't accept it after a certain point because those mistakes should cost you *something*.

And, yeah, I've taken a look at my grades, gone "Damn, Chelsea should be getting an A, what happened?" and taken a look at how to fix it. Not to the degree that Bennett did, obviously; his shit was pretty egregious no matter how you look at it. But I can't pretend I don't get it. Because grades are arbitrary. Period. We shouldn't pretend otherwise.

On Intimidation

August 13 2013

And suddenly, now, with just barely over a week left until school starts, I'm stressed out.

The worst teacher I ever had– by such a margin that the title is not even in question– was my freshman honors Algebra teacher. I got a D in his class during the third quarter; I don't remember the grades in the other three, because the D was so shocking. It was not only the only D I got in my entire academic career, I'm almost certain that there weren't even any Cs to keep it company.

After every test, he would change the seats. He'd arrange everyone by grade, with no attention paid to any other aspect of seat arrangement– such as, say, whether you could see the board or not. The lower your grade got, the closer you were to the front of the room. The very worst grade in the class was reserved for the front row, right by his desk.

He let you retake tests for a better grade. The retake test would be from a different textbook, though, and if you were retaking Chapter Four's test, you'd better hope that Chapter Four from that other textbook covered the same material or something you could handle, because if not, too bad– he *averaged the two grades together,* meaning it was entirely possible to pull your grade down for the retake. Weirdly, most of the kids in his class hadn't figured out how he was coming up with these new tests; I think most of them just thought either he was really hard or they were stupid. No, he was stupid. And lazy, and destructive.

One of my finer moments in my freshman year– and, honestly, there weren't many; most of my freshman year memories are painful in some way or another– was figuring his game out halfway through

255

a test retake that I was utterly bombing and, instead of turning the thing in at the end of the hour he'd given us after school, ripping the thing to shreds and throwing it away instead. Minor rebellions, obviously, but it felt good: *I figured out your game, dude, and you can go fuck yourself.*

I hated him. Now, twenty-two or so years later, I'm teaching his class– my honors 8th graders are taking freshman-level Algebra. I have the textbook right in front of me. Now, mind you, I *know this shit.* I made it through the year and I have repeatedly demonstrated over the course of the intervening years (if nothing else, by passing the PRAXIS; I was in the top decile somewhere) that I can handle this material.

But man, am I suddenly sweating *teaching* it.

Flipping through the book has been intermittently terrifying in the way that flipping through math textbooks is always terrifying; looking over what I'll be covering in the first six weeks revealed a couple of vocabulary words that I didn't immediately remember the definitions of but produced an "Oh, *that*" type of reaction when I found the definitions. Most of it really isn't so far from the math I'm teaching. But I don't want to be adequate about this. I want to *already be* the best Math teacher these kids have ever had, and by the end of taking their second Math class with me I want to be *even better.*

Terror! Whee!

One other thing that's hammering on me, here, is the teacher I had for *sophomore* year math– Geometry, in other words. At the time, he was the best Math teacher I'd ever had, and one of the best teachers, period. Then I had him again for Calculus senior year. And it wasn't the same. I don't know what changed, really; if I just had really bad senioritis and I wasn't prepared to take his class as seriously as it deserved (I was also taking Physics, which was kicking my ass just as hard as Calculus was, but I was *excelling* in Physics despite the workload) or if he didn't feel as confident about the material, or if he was trying to Hold Us to a Higher Standard and it just wasn't working out, or what. But it wasn't the same. If I'd only had him for Calculus, I'd have forgotten his name by now, and honestly my goodwill toward his class would have worn out a hell of a lot sooner. I only made it as far as I did because I'd liked him so much sophomore year.

These kids loved me when they had me in sixth grade. (Something like 30 of the 33 kids were in my class that year; this isn't an exaggeration.) Now they've got me two years later, for what should be a much harder class. This isn't exactly a shaky analogy I'm constructing here.

Not only do I have to do better than one of the worst teachers I ever had, *at the material he was supposed to teach me,* which is intimidating enough, I have to outdo one of the *best* teachers I ever had, by being better than he was the second time around.

I ain't saying I've bitten off more than I can chew; I don't think I have. But damn, does my mouth feel full right now.

On Open House

August 20 2013

Parent Number One accosts me as I'm going to my car to get a change of clothes, half an hour before Parent Night. She starts screeching at me about the class her daughter has been put in. I am not her child's teacher– have, in fact, never had either of her children in my class– and couldn't change her child's class if my career depended on it. She also doesn't want the daughter in question to be in my class. I'm not sure why it's my problem at all, to be honest; this literally has nothing to do with me at all and once I tell you who to bring your problem to our conversation ought to be *over*. Further elaboration isn't doing either of us any good and is wasting my time. I need every second between now and Parent Night actually starting. She ends the conversation– well, technically, *I* do, by saying I have to go and leaving– by suggesting that her daughter is in the class she's in because they're "giving all the goddamn poor kids vouchers," which makes exactly as much sense as you think it does.

Conversation with Parent Number Two starts well, but then veers off into crazytown. I had her daughter in sixth grade and got along with her well; Mom starts complaining about her daughter's troubles with her *fifth* grade teacher and then segues immediately into how she was personally responsible for getting our previous principal fired. I gently suggest that our principal was chosen by the school board to take over and improve a school that was in substantially worse shape than ours was; I leave out the fact that they nearly doubled his salary when he moved, that he's currently the highest-paid principal in the district, or that they've literally (and I'm not misusing this word) given him anything he wanted in his new position, which is a mildly idiosyncratic definition of *fired*. Mom

259

assures me that she knows the right people and has influence in the right places. I think to myself that I'd like to get fired the same way he did. Carte blanche and twice the money sounds just horrible.

I walk into a conversation Parents Three and Four are having with another teacher so that I can introduce myself; they haven't come down to my room and there's not much time left in the Open House and I'd like to speak with everyone I can. I walk into what turns into an extended ten-minute rant about how another student in the same grade as their child "mercilessly bullied" their son on the bus "every day" all last year and no one ever did anything about it. The following are facts: 1) I know both children involved; 2) They provided an accurate physical description of the bully, so I know that this is not a case of mistaken identity; 3) I am the bus supervisor for the entire building and *every single* accusation of any form of misconduct on the bus comes through me before any administrator sees it; I heard *nothing* of this situation from anyone involved at any point last year, despite multiple conversations with the accused child's bus driver *about that child*; 4) The two students *do not ride the same bus* and never did; 5) the bully in question spent most of the last half of the year on half-days and during that time arrived at school at 8:30 or so and left by 11:45– in other words, he never rode the bus *at all* for nearly the entire second semester.

This story cannot possibly be true.

Furthermore, the two boys were in different classes and would, to the best of my knowledge, have had rare chances to encounter each other during the school day. (I will admit I can think of one way in which that statement may not be true; the numbered items above are indisputable.) I spend a few minutes wondering if these people know that they're lying or if they're far enough gone that they've convinced themselves this impossible tale is true. I reflect on the number of stories you see and hear about vicious bullying in schools that "no one ever did anything about," and the number of times I've been directly accused of same, under similar circumstances, and briefly consider quitting my job.

Parent Five pulls into the parking lot as I'm walking out of the building. Parent Night has ended at 6:30; it is 6:40. She has her son, a fifth-grader–the youngest grade in our school– with her. I tell her that the Open House has ended and that she is not going to be allowed into the building. She starts off very angry, but calms down

260

as I talk her and her son through the procedure that we'll be following in the morning. I tell him my name, make him repeat it a couple of times, and show Mom what door to drop him off at and make sure he knows where to go when he gets inside the school and that they both understand what time they're supposed to be there. I tell him to come find me when he gets into the gym and that I'll show him where he's supposed to sit, and answer a few other questions from her about other things that will happen during the day and how much interaction he'll be having with the seventh and eighth graders, a subject she seems especially tense about. By the end of the conversation, she's smiling and the boy actually tells me he's excited about school tomorrow before they drive off. As they leave, I realize that I never actually got *his* name. No worries; he says goodbye as they pull out and repeats my name back to me.

I suppose it could have gone worse.

On Progress and Discipline

August 22 2013

I don't normally bleed at work, and I'm not terribly fond of it, but I managed to be bleeding before the first bell even rang this morning. I broke up a fight– or, at least, what was about to be a fight– and one of the combatants managed to scratch my finger in an annoyingly painful fashion while I was separating the two of them. I spent most of the rest of the day telling my boss that he owed me workman's compensation once my finger fell off. I didn't know one of the kids; he's relatively new to the building (possibly this year, but I think he came in late last year) and the other one was an eighth grade kid who I've been having irregular run-ins with since he was a fifth grader. I've broken up more than one fight he was in and manhandled him into the office on more than one occasion.

The weird thing? I actually get along with him fairly well, all considered. He didn't start this particular brawl, and the fact that he let me get in between the two of them and separate them actually represents progress. I'm not going to go so far as to say that I've made a connection with him– I honestly don't think *anyone* in the building except maybe for the football coach can say that, and I'm not even sure about him– but I seem to have figured out how to finesse him to get him to do what I want. I grabbed him in the hallway later that day and let him know that I'd put in my write-up that he wasn't the guy who started the fight, and talked to him again at the end of the day to make sure that there wasn't any ongoing beef with the kid who had been messing with him. He said it was going to be okay, and I figured he was telling the truth.

Then his bus was late. The buses are terrible this time of year, and this was a perfect example of why: when the bus finally showed up to school, there was still an elementary school kid on the bus, who either didn't know his address or had gotten on the wrong bus or *some* piece of nonsense that was keeping the driver from dropping him off at home. Complicating things, the driver's radio wasn't working properly for some reason and she wasn't able to get in touch with anyone at the little guy's school. So the kids all filed outside to get on the bus and then the driver had to make them all wait (outside, in drizzling rain) while she went inside and made some phone calls to try and figure out what to do with the kid.

This didn't set well with him. So he and another kid (his girlfriend, maybe? And as I'm writing this it occurs to me to wonder where his little brother was…) decided to walk home.

They can't walk home if they're supposed to ride the bus, even if the bus is late. There are massive legal issues involved; if they're bus riders, they ride the bus. Period. Is it unreasonable? Yeah, probably, on some level or another, but it's still the rules and I've got to enforce them. I managed to get him to head back into the building, but he wasn't happy about it.

"This is fuckin' bullshit."

One of our new paraprofessionals overhears this. "What did you just say?"

"Fuckin' Christ, dude, leave me alone."

He takes exception. And I did something I haven't done before: I actually *waved the guy off,* letting the kid go into the building unmolested and holding the para back (not physically, mind you) to convince him to ignore a fourteen-year-old not only directly disrespecting him but doing so in an impressively profane fashion.

And the interesting thing? By the end of the conversation, the guy agreed with me. The kid, meanwhile, went inside, like I wanted him to, and while he was the last to sit down like he was supposed to, he *did it.* The thing about this kid? He's all street, and has absolutely no parenting whatsoever at home. His mother's worthless– another teacher in my building, who has his little brother, and is new to the building, met her the other day and said she was the rudest person she'd ever met. I have absolutely no idea where or who his father is. For all I know, neither does his mother.

This kid is *not going to back down to anyone,* and he's even less likely to do so when he's already had a shitty day. There are things I need him to do, right? I need him in the building, where I'm not going to get my ass sued off if he gets hit by a car while he's walking home or just never goes home at all. I need him sitting down and being with everyone else (granted, this I need less than I need the first thing) and I need him back on the bus in a few minutes and not in a screaming match with the driver who's keeping him from getting home on time. And a stranger (remember: new paraprofessional) getting all in his face about how he said "fuck" a couple of times is not going to make any of those things happen.

So I basically let him get away with dropping the F-bomb a couple of times. Maybe I'll talk to him about it tomorrow. Today, this afternoon, wasn't the time, and doing it in a confrontational manner definitely wasn't going to work. Confrontation itself doesn't work with this kid. The only thing I've seen work with him is quiet, calm conversation and simple, direct requests, which he'll usually comply with, and ignoring his occasional outburst.

Is this doing the right thing? Or am I guilty of not having High Standards of Behavior now? Have I Done Nothing to punish his profanity if all I do is remind him about how to talk to adults tomorrow? Is a lunch detention really gonna make any difference?

More on this tomorrow.

(PS: I'm not demeaning the para, by the way, who so far I like a lot. I might very well have reacted in precisely the same manner he did if it was a *different kid*, one who being a bit more confrontational with had a chance of being effective. But it was never ever going to work with *this kid* in *this set of circumstances*. I don't want to make him seem like a bad guy– he just made the wrong call in a snap decision.)

On Being Surprised

August 30 2013

I had been thinking that the challenge this year was going to be the Algebra class. Two weeks in, I'm pretty sure I got that one completely wrong. Granted, we're still mostly in "review" territory, but the Algebra kids are moving along swimmingly; if anything I could probably be pushing them faster if I really wanted to.

No, the problem is going to be third and fourth hour. First and second hour are just a roomful of kids. Granted, they swing toward the knuckleheady, and there's more of them (32 or 33, I think) than I want there to be, and I'm sure there are going to be days where I hate them– but functionally they're no different from any number of other classes of kids I've had over the years. They're going to do well on some things and not so well on others. They're going to be challenging, because teaching anyone anything is challenging, but they're not going to be *challenging,* if you know what I mean.

On Tuesday, the school counselor walked into my room, shoved a roster under my nose, and told me to eliminate six of my kids.

"Permanently?" I said, eyeing a certain set of the roster.

"To (other teacher's) room," she said, and I started looking at a different set of kids. She then showed me a different list, which contained the six kids that she was moving *into* my room– special-needs students, each and every one of them. Turns out that it had been decided that I was going to co-teach with one of our special ed teachers during those class periods, and they'd decided to consolidate all the available special education students into my room out of the two seventh grade math classes that were available.

267

(Weird, true fact: There are two different kids who would have been on my list if I was consigning them to the flames, but were not on my "willing to send to someone else" list. I'm not sure what that says about me. Certainly not that I'm sparing the other teacher. The impulse is more "no one is your math teacher but me" than anything else, and I certainly insisted on protecting the kids who I had last year. I dunno.)

Teachers who read this will all recognize this anecdote: you know how sometimes you'll get a writing assignment turned in from a kid, and it's so bad that you literally don't have any idea how to correct it? That the only thing to do is start over completely, and by "start over completely" I mean "wipe the kid's brain, send him back to kindergarten, and reeducate him entirely"? Where there's simply no way to *correct* the thing without entirely redoing it?

I've had that impulse in writing classes many, many times, unfortunately. I have never had it in math before, in twelve years of teaching, until this week– and this week I had it with *four different kids*. I have two students with sub-60 IQs, and another pair of boys who I don't even want to talk about on account of their plethora of learning disabilities and neurological disorders. Plus at least four kids who are *severely* autistic (two of whom, just for the record, aren't actually in this class) and two with massive behavioral disorders.

I've never co-taught before; I don't know precisely how it works, and the special ed teacher, who has spent all week buried in beginning-of-year paperwork, has been content to sit back and let me drive the bus for now, although that will probably change as we get to know each other and find some time to actually collaborate. And I've never, ever had a class this *low* before. I've got two kids in there who were among my lowest students last year (although they both showed genuinely impressive gains over the course of the year) and this year *they are the smart ones*.

Good to know I'm going to have an easy, relaxing year, right?

On Basic Human Courtesy

August 31 2013

I have a stupid job, or maybe I have a nonstupid job and I'm just a stupid person.

As I was driving to the gas station on my way to my other job this evening, praying for the fumes in my gas tank to keep the car moving until I got there, I drove past a couple of my students. They all know what my car looks like, so I honked the horn and waved and pulled into the gas station, maybe a block or two farther down the road from where they were.

Two minutes later, as I'm filling the tank and cursing how much the price of gas has jumped over the past week or so around here, they come running over to say hello. They ask where I'm going and I tell them OtherJob; they say they're on their way home and are supposed to be home by five.

I look at my watch. It's not too far from five already. Coincidentally, this is also when I need to be at work.

"Soooo…." one of them says. "Can we get a ride home?"

And here's where my job is stupid. Any other person in any other situation upon running into a couple of people who he knows and likes and who happen to live along the way he's already planning to go would say yes to this *instantly*. It's common bloody goddamn courtesy. But since I'm a teacher I have to go through this stupid mental calculus where I weigh how much I trust these two girls and whether I can trust their parents to not be stupid idiots before I throw all that to the wind and decide to treat them like they're people and not my students and agree to give them a damn ride home, like somebody who isn't a complete asshole.

Note that this may actually have *broken the law*. Not a joke.

269

Luther M. Siler

It isn't until I'm pulling out of the parking lot that the *real* bullshit of this transaction hits me: I've just had two teenage girls run up to me in the parking lot of a gas station, they've gotten into my car, and I've driven away. I make a joke about it and look around for blue-and-whites; luckily, no one official appears to have noticed. Which is a bit of a relief.

The drive home takes all of five minutes and is uneventful. Then I nearly kill one of the little idiots when she darts in front of my car after getting out instead of going around behind it like a sensible person.

That would have been fun.

In Which I Memorize Things

September 6 2013

We've just finished the third week of school, and I've probably spent most of the past three weeks breaking the law in some form or another. I have a thick yellow folder in front of me right now, a folder that is full of special ed documentation about my many, many special education students. There are, right now, 22 dossiers in that folder, ranging from three to thirty-some-odd pages long. Some are for students I don't actually have in my classes and have never met. I'm legally responsible to have read and understood (and "understood" in this case should be taken to mean "memorized") the documentation on each of those kids. And I am *absolutely certain* that I don't have all of my IEPs yet, and am even more certain that I don't have all my BIPs yet, as I don't have any at all from seventh or eighth grade.

Here's the thing: special ed paperwork, and the idea of an "individualized education profile," or IEP, is a very good idea in theory that has gone *terribly wrong* in practice. The idea that a student with disabilities shouldn't be educated in the same manner as a student without those disadvantages is a good one. The idea that special education students deserve the same access to a quality education as other students is a good one.

The idea that I'm supposed to memorize, on average, fifteen pages of accommodations for each of my twenty-some odd students, and that one person is supposed to *write* these IEPs for what could be dozens of kids with special ed needs in a low-income building, is *insane.* It can't be done, and *great* special ed teachers are getting driven out of the field because half of what they do now is push around stacks of paper, and then endlessly revise those stacks of

271

paper based on federal and state and local guidelines that can't ever seem to stay consistent for more than a week or two at a time. It's freaking madness.

And then there are the BIPs, or Behavior Intervention (I think) Plans. I support the concept behind the IEP, if not the way they're implemented. Half the time I think BIPs are bullshit. I'll be honest: I still haven't sussed out what the distinction is between a kid who ends up with a BIP and a kid who is an asshole. It probably has something to do with whether they think the kid's assholism is an *actual disorder* or not. What they basically are is a list of steps that you're supposed to follow with Little Johnny Special Snowflake when he's fucking up so that you can get him back on track– steps that don't have to be followed for any other student. While it's not supposed to mean this, frequently in practice a BIP means that LJSS can get away with shit that would get other students literally crucified– because LJSS is *just too much of an asshole* to be expected to conform to regular behavioral norms.

But whatever, right? I adapt my disciplinary methods to the individual student I'm dealing with all the time. In other contexts– hell, right here in this book, a couple of chapters ago– I've defended not nailing a kid to a wall for something that might have me reaching for a hammer with another student. I *get it,* even though it annoys the piss out of me.

Here's the problem: BIPs have to be seen and signed by *every adult who works in a school* who could conceivably come in contact with a kid. Not just the teachers. Every *adult.* So, like, bus drivers and cafeteria staff and custodians and the lady who does photocopying on Wednesdays are in theory supposed to have read and memorized the BIPs for every student who has one that they could possibly come into contact with. Some of us (me, for example) could theoretically come into contact with *every single student in the building.*

I have BIPs in this folder for students who I have literally *never met,* who are not in my grade or my wing of the building, who I may never have in my class. I may not be able to pick Jenny Fucknut or Johnny Fingerbang out of a lineup, but I'd sure as shit better know their BIPs so if I happen to encounter them freaking the fuck out in the hallway I can calmly redirect them or go through their deep breathing exercises or whatever the fuck; it's not like I've read the damn things yet. All of that without knowing their names, because frequently when these kinds of kids do lose their shit they're likely to tell me that their name is Go Fuck Yourself, and I don't have a BIP for him.

Seriously; the people in the cafeteria line are expected to know these things. Gimme a fucking break.

(The good news? I have very little grading to do this weekend, and my lesson plans are done for next week, so at least there's a chance in hell that I'll end up getting to them at some point.)

SPIDER!!!

September 11 2013

I love my homeroom, right? They're wonderful kids and I would keep them forever and ever if I could, but sadly they're only my homeroom and I don't have them for half of the day like I did last year. I have duty in the gym in the morning, so often my girls are already waiting at my door for me when I get to homeroom– my unofficial rule is that I don't care when the bell rings, if you *beat me* down to my room (which is out in the sticks) then you're not tardy to class. Anyway, one day a week or two ago I'm letting the girls into my classroom when I hear a *piercing, blood-freezing scream* from one of them– a kid who I like a lot but who could very justifiably be accused of being slightly high-strung.

I spin around. Note that at this point I'm not even raising my voice. "Nefertiti, what in the *world* is wrong?"

She points at the *tiniest arachnid ever*, which is toddling across the carpet and minding its own damn business. She's still shrieking. "THERE'S A SPIDER!!!!"

At this point I lost my temper a little bit, I admit it– I don't like *horrifying piercing noises* first thing in the morning, and drilling my ears for no reason is *worse*— and I snapped at her– loudly– before I really even realized I was doing it.

"Child, unless that stupid thing has *laser beams* coming out of its eyes that I need to know about, you'd better leave it alone and get your butt into my classroom before the bell rings."

And that was it. I've yelled at one kid this year and it referenced spiders shooting laser beams.

I think I can live with it.

On Putting Out Fires

September 20 2013

I spent all day today putting out fires, and right now I'm split between basically writing a short-ish "YAAR EXHAUSTION" type of story or going exhaust*ive* and giving you a moment-by-moment breakdown of the horror that was my day. I think I'm leaning toward exhaustive– after all, I'm at my other job, my lesson plans are already done, most of my grading is already done, and it's been raining all day so there really isn't much else to do.

It is entirely possible that this will end abruptly with "fuck this, you get the idea" or something similar; please don't hold it against me.

BEFORE SCHOOL: I wake up on time, but somehow going into my office to check and see if my paycheck came in and my union dues got paid takes half an hour. I have no idea where the time went; I rush through my shower and manage to forget to eat breakfast before leaving the house. I do manage to pack a lunch, which is an unimportant detail except insofar as it indicates that I was *in the kitchen* while I was forgetting to eat. I manage to make it to work on time.

AT SCHOOL, BEFORE SCHOOL STARTS: As I've mentioned many times, I cover the gym in the morning. There are a couple of other adults in there with me by the time the lion's share of the kids are at school but it's not uncommon for it to be me and two hundred kids. Today, our assistant principal (new to the building this year) comes in and asks me in a rather pointed fashion what the building policy is on cell phones. Note: she is *fully aware* of the answer to this question, which is that the kids basically aren't supposed to have them, ever, and if they do they're to remain in

277

backpacks until such time as they are placed in lockers, and at all times they are to be off.

I explain to her that *my* policy on cell phones is You Don't Want None There Won't Be None; I ignore anything that is plainly related to listening to music, force phones to be put away when anything that could involve taking pictures is taking place, and tend to react reasonably, but harshly, to kids who are actually talking on them– which is rare. The main reason is that every second kid in the gym has a cell phone with them and if I start taking cell phones away (which I am fully empowered to do by district policy) I will do *nothing but* take phones away and fight with kids every morning, all morning. I fully understand why this is the policy in *class* but it is virtually unenforceable when the ratio of kids with cellphones to teachers doing something about them is literally a hundred to one. I am not interested in that fight every day, and kids who are being reasonably discreet are going to be ignored.

She does not appear happy with this explanation until I look around and find five kids who are quietly listening to music and ask her which one she'd like me to take a phone away from first; that child will immediately find the other four and ask why I'm not taking *their* phones away instead of whoever I'm talking to. They will then report to their parents that I'm picking on them. No thank you. This appears to clear the fog a bit and the conversation ends with no directive to change my policy.

The kids are on edge in a weird sort of way but there aren't any fights or any real threats of one. But there's a weird vibe in the gym that I don't like.

HOMEROOM: The bright spot of my day, once the girls are done screaming about another spider in the hallway, which is quickly becoming the theme around here lately. We do a Word of the Week; this week's word was "ration." The kids are supposed to write a sentence for me; I select the best two or three and send them to the librarian, and he names a victor for each grade level. One of my girls wins today. If her name was Charlie, this would be the sentence: "Mr. Siler told me that he has a ration of Charlie that he is allowed every day, and I don't get to talk to him again until tomorrow."

I am beloved, obviously.

SUCCESS: (It's between homeroom and first hour, I didn't name it, shut up.) I'm ten minutes into my lesson when the teacher next door asks if she can borrow me for "a minute." There are two teachers in the room for Success so I have the other one take over and go into the hall. There is an eighth grade girl who I only know by sight (new to the building this year) pacing and muttering angrily in the hallway with her fists clenched and tears in her eyes. I get over my initial *why the hell is this my problem* bewilderment and ask her what's wrong.

Here's a thing: Seventh and eighth grade girls are *really fucking easy to manipulate.* I don't know if you knew that but holy Christ is it true. Some fifth grader– a bloody *fifth grader*— on the bus asked her if she thought she could beat up some other student, and now she's angry because she has to fight this other student. Who, as it turns out (and unbeknownst to the teacher next door) happens to be in my room at that very moment. I spend a few minutes trying to calm her down and then call the other student into the hallway. They are *both* saying stupid shit like "I don't wanna fight her, but if she hits me I'm gonna kick her ass," and pointing out that *both of them are starting their sentences with saying that they do not want to fight* is not doing the job it should of convincing them that, no, nobody's actually going to fight here.

This conversation literally costs me the rest of the period. By the end of it I'm reasonably convinced that I'm not going to have to break the two of them up at any point today and I'm ready to break the fifth grader's head myself. Then the teacher pulls *another* student out of her classroom who I have to convince that none of this shit was his business and he doesn't need to threaten the first girl because nobody wants to fucking fight here so stop being a damn asshole. I make a mental note to have a stern word with the fifth grader and bemoan the critical thinking skills of everyone under 30. I do virtually no teaching in my first class of the day.

FIRST AND SECOND HOUR I have to spend keeping an eye on one of my autistic kids because he's making his para insane and in general the kids are being weirdly dependent and pretending to not be as bright as they are. This is an affliction that is not at all specific to them but they're bad about it; I need to break them of this habit. I have deliberately put a review packet together for my kids today because I have a crapton of desk work that *must* get done by the end of the day and my prep period was full before I even walked into the building.

(Note: this is something that most people don't realize about teaching. I have virtually no time to do anything during my day that isn't teaching. Any paperwork of any kind, including *all* of my grading, gets done on my own time. It had piled up too much by this point. It was time to have a work day.)

At any rate, this plan didn't work out, because the kids had way too many questions. I got a bit done but not as much as I wanted.

THIRD AND FOURTH HOUR was when all hell broke loose. Third and fourth hour contain The Twins, who are several essays unto themselves and who I will talk about in more detail when I have the mental energy. And if I'm being honest this is already a fourteen hundred word essay and I haven't even *gotten to the stressful part.*

So, yeah: I'm gonna abbreviate. A *lot.* The twins are, very soon, gonna get the shit kicked out of them, and it's going to be their own damn fault– and that is not something I am prone to say about my students, particularly students who have obvious developmental issues. I suspect fetal alcohol syndrome; this is unconfirmed. But they piss off everyone they come into contact with, more or less *deliberately,* and then they tattle on the kids they've pissed off.

For example: if walking past the desk of the biggest gangbanger in the building, a kid who was in *jail* before he got expelled from his previous school and sent to us, maybe you don't knock his shit on the floor on purpose. Because he might literally *kill you.*

It's happened *twice.*

The kids nearly caused *two different fights* today, and that's not counting the number of students they got pissed off at *them.* I ended up sending them out of my room with my co-teacher for their own safety and not only arranged for them to not be in the halls during passing period for the rest of the day but literally created a security detail to get them to their buses at the end of the day so that they didn't have to be in the gym with the rest of the kids.

I fully expect to find another article in the paper in a few months about how I didn't do anything about the way they were mercilessly bullied, by the way. I'm at 1700 words; this would be twice as long if I *actually talked about* all the nonsense they created today.

And that was before my fifth and sixth hour got into my room.

God, I'm tired.

Trans-Abdominal Reverse Blowjob

September 24 2013

I'm in the gym this morning when a couple of sixth graders, both girls, run up to me. I know one of them fairly well, at least for a kid who's never been in my room, and know the other one not at all. They hand me a note that the one I don't know found in her locker at the end of the day yesterday.

"I didn't write it," the one I know says, which is kinda weird because I've not accused her of writing it yet.

I read the note. It may be the most obscene, sexually explicit thing I've ever seen in a school before. It's from another student– presumably, another sixth grader, who bills himself as this other girl's secret admirer. It begins by talking about how much he'd love to put his fat dick right into her mouth and have her suck on it for a while, and by the end of the note he's fucking her in the ass so hard the tip of his dick is coming *out* of her mouth. At the end it asks her to write back and put her response to this well-considered proposal into a nearby locker– which, as it turns out, is the locker of the second girl– thus the panic about me accusing her of having written it. She volunteers to show me a sample of her handwriting; I decline the offer.

Perhaps the worst thing about this is that I genuinely can't tell whether this note is meant to be sincere or whether the writer is trying to make fun of the girl or hurt her feelings. It's obviously horrifyingly inappropriate, and *God how big of a fuckup as a parent do you have to be* that your kid thinks it's okay to write notes like this to someone– but what makes it worse is that I think he thinks it's going to *work*. The kid's not trying to scare her or harass her– he may actually *think this is a love note*. Which may be the most

283

Luther M. Siler

fucked-up thing I've ever encountered as a teacher. Honestly, I think
if it hadn't referenced the other girl's locker I might never have seen
it. The girl who brought it to me seemed a little grossed out but
otherwise wasn't as bothered by the note as I was.

Sixth graders. And sixth graders in *September*, which is
important– this is a year with *a lot* of development happening. This
would still be surprising in May but not nearly as much. And, again–
this note is beyond the pale even compared to the other shit I've
confiscated over the years.

I bring the assistant principal over and hand the note over to
her. We both suspect that we can catch the culprit with the cameras;
I haven't followed up yet to find out if they caught anything.

I promised a funny part.

The last line of the note– before the "Please reply in locker blah
blah" part, and right after the bit about the trans-abdominal reverse
blowjob– is "If it's okay with you." One sentence. All by itself.

I'm going to fuck you in the ass, eleven-year-old, until my
dick *comes out of your mouth...* but only if you think that's okay.

Yeah.

On Being Smart

September 28 2013

One of the things that's really hitting me with my Algebra kids this year is just how unused they are to having to *work* in class. These kids are smart, right? And they're used to being the smart kids, and with only a couple of exceptions they're used to *thinking of themselves* as smart kids; it's part of their self-identity; something they're proud of.

Smart kids are supposed to get stuff. School's not supposed to be *hard* for smart kids.

Literally the first thing I said to these kids when they walked into my room on the first day of school was "Welcome to high school." I'm walking a fine line here; I'm trying to push them as far and as fast as I can without breaking any of them, and it's an interesting and delicate dance to be involved in. I'm thinking about this because I graded a mid-chapter quiz today, and I'm trying to figure out what to do with the kids who didn't do well– some of them are *clearly* smart kids (remember, I've had everyone in this group before except for about three of them) who are so unused to having to ask questions in class that I think they're actually ashamed to have to do so. I gotta work on that. By and large, considering the volume of stuff I threw at them in the last three weeks, they did well. It's just the handful that didn't that I need to figure out how to handle.

Getting a new student on Monday. I can pronounce neither of her names, and I only know she's a she because I looked her up. My wild-ass guess is that she's Kenyan. This should be interesting. (Kenyans speak, what, English and Swahili? With maybe French as a distant third? Hopefully there's not a language issue.)

285

So, yeah. Smart kids. Then there's whatever is going on in that picture there, which I took in my classroom on Friday after a student *volunteered* to do that problem on the board. Now, this is my special ed group– don't get me wrong, I'm not in any way trying to *make fun* of this kid, just to give you an idea of the range of abilities I see throughout the day, because after this kid leaves my room I get the Algebra kids, a group that contains a kid who got a *perfect score* on his math ISTEP last year. I was trying to demonstrate the various algebraic principles; the problem on the other side of the one on the board is 4x(6×5) and the idea is that they're supposed to notice that both equal 120 regardless of where the parentheses are. Note that this does *not* represent multiple attempts to solve the problem. He did the green part first, where rather than multiplying four by six (or adding it six times, which would have been fine) he tried, unsuccessfully, to raise four to the fourth power. Then he switched to a blue marker, getting into an argument over whether it was "his" marker in the process, added six to itself four times and got 24. What caused him to privilege the 24 over the 32, I'm not sure, although this kid is prone to giving me multiple choice answers on assignments– he'll literally write "3 or 30 or 4 or 17″ next to a problem. The blue squiggle next to the 2 under the actual problem is supposed to be a 4; there are also huge handwriting issues.

Then he switched to a *red* marker and tried to multiply 24 by 5. Note that he's first tried to add it, but only four times, and that the presence of a tens digit has utterly confounded him– he's added the two pairs of fours to get two eights, then added those and gotten six instead of sixteen. This isn't forgetting to add a digit; I was standing behind him watching this performance and he actually said "four plus four is six" while he was writing. He then turned around and told me that the answer was six, at which point I took this picture, erased the whole mess, and walked through everything with him.

I do this often, by the way– letting a kid dig himself into a hole can frequently be useful because it gives me insight into how they handle mathematics. Unfortunately, for the second time this year, I'm looking at this and getting the "holy shit, I can't fix this" vibe that I get from writing sometimes. The kid can't handle basic multiplication on his own, and even with other adults in the room I can't get around to them often enough to help him with everything he needs help with. Luckily, he has involved parents; I can't imagine what he'd be like otherwise, as this is what he is like *with help at home*.

I'll figure it out– I'll figure *him* out, I always do– but Christ, do I have a headache right now.

On Teacher Pay

OCTOBER 3 2013

I voted to approve the new teacher's contract, but I'm not terribly happy about it. Oh, it's not bad, as they go– we're getting a small stipend this year basically just for the hell of it and we actually get our first real raise in seven years (two whole percent!) next year, that is assuming we don't get placed in one of the two lowest evaluation categories. More money is good. I like money, even if 2% after having frozen salaries since 2007 is kind of bullshit. It's still better than the no-money we've been getting on the last several contracts.

The problem is that this round of negotiation really has driven home one important fact for me: That two percent hike got eaten by inflation years ago. We are *never really getting a raise again*, and by "we" in this case I basically mean all of Indiana's teachers. The way things used to work, we got yearly step increases until you hit sixteen years of experience and after that you were depending on actual increases to the pay scale (ie, "raises") for any further increase in salary. What this meant is that if you stuck it out long enough eventually everybody made the same amount– sixteen years is a long time, granted, but it leveled you out sooner or later, barring differences in how many degrees you had.

Now? Anyone in my district who makes more money than me right now *is going to make more than me forever*, and anyone under me– particularly anyone unfortunate enough to have started in the last few years since even step increases became impossible– is going to make less than me forever. There's no merit pay of any kind that can increase salary– not that I even think that's a good idea, mind you– and no bonuses for good performance. There's only the stick;

289

you don't get any raise of any kind if you end up in the lowest two evaluation categories, but it's not like you get *more* money if you get a superior ranking.

It's unfair in a way that I really, *really* don't like. Teaching is already a career with effectively no mobility– a teacher is a teacher is a teacher and while most districts do name team leaders and things like that (a job I've held myself on a few occasions) there is no actual salary increase attached to that. As a teacher, I'll never be anyone's boss unless I move to administration– which *isn't teaching*. There's literally no way to be *promoted*. Which means that the fact that there are teachers in my district who not only make ten grand more than me but will make ten grand more than me *forever* really stick in my craw. Similarly, I'm mentoring a first-year teacher this year. I make fifteen thousand dollars a year or so more than she does and I will make fifteen thousand dollars a year or so more than her forever, until she wises up and realizes that spending her entire life making $32,000 a year is untenable. (She gets a raise to $34,000 in 2014-15; the poor schmucks stuck in the bottom two pay steps get a little bump. But she'll be stuck there forever.) Once she realizes that she can make better money and have *much* less stress in her life doing something else, she'll be gone, and she'll be replaced by another 22-year-old making the same $34K that she did until she quit.

Note, also, that while teachers making more than base pay will be *quitting* a lot, or retiring, they will only be being replaced by teachers making base pay. Which means that you travel far enough down the road– and I bet it won't be more than seven or ten years– and something perilously close to all of us will be stuck at that base pay level. Which people will put up with until they have kids, then they'll move on to jobs where they're actually treated like educated professionals, and kiss teaching in a public school district goodbye.

Which is a feature, and not a bug. This is what they want, and this is what state law is written to do.

I fucking hate Indiana.

Homonyms are Complicated

OCTOBER 4 2013

Under ordinary circumstances, I'm not really the type to bribe my classes with candy. I hand it out now and again, certainly, and will use it as a minor incentive for minor stuff that they would be doing anyway. For example, we write every Friday morning; I give the kids who read what they write a Jolly Rancher. Sometimes I give them two if whatever they wrote manages to entertain me. I used to do a trivia question every week that was due Thursday; kids who got it right got a piece of candy on Friday. (You may be seeing a theme here.)

I've been trying to give away the same container of Jolly Ranchers for a while now, to the point where I thought they were getting old– at least to the extent that it's *possible* for Jolly Ranchers to get old– and I decided that today I was finishing off the container no matter how ridiculously contrived the reason for handing out Jolly Ranchers was. Making this easier was the fact that most of my knuckleheads in first and second hour are suspended right now, so the kids were much more likely to behave than normal.

"Work on this assignment," I declared grandly, "and I shall reward those of you who do not annoy me with these Jolly Ranchers. Perhaps more than one, if you please me greatly and are not otherwise foolish."

(Yes, those exact words.)

Fifteen minutes later, they were noisy. "Remember, folks, Jolly Ranchers are at stake here," I said.

...

One of my smarter kids– I *swear*, one of the *smarter* ones– puts her hand up.

291

"Is you sayin' you gonna give us steak, too?"

(I'm reproducing her words precisely. She actually generally doesn't talk like this; her speech gets more slangy when she's expressing surprise. True story.)

For a moment, this confuses me.

"No. What? Jolly Ranchers. No steak."

The students go insane. There is a chorus of complaints. I remain bewildered.

"You said Jolly Ranchers and steak!"

Sigh.

There has to be a factory somewhere that's actually hiring, right?

I'm In this Job for the Paperwork

October 17–18 2013

It's bullying awareness week, or some such bullshit. Or maybe it was last week; I'm not aware enough to be sure. Here is how most people think bullying works: A bunch of children mercilessly pick on one poor bullied student, causing him to be very sad and blah blah blah. Here is how bullying actually works, most of the time: *everyone involved* is an asshole and a bad actor and everyone involved is doing their best to make everyone else involved miserable as best they can, and the ones who are either the sneakiest or the quickest to file paperwork get to be the "victims" while everyone else gets to be the "bullies." Oh, and every time the word gets used I have a legally-mandated two days to "do an investigation" and a bunch of complicated paperwork to fill out, only to find out that Suzie told Allie that Shelly said that Sammi said that Sharon said that Allie said that Sheryl was a slut, only it turns out that Shelly didn't actually say that, Sharon said that Allie said that to Shelly but Suzie is dating Sammi's ex-boyfriend and Sharon's mad at her because of it so Suzie *actually* said that Sammi was a slut because she was defending her on Facebook and today this is a world-ending crisis and the *very second* I'm done with the paperwork they'll all be best friends again and oh never mind we worked it out until they hate each other again next week.

If you think I'm exaggerating, you're *not a teacher*. I have been doing this job for twelve years and I can count the number of unambiguous instances of clear bullying that I have witnessed on *one hand*. Everything and I mean *everything* else has been mostly-mutual teenage bullshit of some kind or another.

293

That said, one of the events I'm about to describe so far may actually be pretty clear-cut, but I haven't done my *investigation* yet.

Keep in mind, by the way, that these are seventh-graders. Thirteen-year-olds.

My third and fourth hour got wrecked because of some vile combination of the following events: 1) One student suggesting to another student that she'd be open to a threesome with her ex-boyfriend and one of his friends; 2) That student reporting to the ex-boyfriend and the buddy that said threesome was a possibility; 3) Upon being asked about the possibility of said threesome via Facebook message (I've not seen this message, but other staff members have) the original young lady replied "No... well, maybe... LOL" and then was 4) *surprised somehow* when the two young gentlemen in question told *everyone they knew* that this was going to happen. And then during art today there was apparently 5) an attempt to get the threesome bargained down to some oral sex for the non-ex-boyfriend while the ex-boyfriend, apparently, watched. Throw in a different ex-girlfriend of the same dude doing her best to keep her nose in their business and one of the two guys deciding to try to get everyone to ostracize the second girl in the first conversation and you have *eaten my entire day,* as all four of the principals involved are in my third and fourth hour.

Note that, legally, this *isn't bullying*, and I know this because we just had a meeting where we went over the legal definition of bullying in great detail. And also note that *nearly none of it* took place in school and yet it destroyed not only my entire day but at least two other staff members' days as well. (And while we're noting things, note that this still qualifies as sexual harassment and it's not being ignored.)

I'm leaving the school counselor's office after spending the first half of my prep period with her and one of my paraprofessionals hashing all this out and making sure we've written down everything and notified everybody we need to notify. I've done no actual *preparing* during my prep period. I *never* do any preparing during prep; that's Fireman Hour.

I walk to my room, sit down at my desk, and start composing an email. The teacher next door walks into my classroom with another kid in tow– a student who I had in sixth grade two years ago who I just last week had referred to a risk-assessment psychologist on account of she's cutting herself. The student is being disruptive and making her job impossible and can she stay in my room for a bit? Sure, why not, this email's gonna take me a few minutes and I'd prefer to have a good excuse to stay in my room if I can have one.

Less than five minutes later, I'm taking her back to the nurse because she's started shrieking and ranting about how ridiculous it is that anyone thinks they can stop her from hurting herself because it's *her body* and she's gonna hurt herself if she wants to. Well, fuckin' great, let's go talk to that psychologist again. I go get the counselor (whose office, remember, I've just left) again and that eats another fifteen minutes of the only break (to do *everything else I have to do but teach*) that I have each day. I have just enough time to run down to my room and get something that I need to have photocopied by the morning; I make it down to the photocopier as the bell is ringing and discover that the photocopier is broken.

Well, great.

Off to the gym, where I make the seventh and eighth graders sit where they're supposed to and call off buses as they arrive. I spot one of my (7th grade) homeroom girls, normally the sunniest, biggest-smiled kid you've ever seen in your life, sitting in the stands, bawling her eyes out.

No goddammit don't ask this can only cause trouble what are you doing jesus this day is long enough don't you NO GODDAMMIT YOU DON'T WANT TO KNOW WHY ARE YOU WAVING HER OVER JESUS STOP IT NO NO

"What's wrong?"

"Nothing."

I consider simply replying "Bullshit" and don't; there are a few buses gone by now and there are a bunch of other teachers in the gym, so I can pull her into the hallway without officially abandoning what I'm actually *supposed* to be doing.

We go into the hallway.

"Let's try that again."

She takes a deep, shuddering breath. Sobs again.

"Sweetie, there's *absolutely no way* I'm letting you get on the bus like this. Tell. Me. What. Happened."

"(Eighth-grade boy) won't leave me alone. He asked me out yesterday and I said no and he just *keeps asking* and he's been bugging me about it all day. I can't get him to *stop*." And she starts bawling again.

Which: again, *not bullying*. But is, again, at least at first blush, a pretty damn clear-cut case of sexual harassment. By some sort of divine providence, the boy in question is part of the reason that the wrist-cutter earlier got put into my classroom; the two of *them* were feuding about something too.

I note that he's already left and ask her if he has her phone number and if she thinks he'll be calling or texting or Facebooking or anything like that tonight or if he knows where she lives or if she will be quit of him until school starts tomorrow. She confirms that he has no way to get in touch with her and I tell her that we'll talk about this tomorrow morning. I reflect that she has *many* older brothers (like, seriously, at least four, plus at least one sister) and consider simply making sure that *they* have this kid's address.

I put her on the bus and stop in the counselor's office on my way out, asking her if she has any room on her lap left, and (as I am mandated to do by law whenever I encounter instances of sexual harassment or bullying) notify her as to the content of the conversation I've just had and that I'll be following up with my official within-two-work-days investigation during homeroom.

At least I know what I'll be doing during seventh hour tomorrow.

I end the conversation with the counselor early because there is a parent in the office who is *screaming at the attendance secretary* so loudly that I can hear it halfway down the hallway through *two* closed doors. As it works out, both the principal and the assistant principal have been out of the building all afternoon at different meetings and so there is really no one in the office who the secretary can refer her to.

"Yeah, I'll talk to you tomorrow, I'mma go deal with *that*," I tell the counselor, and leave her office, attempting to summon my Calm Face. Luckily for (very likely) everyone involved, by the time I got down there another teacher had intervened already and maneuvered the lunatic into the hallway and out of the office. As it turned out he was apparently who she was looking for anyway; I hung around for a minute until I decided he didn't really need any help (turns out that kids who are angry psychotics tend to have angry psychotic parents; who knew?) and went down to my room to get my stuff, the music of her discontent accompanying me the whole way.

The end.

In Which Something Entirely Unexpected Happens

October 18 2013

Have you read the previous chapter yet? Of course you have! You read books in order, right? Sure. So you know all about the sexual harassment issues that blew up my third and fourth hour and then ate most of my prep.

Remember the bit at the beginning, the bit that I almost deleted on account of it was the Same Rant All Over Again and wasn't entirely connected with the rest of the piece? The bit about how bullying is a Huge Fucking Deal until the very second the kids are best friends again and then oh, wait, we were filing formal complaints on each other? *Never mind.*

Yeah, keep that shit in mind.

Today's highlight involved confiscating a note from the threesome-wanting blowjob-denier in the first story, who threw the whole school into a tizzy and wasted several hours of the time of at least three different staff members by filing a formal complaint of bullying against two other students, one of whom was her ex-boyfriend and the other of whom was his best friend.

The note was passed through the *second* girl in the first story– the one who everyone was mad at because she supposedly started everything– to the non-ex-boyfriend, to be given to the ex-boyfriend.

Note that I barred the two boys from class today, hoping that a day without them would help to calm things down a bit.

The note was asking the ex-boyfriend to please please please take her back so that she didn't have to give up on true love.

I took it to the counselor.

297

"I cannot deal with this without using words like *idiot* and *moron*, and I probably also cannot deal with this without pointing out in clear language to this young fool that this boy thinks of her as nothing but *pussy*. It is therefore your problem."

I have nothing else to say about my day.

See If You Can Make Me

October 24 2013

First things first, because this is going to be a bit of a downer and you deserve something at least a little funny: I somehow managed to make it through the *entire day* with a massive hole in the crotch of my pants that I didn't notice until I went to the bathroom during my last-hour prep period. I assume no one else noticed it; I can't imagine a universe in which I don't get the hell mocked out of me for it if they did.

I did something I've never done today: got pissed off and stormed out of a faculty meeting.

(Second disclaimer, and lemme put this right up at the top so I'm not misunderstood: I am manifestly *not blaming the people* who brought me the information that caused me to storm out of the faculty meeting today; I am not shooting the messengers and they were just doing their jobs. Nor am I pissed at my boss. The fact that at least two of the people involved may well *read this* is in no way related to the early disclaimer.)

I'll try and nutshell the background for those of you who aren't teachers: Every three weeks our students get a math test and a language arts test. The tests are the same across grade levels– in other words, every seventh grader takes the same math test– and are *supposed* to be the same across the corporation as a whole, although I'll admit right here and now that the math team at my school has altered individual questions that we thought were unfair or poorly written in some way and we didn't bother getting permission for it. We're required to display the results of these tests on what are called *data walls*, because us educators like having complicated names for things. I generated an Excel document for

299

everyone that takes the test results and spits them out into pie charts that are broken down for the test as a whole and each individual math objective (generally, three) that is being tested. The data is genuinely useful; I can keep track of where my kids are at relative to each other, to the grade as a whole, and I can see where my instruction doesn't seem to be working– if my kids bomb one objective that the other teachers did well on, that may be an indication that I'm doing something wrong, or that the other teacher has an exceptionally good technique for something that perhaps I might want to steal.

The data, again, is displayed *on a class level* in the classroom. No individual scores, no names. Just how each *whole class* did.

Apparently some lord high muckety-muck downtown has decided that that's not good enough. We're now required to do "student-centered" data walls; the charts aren't enough.

A "student-centered" data wall is one where the kids are posting *their* results on the wall– supposedly thinly veiled by using student numbers instead of names or some such shit like that. The idea is that the kids are "aware of" and "own" their results, which somehow isn't the case when I *give them their tests, discuss them, and then discuss the class results with them, which I do every time I give a test.* We're supposed to create some sort of bulletin board somewhere in the room where we can have the kids put their little name-tag *thing* up in the band (red, yellow, green) where their score landed. In case it's not obvious, green kids did great, yellow kids passed, red kids… didn't.

I've talked about him before: my freshman year Algebra teacher was the worst goddamn teacher I've ever had in my entire life, and a large part of what made me hate him as much as I did was his practice of rearranging the seats after each test– *by test score*. The kids who did the worst would be in the front row, all the way back to the kids with the highest scores, who ended up in the back. The very worst score in the room would end up right in front of his desk. And you'd stay there until the next test, when, more than likely (because he was a shit teacher) you'd get planted back in the front row *again*.

I spent a lot of time in the front row my freshman year of high school, and over *twenty years later* I can *still* feel the humiliation. Note that I *teach* freshman algebra now, so this clearly wasn't a result of my poor math abilities. I literally teach the same class I flunked when this asshole taught it. And I do it better than he did.

Anyway.

Here's what this means: you fail a math test in my class, not only do you *fail a math test in my class*, but you are supposed to *get up and move a doohickey* (that is supposedly, but not really, safely anonymized) so that not only do you get to be *reminded* that you failed every fucking time you walk in the room but everybody else gets to know about it too. If you're the only kid in a class who failed? You get to be down there in the red zone all by yourgoddamnself and if the class doesn't already know who the one kid who failed was they're sure as hell going to do their best to find the fuck out.

I'm not doing this.

No.

Fuck you. And fuck *that*.

I put my hand up and said, out loud where everybody could hear me, that I don't like this goddamn job enough that I'm going to humiliate kids in order to keep it. And then I left the meeting.

I don't know what happened after I left; I don't know if there were further riots or not. But I'm putting my foot down on this one: I *will not do this. Not under any fucking circumstances, period.* And if they don't like it they can fire my two-time Teacher of the Year ass and I'll go to a district that isn't *fucked in the fucking head.* Or just get the hell out of this demeaning fucking career altogether and leave the public school system to fucking *rot* like the Indiana public clearly wants it to anyway. Fuck it. My job isn't worth this. No.

In case you can't tell, it was a long fucking day.

On Calculators

OCTOBER 25 2013

A friend on Facebook just pointed me at this article from the Atlantic. Well, not me *specifically*, but… y'know. Entitled *The Great Forgetting,* the article discusses the ways in which computer automation of various tasks has affected the ability of us reg'lar folks to learn and remember how to do complicated tasks. The article begins by discussing a few recent plane crashes in which the autopilot failed and the pilot, panicking, did *exactly the wrong thing* and ended up crashing the plane.

What really caught my attention, though, was his comment that the article made an argument against use of calculators in math classes. I'm not convinced of that. I don't doubt that the author's basic premise is strong; automation *has* eroded our ability to do certain things. To pick a less important example, I used to have dozens of phone numbers memorized; nowadays I'm only able to recall my wife's with difficulty, and I couldn't tell you anyone else's if my life depended on it. Now, of course, I'm certain I could recapture this ability; I simply haven't *bothered.* The author also mentions things like map reading; I'd be more inclined to buy that if I thought most people were *ever* able to read maps. Most people were never able to read maps.

(Similarly, spellcheck. No, spellcheck isn't eroding our ability to write. Over all of human history, most people haven't been able to spell or write worth shit. Spellcheck has manifestly *not* made this worse. What *has* happened is that the digital revolution has exposed us to much much much more of our fellow humans' shitty attempts at writing. I can show you some documents in Biblical Hebrew with misspellings if you don't believe me, and for those fuckers writing was their *job*. Why was it their job? *No one could write*. This is not at all new.)

Another interesting example he brings up, albeit briefly, is surgeons using machines. I am not a doctor, obviously, and if I'm getting this wrong feel free to correct me, but I believe that most surgeries that are being done via computer nowadays are surgeries that are *too goddamn complicated* to be done by regular humans with our clumsy hands. My mother had surgery done on her lower spine a few years ago. The surgeon was startled at the extent of the damage, and likened fixing her back to peeling apart soaked sheets of wadded-up tissue paper. There is simply *no fucking way* that a doctor could have uncrushed her spinal nerves and delicately teased everything apart and put it back in the right place with our clumsy human monkey paws. The surgery didn't replace human skill; the surgery *enabled* the human skill. Call me when we can't set limbs because the computers do it better. (Which might actually be coming: I've seen a few articles on 3D-printed custom casts, which look like spiderwebs and are pretty freaking awesome.)

I would argue that, *used properly,* calculators are less like digital address books and more like surgical tools. I want my kids to be able to do math in their heads; you're just going to have to take that on faith. I would *much rather* work with kids who don't ever feel like they need calculators. But the simple fact is that (particularly in my special ed class, but not limited to them) I have a number of students– hell, probably *most* of them– who are uncomfortable, to put it mildly, with basic math facts. I have a few who do not appear to know they exist. In some cases, it's probably because the kids are just lazy and/or disengaged from school. In several it's because they have sub-60 IQ's and are *never going to be able* to memorize basic math facts. It's just not gonna happen.

Here's when I allow calculator use in my class: whenever the calculation *itself* is not the point. If we are working on multiplying decimals, for example, I refuse them calculators. My more severe special ed kids will get cheat sheets for these, but no calculators. Any other time, though, when there's *process* to be learned, I allow calculator use– because otherwise the calculation *gets in the way* and actually inhibits learning of the material I'm trying to teach.

A specific example, because we actually just finished this: the math my seventh graders were covering for the last few weeks involved similar triangles and metric and customary conversions of length, mass, and capacity. So, for example, I give you one triangle with legs that are 11 and 5 inches and a second where the long leg is 18 inches and I want to know the shorter leg, or I tell you that a given length is 12,203 feet and I want to know how many miles it is, rounded to, say, the nearest hundredth.

This is complicated math if you don't know how to do it. It has the power to break their brains– even the smarter ones– early in the process before the methods involved really sink in, and if they are already struggling with basic facts it is *manifestly impossible* without a calculator. If you're struggling with 5 x 7, you are *never in a million years* going to be able to divide 12,203 by 5,280. Even the kids who are *good at math* revolt at that kind of long division, with good reason: it's a huge pain in the ass. It also introduces a whole bunch of new sources of error, all of which inhibit their ability to learn the *actual material I want them to learn.* I need them to learn how to set up equivalent fractions and figure out that 18 is (checks calculator) 11 x 1.63 repeating and that therefore you ought to multiply 5 by that same number to get the bottom leg, or that since you're converting from a large unit to a small unit you need to *divide* and not multiply and then to (hopefully) remember or (acceptably) accurately look up that there are 5,280 feet in a mile and divide the two numbers in the right order– because that's a mistake they make too, and if they divide 5,280 by 12,203 I need them to notice that the answer doesn't look right and figure out *why.*

One check I've been using with similar triangles all week is to divide the long leg by the short leg of both triangles once they've got them figured out, and to make sure that they get the same number both times. The smarter kids took to this right away; the ones who are still struggling resist double-checking their work, but will when I remind them. This is *already* a fight, in other words– why would I make it twice as bad by insisting that they do both of those long division tasks manually? No way. They just *won't do it,* and they'll not be attending to their own precision with the rigor I need from them. Even with my brighter kids who might not *need* them, the sheer speed advantage calculators afford means that we can do *more* work with complicated mathematics than we might otherwise be able to if I had to wait for them to manually do every step of the problems.

In an ideal world, none of this is necessary, because my kids all love math and don't have any preexisting disabilities (or just

305

disinclinations) with math and I don't ever have to worry about it. Or, in a slightly less ideal world, I have the time to work with these kids individually or in small groups and I can magically get them back on grade level by the end of the year. And I have some success stories in this regard– I can think of about half a dozen kids who were low but not necessarily special ed who were constantly insisting on calculators in sixth grade and now 25% of the way through seventh grade really don't seem to need or want them anymore most of the time.

But for a lot– arguably too many– of my kids, and for millions of kids across the country, that's not the case and it's never going to be. I *have to keep these kids on grade level* as much as humanly possible. And regardless of whether I like it or not, that is just not possible without calculators.

Paprika

November 12 2013

Speaking of calculators…

Let's tell a nice story for once.

I have this girl in my class; let's call her Paprika, which is close to her actual name in a fashion that has me cackling just a little bit right now. Paprika was one of my kids last year, too. She's not special ed, but she's *low*– low enough that she probably got tested for special education at some point and just missed the cutoff. I like the kid; she's a sweetheart, if perhaps a bit too obnoxious at times, but she's never going to be a Rhodes scholar.

Last year, at the beginning of the year, this kid literally *refused* to do any math at all without a calculator next to her and a pregenerated math facts list. Flatly refused. She didn't get it, she didn't know, she's never been *taught that* before, every excuse you can imagine. I worked and worked and worked with her on basic math facts last year to the point where by the end of the year she was occasionally forgetting to ask for her crutches– and I was rewarded with one of the higher ISTEP gains I got out of my kids last year. She still didn't pass, but she did a *lot* better.

She broke a couple of fingers this week– I'm not sure how, but her writing hand is wrapped to hell and back and she's got at least one solid brace in there, but she's got some pincer mobility with her thumb and index finger– the affected fingers are the middle and ring fingers on her right hand.

We were doing some calculations today and she called me over to ask a question. I answered it for her and then *literally instructed*

307

Luther M. Siler

her to "check that with your calculator" to make sure it worked as we expected.

She, with a *broken hand* and a calculator sitting three inches · away, pulled out a piece of paper and solved the problem manually.

Every so often– not often enough, unfortunately, but every so often– they make me proud of them.

In Which I are a Perfessional

November 20 2013

Had an awesome couple of minutes as an educator this morning. I was up at the front of my classroom (which is at the opposite end of the room from the only door) teaching my kids during first hour when one of the 7/8 language arts teachers skipped (literally!) into the room and grandly waved a gift at me: a McDonald's apple pie. I smiled and nodded and she left it on my desk and then skipped back out again without saying a word. I mentally filed "eat tasty treat" away on my List of Shit to Do and went on with my class.

Skip ahead forty minutes or so and my kids are (mostly) seated and (mostly) quiet and (mostly) working on their homework/end-of-class assignment and I decide that it would be a good time to eat my tasty snack treat, which was *probably* still warm and thus should be expected to be edible.

Allow me to pause here: as a reward for doing well on a test we took last week, one of the paraprofessionals in my classroom has agreed to bring Reese's Peanut Butter Cups to the kids in my room. He has produced said Cups this morning; the kids know they are on my desk and have been told that they will be distributed closer to the end of the period.

(If you are inclined to now begin a conversation about whether Rewards with Candy are appropriate for the middle school setting, be aware that I hear you, and that at the moment I don't much care. This is the *least* of my various inappropriatenesses. Which is a perfectly cromulent word.)

I pick up my apple pie and slide it out of its cardboard box (all good food comes wrapped in cardboard) and take one single bite. A

Luther M. Siler

student sees me do this and asks me, rather loudly, why they don't all get apple pies and why I get to eat in class.

I have my back to the door.

"Because I am better and more important than you, my dear," I say. "It is my great specialness that entitles me to this tasty treat. Watch, while I eat it right in front of you."

(Yes, I talk like that. Not always, but when the mood strikes me.)

And then I turn around.

And discover that the director of math instruction for my corporation has somehow ninjaed her way into my classroom, is standing *right the hell behind me,* and has a giant, shit-eating grin on her Ph.D-havin' face.

My kids, by the way, have no idea who she is; they have about as much understanding of the higher echelons of our corporation as you did at that age. They just know an adult has busted me. Now, I'm not in *trouble,* mind you; I have a good relationship with this person and she wasn't in the room to bust me or anything like that. But it was a lovely "Oh, you have *got* to be kidding me, November" moment to add to the tree that killed my fence and my mother-in-law's stroke and my cat nearly dying. November *fucking hates me,* people, and getting formally reprimanded for mocking my kids while eating preservative pastries woulda just been the icing on the cake.

She thought it was hilarious.

We talked for a few minutes about the various things she'd come to talk to me about, and then one of my kids interrupted us to ask when the hell he was getting his damn candy (okay, he didn't swear, but it came across in the tone) and well *that didn't help either, now, did it?* And since my Big Lord High Muckety-Muck Boss was in the room (as opposed to my regular boss, who I will happily threaten children in front of) I couldn't really do anything about it.

Let me remind you that I am literally on a committee that helps retrain struggling teachers on how to do their jobs right, because I am a professional.

Oh, also I was wearing jeans. Which I do every day, but still.

Sigh.

(Later that day, during third hour, my *assistant principal* also managed to ninja her way into my room without me noticing. I had a better excuse this time, as I was crouching next to a kid helping her

with something, and wasn't doing anything embarrassing this time,
but I seriously thought about hiring a guard for the door.)

Whatever Works, I Guess

December 6 2013

I have a handful of severely autistic students. One of them in particular has been a major behavior issue as of late– he's been running out of the classroom, throwing things, saying crude sexual insults to the girls, and trampling people in the hallway. We are trying, for a variety of reasons, some good, some not so good, to keep him in our building and not have to move him into a residential placement of some kind somewhere else. His issues generally begin when he gets into the building, amplify during Success period, and by the time he gets into my room for Math he's completely uncontrollable and acting out.

I met with the corporation's autism consultant on Thursday, and she was in my classroom observing me/him/us today. (Sidenote: all three of my classes *killed* their math tests this week; I'm super happy about how they did.) We've been working on solving two-step equations and linear equations for the last few weeks, and so they've been hearing me say the phrase "work backwards" or "do the opposite" over and over and over and over again. (In other words, 4x = 12 is a multiplication problem; you need to do the opposite, division, in order to solve it.) Well, everybody *but* this kid has; he's spent most of his time either sitting in the hallway or in the main office or the counselor's office.

He has to take the same tests as everyone else, so the autism consultant and his usual paraprofessional worked with him in the back of the classroom. I heard them repeating my instructions and going over procedures to solve problems, mimicking the language I'd been using. The kid actually did pretty well.

For the last ten minutes of class, the autism consultant and the paraprofessional disappeared for some reason and left the kid in the room with me. I noticed after a minute that every time I gave the class an instruction he was doing something else. *Oh, great,* I thought; *last thing I need is a meltdown when the two people who are here to observe him have left for two minutes.*

"What are you doing, Jim?" I asked. (Jim, obviously, isn't his name.)

"The opposite," he said. "They said I'm supposed to do the opposite of everything you say." Big, toothy grin on his face.

Parts of my head screamed at other parts of my head.

"Stand up," I told him.

He sat in his seat.

"Make as much noise as you can until the bell," I told him.

Complete silence.

"Don't do any of your missing work, *at all*," I told him.

Out comes his math workbook.

Ah, *autism.* Every day can be Opposite Day from now on.

Santa

December 9 2013

I'm teaching first hour today, *as I do*. I'm expecting a pretty good day– a number of my usual discipline issues are suspended or out of the building for some reason, so, oughtta be peaceful, right?

Sure.

We're midway through first hour when It Happens. One of my girls– normally not a dipshit– looks out the window. Note: it is snowing today. It's not super bad, certainly not anything to compare to what's hitting the East Coast right now, but there's definitely precipitation happening.

"Santa!" she squeals.

Uh, what?

Other kids are running to the window.

"Santa! Santa's outside!"

Note that this is a seventh grade class. These kids, if they *ever* believed in Santa, don't anymore. And they are all hollering to me that Santa Claus is outside.

I look out the window and there is a goddamn fat person in a gigantic bright red coat with white fur lining the edges in the field outside our window. He or she– I can't see a beard, and something about the person scans female, but I can't tell for sure because of the gigantic coat– is walking a dog. The dog is *wearing goddamn reindeer horns.*

Dude/ette spent twenty minutes outside my room, just fuckin' walking around in circles– I don't know if the damn dog was constipated or what but it was freaking below freezing outside and by the time he finally left I was about to just send the kids outside with him. Because *holy shit you people can be distracted by anything.*

315

Luther M. Siler

I have a silly job.

Story Problem Time!

December 12 2013

Have a math problem:

A boat travels 60 kilometers upstream against the current in 5 hours. The boat travels the same distance downstream in 3 hours. What is the rate of the boat in still water? What is the rate of the current?

If you are a reasonably mathematically talented person, you should be able to make headway with this fairly quickly: the boat travels 12 km/h upstream (60/5) and 20 km/h downstream (60/3), which means that the boat's speed in still water is the average of the upstream/downstream speeds, (20 + 12)/2 km/h, or 16 kilometers per hour, and the current is 4 km/h, which is the difference between either of the measured speeds and the average.

I spent about half an hour last night texting back and forth with a former student trying to work her through this problem and becoming more and more bewildered about what it was she didn't get about it as the conversation went on. She *got* the math– the math isn't really that complicated, right? Just division and an average.

What she didn't get? *Rivers.* As it turns out, "downstream" and "upstream" are not terribly salient terms to kids who have lived in *cities* all their lives– and the terms "downstream" and "upstream" hadn't managed to really ensconce themselves in her vocabulary as of yet.

This young lady is generally one of my brightest kids, mind you. I'm not mocking her at all here, although maybe she deserves it a little bit– but the entire conversation got me thinking about how *incredibly easy it is* to write standardized test questions that you *think* are questions about math but turn out to hinge on some

317

Luther M. Siler

other kind of non-mathematical knowledge. She could *not* wrap her head around the idea that the boat wasn't going at its full speed "downstream" and that the current wasn't slowing it down by (20-12) 8 km/h going upstream. Which, of course, was one of the answers, because whenever anyone with half an ounce of sense writes a multiple choice test, one of the horrible tricks you do is thinking "Now, how might the students *screw this up?*" and then writing answers that match what they might have gotten if they did something predictable wrong.

The math? She's got it. The *geography lesson* that the writer of the question no doubt didn't realize was embedded into being able to get the question right? Not so much.

Luther M. Siler

other kind of non-mathematical knowledge. She could *not* wrap her head around the idea that the boat wasn't going at its full speed "downstream" and that the current wasn't slowing it down by (20-12) 8 km/h going upstream. Which, of course, was one of the answers, because whenever anyone with half an ounce of sense writes a multiple choice test, one of the horrible tricks you do is thinking "Now, how might the students *screw this up?*" and then writing answers that match what they might have gotten if they did something predictable wrong.

The math? She's got it. The *geography lesson* that the writer of the question no doubt didn't realize was embedded into being able to get the question right? Not so much.

318

We're Brainless!

JANUARY 9 2014

I have officially survived the first day back from winter break without, really, anything of note to gripe about; anytime I get through a day with no disciplinary intervention more serious than having to swap a couple of seats, it was a good day.

Sadly, I had to watch my third and fourth hour class pull their "We're brainless!" move, which is *absolutely my favorite thing* as a teacher; we got through the first class period okay and then I just-about-literally *watched* their brains leak out of their headholes as we moved from basic geometry (areas of circles, triangles, rectangles, parallelograms, and trapezoids) to composite shapes. Composite shapes are, just for example, an arrow or "house" shape, where there's a triangle sitting on top of a square or rectangle, or an L shape composed of two rectangles. The idea, basically, is that the kids take basic planar geometry and extend it by recognizing simpler shapes inside of a complex one and know to add them together, or sometimes subtract out a shape that is designated as a "hole," along with sometimes having to reason out what the length of an initially unknown side is.

My kids– especially my special ed ones– are generally not very good at this, and they're sure as hell not going to be good at it on the first day back from winter break, and they're *surer* as hell not going to be good at it when the first day back from winter break is the first day I cover the material. But third and fourth hour, particularly, were playing the Moron Game, where we pretend that we don't understand shit that we literally *just did* three minutes ago, and where we can't find an answer that is *on the board and I'm pointing at*, because we

Luther M. Siler

don't want to think and we think if we filibuster long enough the
teacher will give up and call on someone else.

This strategy *never, ever, ever works* on me– believe it or not,
after twelve goddamn years of working with recalcitrant middle
schoolers I can *tell the difference* between a kid who legitimately
doesn't understand what I'm talking about and a kid who is being
lazy. It's a real good way to get my dander up if dander is what
you're looking for, though; the good news is that they pulled it
during the ten minutes before lunch and managed to pull their shit
together before they came back into my room. So, yeah. If
tomorrow is as good as today I'll call the week a win, I think.

On 8th Grade Boys

JANUARY 15 2014

Here is what teaching 8th grade boys is like.

Yesterday's classes were pretty simple: one period of instruction and one period of more-or-less guided free time; in other words, "so long as you're working I'm going to leave you alone," and oh by the way all late work for the quarter is due by the end of the period or you get to keep those zeroes in my grade book.

So the kids are chatting, right? My 8th graders (also known as my honors Algebra group) are actually a pretty pleasant group most of the time, and I'm rarely the type of teacher to insist on absolute quiet unless I'm directly instructing the class. I'm at my desk, intermittently helping kids who need it and working on some grading and lesson planning and email and whatever else it strikes my mind to get accomplished while I actually have some time.

The phrase "hydraulic butt" floats into my ears.

I have a brief moment of no, you did not hear that, and even if you did hear that, you didn't hear that, and you don't care. Keep your head down and keep doing whatever you're doing.

I ignore my brain and look up. There's a table of four kids sitting near me. Three of them are staring at me with horrified looks on their faces. The fourth is doing his damnedest *not* to make eye contact, but has perhaps the most coprophagic shit-eating grin on his face I've ever seen.

A brief note on this kid: I love the hell out of him. Smart as hell, funny, athletic (wrestling, football, and I *think* whatever running sport– track or cross-country– doesn't interfere with the other two), polite, and– not for nothin'– a bit of a heartthrob as well. I'd let my daughter date the kid, if I had one.

He continues to deliberately avoid looking at me. I hear the sound "Pzzzzzzhoooooooooop!" and the right half of his body, butt-cheek first, raises off of his chair.

He holds this position for a moment.

"Pzzzzzhoooooop!" again, and the *other* half of his body raises out of his chair. At this point, for no clear reason, the room has fallen completely quiet and everyone is staring at him. He is, at this point, balancing in what looks like a seated position but he's actually got his ass hovering about four inches above his chair, which I imagine involves rather impressive control of his leg muscles.

I do not speak. Neither does anyone else.

"Psssssssssss....." and he slowly lowers himself back into his chair.

And, on cue, the boy sitting across from him *farts*. Explosively. Like, loudly enough that we'd have heard it even if the room hadn't been utterly quiet.

I want to teach at an all-girls' school.

On the Teacher's Lounge

February 15 2014

I have, for whatever reason, encountered several discussions of teacher's lounge culture on our Internets lately.

Twice I have seen the phrase "den of negativity" used, which as descriptions go isn't quite "wretched hive of scum and villainy," but may as well be. That description is both fair and accurate. It also *completely misses the point* of the teachers' lounge, and misses it in a way that's hard to describe to people who aren't teachers.

Yes, the teachers' lounge is a den of negativity, and a place where people, usually teachers, are occasionally prone to say *terrible, horrible things* about the children who are in their charge. But here's the thing: *don't worry about it.* What y'all need to realize– and I'm generalizing now because the one that set me off is *far* from the only essay I've seen discussing teachers' lounge "culture"– is that my twenty-five minutes in the teachers' lounge is literally the *only 25 minutes of my day* where I get to interact with adults when I'm not on the job. Even if I have a co-teacher or paraprofessionals in my room, I don't get to have "off-duty" conversations with those people while they're in my classroom, and I'll admit to being rather cold to people I shouldn't have on the rare occasions where they *tried* to have a conversation unrelated to what was going on in the classroom. That's not the place.

The teachers' lounge *is* the place. During those 25 minutes I need to a) eat lunch, b) find a way to relax a little bit, and– and this is the important part– frequently I, and everyone else, need to c) *find a way to blow off some steam.* That's a lot to do in 25 minutes, and I can build up a *lot of damn steam* in the first four hours of my day.

I'm sorry if it sounds terrible, and it probably does, but if calling Jimmy a stupid brain-dead motherfucker in the teachers' lounge keeps me from *treating Jimmy* like a stupid brain-dead motherfucker *in the classroom*, I'm going to run my mouth about him– to people who know him, and who *understand*, mind you– in the teachers' lounge, and I'm not going to feel too bad about it.

Wanna see something interesting, though? Watch what happens if a *sub* tries to talk shit about our kids– or anybody else other than us who may happen to be in the teachers' lounge at that time. Every adult in the room will jump to the defense of a kid who we might have been perfectly happy to joke about the suspect parentage of five minutes ago. Why? He's *ours*. We can talk shit about our own kids. Nobody else gets to. Period. And everybody in that room who *hears me* call Jimmy a stupid brain-dead motherfucker knows that I'm about to walk back into my classroom and work my *ass* off to teach the belligerent little shit some math.

Are there teachers who are complete burnouts, like she describes? Absofuckinlutely. I've come dangerously close to it at any number of points in my career– hell, the last two weeks have not been pretty; I *really needed* the last couple of days to go well and I'm glad they have, but I got home on Wednesday griping that I needed to find something else to do with my life, and not remotely for the first time. But you identify a burnout by what they do in the *classroom*, not what they say in the teachers' lounge.

We *all* sound like assholes in there.

I Cannot Even, Not Anymore

FEBRUARY 6 2014

It has not been a good week. I've been tired, sick, crabby, stressed out, and not reacting to the kids well at all, and the fact that in general they've had a bad week *themselves* has not led to anything good happening in my classroom. We had school today; I'm still crossing my fingers that we'll be off tomorrow morning since it's supposed to be a bazillion below zero again, but we were open today.

A bit of good news I just discovered: the state board of education has voted to extend the testing window for the first ISTEP test by a full week and a half, which is *fantastic* news. Means that all the snow/weather delays won't kill us. Great news.

Anyway: good news aside, shit like this doesn't help. I took my morning class on a bathroom break this morning. I generally follow the boys into the bathroom because if I don't they fuck around and make a lot of noise and generally act like assholes; once everyone's occupied with actually doing what one would expect one to do in the bathroom, I head back into the hallway.

I discovered another student– one of mine, but not in my first and second hour class (so he was out of someone else's room)– trying his damnedest to *climb over the stall door* into the handicap-accessible stall. You read that right. Climb *over*. Which, the way our bathrooms are designed, would have required him to haul himself seven or so feet off the ground. He is not *remotely* athletic enough for this task. He's hanging by his hands, scrabbling with his feet and trying to get purchase on the door to climb over.

My response was probably not nearly as profane as the situation deserved. I did *not* ask him what in the blue fuck he thought he was doing, for example.

325

"The door's locked."

I did not ask him if he had considered that perhaps the fucking door was locked because there was a *person taking a shit* inside the bathroom stall. As you would *bloody expect there to be* if a bathroom stall was closed. Somehow, I managed to get through that conversation without swearing or using the words "imbecile," "moron," "fucknut" or "halfwit."

I don't know how.

Later, when he *was* in my room, we're going over some simple bell-ringer work. My kids understand what factors are, and they understand how to do prime factorials, but they frequently forget what they *are*. In other words, it's an annoyingly persistent vocabulary issue and not a *math* issue per se. At any rate, they're supposed to be finding all of the factors of 36 and then doing a prime factorization of 28. I give them a few minutes to do both, ask a couple of kids to explain what they did, correct a couple of misconceptions, and then work both of the problems on the board in a couple of different ways, emphasizing that they need to *show their work* for these kinds of things, even if they're able to rattle off factors of 36 off the tops of their heads, ISTEP scoring demands that they show how they came up with their answers.

I walk past this same kid. Note that I've spent five or ten minutes going over *exactly* how to do this shit and it's *still* on the board. Note also that the problem is on a Powerpoint projected on the board and is manifestly impossible to *miss*.

He has written $35 \times 28 = 7$ on his piece of paper and nothing else.

Again, I do not swear. I do not ask him what in the merry fuck he is doing.

He says– and I swear to God I'm not making this up– "Oh, was I supposed to divide?"

I could have been a doctor or a lawyer, people.

The other thing that happened today was one of my girls from my second math class being pulled out of class to be told that her house had burned to the ground this morning. There are three girls from the same family in my building; I've had two of them, one this year *and* last year and the other three years ago. The fire apparently started in the girls' room, so everything they own is completely gone; the upper floor is apparently a total loss and most of what was on the bottom floor is thoroughly water-damaged by now. All of the humans living in the house are uninjured; to the best of my knowledge they have not found the cats.

I can't even imagine.

Why Standardized Testing Doesn't Work, pt. 8923423

February 27 2014

First things first: I'm pretty convinced there's not gonna be school tomorrow. Again. The prediction for tomorrow morning between five and seven AM has windchill temperatures in between twenty and twenty-five degrees below zero. It's supposed to warm up quickly after about nine or ten o'clock, and be almost civilized by the end of the day, but I just don't see any way that they're making kids walk to school/wait for buses in that kind of wind chill. Twenty below has been the trigger for the last several school closings and there's no good reason to assume tomorrow will be any different.

I had tests planned for today for both of my seventh grade groups but the eighth grade test was scheduled for tomorrow. I spent most of my time in the gym before school grabbing my algebra kids and saying things like "Hey, remember how I said there was a test tomorrow? I lied. It's today." It is either a sign that my kids really like me or that they just don't care that much about their grades that *none of them* bothered to gripe about not having time to study.

My seventh graders, though, *knew* that there was a test today. We've been talking about it for a week and reviewing for a couple of days. And for *both of my goddamn groups* today they knew what slope was and how it worked during the first class period and then *bombed the shit* out of what should have been a pretty easy test during the second. And I have no idea why. I bet if I give it to them again tomorrow or Monday they'll do goddamn fine. But not today, for whatever reason, even though I was getting correct answers to *everything I threw at them* during the first period of class when we were reviewing.

Lesson is: sometimes kids don't know shit, even if they knew shit before, and you can't always predict when those days will happen. My first and second hour kids got the *worst results I have ever seen as a math teacher* on their window test today. And again: it was *not a hard test*. That record lasted an hour and forty minutes, until my third and fourth hour kids took the same test and did even worse. If today had been ISTEP day they'd have fired me already. And the next test we take they might get the highest scores in the seventh grade. What happened? Hell if I know. They knew it and then they didn't. And that's just the fuck how it works sometimes.

We'll post-mortem it on Monday, I guess. Er... well, maybe tomorrow. But I kinda doubt it.

This Story Needs a Witty Title

February 28 2014

Today was… challenging. And I think I actually do mean *challenging*, I'm not using that word as a euphemism for "awful" or anything like that. Today was challenging.

I have two students in my first and second hour class with rather profound disabilities. They're both well into the autism spectrum but there are other issues with both of them as well; one has some serious physical handicaps and one has a deeply problematic home life as well. Of the two, one of them— I'll call him Matt, since without a pseudonym this story is going to be impossible to write— poses a greater challenge. Raymond, the other, is a lovely kid and a hard worker; the main thing with him is being able to get past his disabilities to be able to give him the education he deserves. The other child, to put it kindly, must be *managed*. There are days where he's all there and he's a student. There are other days where it's as if someone has unleashed an untrained, 115-pound puppy into my classroom. I know that sounds cruel, and I don't want it to be, but it's a pretty precisely accurate metaphor.

Matt was a disaster (again) today. We had several weeks in a row where we had his behaviors under control but lately he's been acting up, throwing things, running around the classroom, running *out* of the classroom, lots of loud outbursts, stuff like that, to the point where I've had to have him removed a couple of times. I don't like to do this for a variety of probably perfectly obvious reasons but eventually he hits the point where I need to keep the educations of the *other* 28 kids in the room in mind. He fled the room twice during my first class period. The first time was just for a minute or two and he came right back; the second for a longer

331

period. When he came back the second time, he shoved one of my girls. Now, my kids *know* Matt; they've been with him for at least three years now and some of them for much longer, so they know what he's about and they're not likely to react to him doing things they way they might react to other kids. There's a lot of his behavior that I can redirect or ignore. I *cannot* ignore him putting his hands on people. I tell him I'm going to have to write him up for pushing the girl he's pushed.

"I didn't push anybody!" he screams. *Screams*.

"Yes, you did, Matt, I saw you," I say. The girls by this point are back in their seats.

At this point, Matt starts chanting "MORON!" at the top of his lungs. At me. Okay, fine, that can go in the write-up too. Now, keep something in mind, and I hope this is obvious enough that I don't need to say this: I'm not *mad* at the kid. Getting mad at him is *pointless*, because when he's in his unreachable stages it's just going to make him happy and under any other circumstances it's just not useful. But again: if he's so far gone today that he's shoving people I need to have him out of my room. So I write him up. This takes a minute; while I'm doing this, *Raymond*, who normally is not a problem *at all*, gets angry with Matt. Says to him, in fact, "I'd like to strangle you for what you just said to Mr. Siler."

This is *also* not appropriate. But, again, I'm not mad; it's not worth it. I say something along the lines of "Raymond, threatening Matt isn't appropriate and it's not helping. I don't want you to talk like that."

Raymond tends to be a crier; have I mentioned that? He *really* doesn't like it when he thinks someone is mad at him, so I have to be especially careful on the rare occasions when I have to redirect or chastise him to keep him from getting upset. He gets out of his seat and walks toward me.

Oh, hell, kid, I do not have time for you to have an episode right now.

Keep something in mind: there are *twenty-eight* other kids in the room– well, probably less than that, since it was so cold I had some absences; let's say twenty-three. I'm supposed to be teaching them math right now.

Raymond walks up to me and grabs my hand. Starts shaking it up and down. Starts to say something.

And *goes away*. For, like, fifteen seconds. He's still shaking my hand. A little train of drool comes out of the corner of his mouth.

Oh, *fuck*. He's having a seizure. I call his para over. Nurse. Nurse *now*. His para thinks he's still dealing with *Matt's* shit; I no longer give a damn about Matt.

Long story short; they were both out of my class for the rest of the morning. Matt was moved to an alternate location until he calmed down; I *think* the nurse checked Raymond over and decided he was going to be okay after talking with his father but I'm not sure. Raymond has had issues with seizures in the past but this is the first one I've seen.

Go ahead; ask how much math teaching I got done during that period.

Later in the day; fourth hour. You may recall some references to *the twins*. Originally *the twins* were both in my third and fourth hour block; it's been decided since then that it's best for them to be separated, so I have one first and second hour and one third and fourth. It was explained to me (and not unreasonably, mind you; I didn't fight this plan) that the theory was that this would aid in both of them developing some independence from each other, which they badly need. What it has *actually* resulted in is that I get to have this conversation four times a day instead of only twice:

(Twin brings me a paper.)

TWIN: I'm done.

(I look at paper. It is covered in writing and arcane symbols that resemble no known form of human mathematics in any way; it has no obvious connection to any assignment I have given. I have had the "I'm done" conversation *before* giving assignments before.)

MR. SILER: Did you hear even a *single word* I said about how to do this?

TWIN: Oh. I messed up. (Turns to leave, without asking or staying to hear what he did wrong.)

MR. SILER: (Physically stops Twin.) You need to <insert lesson here.> Do you hear me this time? Repeat my instructions back to me.

TWIN: I need to do it.

MR. SILER: What do you need to do?

TWIN: My assignment.

MR. SILER: And *how* will you do your assignment?

TWIN: I don't know.

Understand, please, that this is not exaggeration, that I have this *precise* conversation nearly word-for-word *at least* once daily with *each* of the boys. Today we were working on creating bar graphs; a simple, one-off assignment that I can toss in on a Friday where we had a math test yesterday and I thought we weren't going to have school. (Yes, it's connected to my current standards, *boss.*) Here was the assignment: 1) Pick a theme; I suggested "favorite X". 2) Poll all of your classmates on their choice to collect data; 3) Turn data into a bar graph and either a histogram or a pie chart; extra credit given for accurate pie charts since they're sorta complicated compared to the other two.

Both of the boys, entirely independently of each other, brought me a piece of paper on which they had recorded *hundreds of votes*. Both of them attempted to walk away *immediately* when I pointed out that there were not hundreds of students in the room with them. Later, one of them attempted to turn in only one of the two graphs, which he'd stapled to his data (which they were supposed to do.) I pointed out to him that he owed me the other chart as well, at which point he *shoved the stapled corner of the pages into his mouth and bit the staple out.*

What is this I don't even.

This is the job, folks.

How to Lose your Shitty Job

MARCH 4 2014

It is fourth hour, just past lunch. I have had a remarkably easy morning; my first class of the day, miraculously, has had so few questions about their assignment that I have been able to– wait for it– *sit at my desk,* and not only sit at my desk, but sit at my desk long enough to sort through some of the ridiculously huge piles of junk everywhere. Did you know I had a desk calendar? Not only can you *see* it, but it even knows it's March now! This is a miracle.

And, of course, I paid for it.

So, right, fourth hour. There is, suddenly, an *immense* amount of yelling coming from next door. Keep in mind that my door is shut and the wall in between our classrooms are made of *cinder block.* I hear swearing. *Really loud swearing.* From *inside my classroom, with the door shut.*

Oh, *fuck.*

I bail on what I'm doing and head into the hallway. The sub is already out in the hallway, *screaming* into the face of one of our seventh graders. Not one of mine, but his sister happens to be in my classroom at that very moment. He's swearing at the kid. Red-faced, practically on top of him. The kid is swearing back. And in tears.

Sigh. Suddenly I really don't want to tell this story anymore. Long story short: I had to physically separate the two of them and I spent at least a few real moments trying to figure out if I was going to have to knock the sub down to get him away from the kid. By that point basically every adult male within a hundred yards, including an armed police officer, was heading toward our part of the building at high speed, and the sub was in the building for about

335

Luther M. Siler

another fifteen minutes before being removed from the premises. It was... ugly.

Weirdly, it's the second time in my career I've been in the vicinity when a sub went insane on a kid. The first time, many moons ago at my first school, started off exactly the same way except this time there wasn't an administrator in the building to hand it off to. I told the sub that I couldn't literally tell him to go home but I was taking over his classes for the rest of the day (at the time, due to the complexities of my position, it was actually possible) and he was to go sit in the teachers' lounge until the actual administrator got back. I remember thinking I was probably going to end up in some trouble for it and not caring.

Yeah. It was a long day.

Another Reason Standardized Testing Sucks

March 5 2014

I walked past the office on the way back to my room from lunch and noticed one of my students and her older brother sitting in there waiting for someone. They're in different grades, so it seemed unlikely that they were both in trouble, and normally she's almost annoyingly conscientious about letting me know when she's not going to be in school, so it wasn't likely that they were waiting for a parent to come pick them up unless something had gone wrong.

I stuck my head in and asked what was going on. She said she didn't know. I glanced at the older brother; he shrugged too.

"Will you be back in class?"

Another shrug. At this point I asked one of the office staff, who gave me a *don't ask right now* look and said that she'd be back sooner or later. Well, okay; not worrying about it right now.

She came back with about ten minutes left in class. Changed her seat to an isolation desk (I don't have assigned seats; the kids can move whenever they want so long as they aren't being disruptive. I'm also free to move them when they *are* being disruptive) and put her head down. She'd been in a perfectly good mood when I saw her last. I was swamped with kids wanting help with various things, so I left her alone for a couple of minutes, at which point it became clear that she was crying.

I pulled her out into the hall to find out what was going on. The crying quickly turned into sobbing hysteria; the kid was completely unable to even get a word out. It took *ten minutes*—during which time my classes switched, and I told my eighth graders

337

to find the next section in their textbooks and teach themselves how compound interest worked– before I could even get her coherent enough to talk. What the *hell* happened down there?

I didn't get much detail, obviously, but apparently child protective services had met with the two of them for some reason (not that I'd share it if I did, but at this moment I have *no* idea why) and toward the end of the interview had either *asked* them if they thought it would be better if they were removed from their home or *suggested* that it might be better. And she, understandably, *freaked the fuck out.* And, again, I have no idea why– I've never seen any real evidence that this kid comes from a fucked up household, although I've also never met or heard from her parents, and she's a good kid so I've not had reason to contact them on my own. I sent her off to the counselor on a pass once I got her calmed down and went on with my day.

This isn't about that. This is about my *reaction* when this sobbing child who has been in my room for a *year and a half,* and who I've watched blossom from someone who insisted on either a calculator or a math facts sheet when presented with the *slightest challenge* to someone who is, two or three days out of the week, one of the best math students in her class, told me that the reason she was crying was because someone had threatened to take her away from her parents.

My first thought was How dare those fucking assholes do this to me the week before ISTEP.

Do this. To *me.* Because clearly if CPS thinks this child has a reason to be *removed from her parents*, that is something that they are doing to *me.* Because apparently there is part of my brain that thinks my fucking *test scores* are more important than this child's basic health and safety.

Fuck standardized testing. Fuck it, fuck it, *fuck it.* And fuck me for a soulless bastard for even *allowing that shit into my head* even if I have the decency to be ashamed of it afterwards.

More Awful ISTEP Bullshit

March 11 2014

Something I *am* going to spend my time worrying about: remember Raymond? Unfortunately, his seizure during class a couple of weeks ago was only the first in a series of them. He's not been in class very much lately as his parents have struggled to find the cause of the problem and adjust medications, but they sent him in today because of ISTEP testing.

He apparently had at least one seizure *during the test* today. He didn't test with me because of his disabilities; he gets extra time and he has difficulty with fine motor skills like writing so he's got a scribe with him for the test. His para told me that there was no point anywhere during the test where Raymond had any idea what the hell was going on around him or what he was supposed to be doing on the test.

I can't get mad at his parents; they were trying to do what they thought they were supposed to do. But I'll be *damned* if I'm not going to raise hell to get that test invalidated, and I hope to hell his parents keep him home for the next couple of days. This is true for obvious humanitarian reasons– this test *is not important enough* for a kid to jeopardize his damn health to take– and slightly-more-selfish reasons, such as the fact that current ed reform theory is that there is nothing more important to student test scores than the skill of the teacher (and I'm certainly the only one who's going to get *blamed)* and I suspect that fuckin' *epilepsy* might have a bit to do with his scores here. I didn't find out about all this until late in the day so I didn't have time to talk to his parents; I'm sure as hell going to be meeting with administration tomorrow to see what we can do about invaliding the test.

I suspect that meeting is going to be fun.

In Which I Travel

March 26 2014

Because it entertains me to do so, and because I just got home from the parent meeting and am too tired to blog, here is the full text (well, almost, and some names altered to protect the innocent) of the notes I just sent home with my parents for the kids going with me to Washington DC next week. Yes, this really is what I'm like.

DO NOT BRING:
- Any electronics that have to be plugged into a TV to be used.
- Laptops
- Flip flops (see below)

These items will be handed back to your parents when your bags are checked, and you will probably be scowled at, but you will still be allowed to go. Do not argue with me about whether your fancy-schmancy laptop-tablet hybrid is a tablet or a laptop. Tablets are allowed but are NOT recommended, and I don't want to hear it if yours is broken or lost.

ABSOLUTELY DO NOT BRING:
- Cigarettes
- Drugs, other than prescription—and those should be given to Mr. Siler
- Alcohol
- Weapons of any kind (I carry a three inch pocket knife. I'm leaving it at home. Do NOT mess with DC security.)
- Anything connected to sex in ANY WAY.

If you have any of these items with you, or anything else not on that list that may cause me to believe that you are planning on making stupid decisions on my trip, you will be SENT HOME. No bus. No trip. No refunds. Period. There is no appeal process and I am not kidding. PLEASE DO NOT TEST ME ON THIS.

Stuff to bring:
- Clothes. This includes pants, shirts, socks, AND underwear. Yes, one pair for each day. We will be on a bus together for four days and you are not allowed to smell bad. Be prepared for a wide variety of different kinds of weather; the East Coast has been just as weird as we have this winter. Pay attention to the weather forecast.
- Bathroom stuff (toothbrush/toothpaste, DEODORANT, shampoo if you're picky)
- A collapsible (very small) umbrella
- At least one decent outfit (shirt with a collar) for Monday.
- COMFORTABLE WALKING SHOES. This may be the most important thing on the list. DO NOT BRING FLIP FLOPS. ACTUAL SHOES WITH TOES AND LACES AND EVERYTHING. YOU DO NOT WANT TO SEE WHAT WILL HAPPEN TO YOUR FEET AFTER TRYING TO WALK TWENTY MILES IN FLIP FLOPS.
- A bathing suit (optional, possibly unnecessary)
- A hat (plenty of places to buy these, but a good idea anyway)
- Sunglasses
- Sunscreen
- Allergy meds, if you have problems—the cherry blossoms can be an issue at this time of year (give these to Mr. Siler)
- Any other medications you need, especially if you are on any kind of ADHD medication.
- A cell phone (essential)
- Chargers for any of your electronics (there should be outlets on the bus)
- A camera, if you are secretly from 1983 and your phone doesn't have one.
- Money for souvenirs (you probably don't need much more than $50 or so, but I won't be checking your wallets)

•Feminine supplies, if feminine (someone will be caught by surprise. I will have extra; you just have to be brave enough to ask.)
•Exactly $3 as a tip for the tour guide. More is OK.
•A healthy amount of patience.

THINGS I WILL HAVE WITH ME:

•Basic medicine (some sort of pain meds, probably ibuprofen; a basic antihistamine, Pepto-Bismol or Imodium)
•Basic first aid supplies
•Sunscreen
•Extra girl stuff

YOU WILL BE GIVEN:

A WorldStrides ID card on a lanyard that has emergency numbers on it and you are to wear around your neck for EVERY SINGLE SECOND OF THE TRIP WHEN WE ARE NOT IN THE HOTEL. You are not allowed to trade this for Jolly Ranchers or let your girlfriend wear yours so that everyone can see how much you love her. In fact, for the four days on the trip you are not allowed to have a girlfriend either.

IS THERE A DRESS CODE?

You are not required to wear your school uniform. You are required to not look like a slob, other than on the ride to and from DC, and I want everyone looking classy on the last day of the trip because we will be touring a graveyard and the national Holocaust museum. Dress respectfully for the final day. Saturday and Sunday I'm not as concerned about other than the "not a slob" rule.

THE DAY OF THE TRIP:

Be at school by 6:00 PM on Friday. The bus leaves at 7:00 and we need time to check bags. Mr. Smith and Mr. Jones will be checking bags for the boys; Mrs. Brown and Mrs. Anderson will be checking bags for the girls.

Bring ANY MEDICATIONS YOU NEED along with clear dosage instructions for Mr. Siler. We will decide on a case by case basis who I am holding meds for and who will be trusted to take them on their own.

Dress comfortably for the long bus ride. The "don't be a slob" rule is suspended for the ride to DC and the ride home from DC. I will be wearing jeans and a hoodie. Sweats/pajama pants are fine for the rides to and from DC only. They fall under the "slob" rule for the rest of the trip. A blanket and a pillow are also a good idea. Note that on the bus boys are sitting with boys and girls are sitting with girls.

FOR THE BUS:

Pack an overnight bag (a backpack) with a change of clothes, your toothbrush/toothpaste, a hairbrush or comb, and your deodorant, along with anything you think you might need specifically on the bus. Some snacks are fine too, although we'll be stopping a couple of times on the way. Everything else should go in a suitcase. There are fairly spacious bathrooms at the Hard Rock Café where we have breakfast on the first day and we will be changing clothes and freshening up there.

WHAT ABOUT THE POOL? IS THERE A POOL? TELL ME ABOUT THE POOOOOOLLLLLLLLL!!!!!

Don't count on it, but feel free to be optimistic. We'll discuss it when we get there.

HOW TO CONTACT ME:

▪My phone number is (something). Send me a text with your name RIGHT NOW (and whose parent you are, if your last name is different) so that I know who you are if you call.

▪You can follow us on Twitter @(address); if you don't use Twitter you can still see the feed at https://twitter.com/(address).

In Which I am Renewed

March 31 2014

I've had two run-ins with former students recently, both while attempting to buy food from fast-food joints. On the first I was in between errands and needed to grab something before my DC parent meeting; the second was simply an issue of my wife and I not feeling like making real dinner. In both cases, the kids recognized me right before I figured out who they were, and in both cases I remembered the kids, although the first one looked different enough that I had to have her remind me of her last name.

The second kid... man, it was surprisingly nice to see him. In his case I was actually in the restaurant as opposed to going through a drive-thru so we had a chance to talk for a minute. He's a senior, graduating in a couple of months (which, God, does that make me feel old) and going directly into the Army after graduation. Which... *whoa.*

A moment after he asked me if I was Mr. Siler, and I blinked at him a couple of times and called him by name, one of the other customers in line looked at me and said "Is he worth remembering?" Yeah, he certainly is; he was one of the good ones. He's apparently working two different jobs right now in addition to school. His younger brother, who I remember being considerably more troubled than he was (and who he cracked "wasn't nearly as worth remembering" when I asked about him) is *also* doing well in school and working more than one job, a fact that warms the heart fairly considerably.

I shook the kid's hand and told him I was proud of him. And I am. It was nice to see him.

345

Fun story about this kid: there was a brief period of time where I was both a computer teacher for fifth and sixth graders and teaching a single, multi-grade writing class, and he was in that class. I was able to basically hand-pick those kids and both he and his brother were in the room. There was a day when I'd had a sub because I had to go to a meeting, and so I had a couple of minutes to talk to the sub about what to expect with my students in the room. "This class isn't going to give you any trouble at all," I said, looking around at my chosen group of perfect angels...

...and this kid *has his pants off* in the back of the room. Well okay, *mild* exaggeration; they were down to his knees. And, in his defense, he had basketball shorts on underneath them. Which had apparently bound up on him, requiring a brief uniform adjustment. Which he had just gone right ahead and done right in front of Jesus and errybody in the back of the room.

At which point I had to, for the first time in my teaching career (but, sadly, not the last,) use the phrase *could you maybe put your pants back on please* in class. In front of a sub, who I had just told to expect a perfectly easy first hour class.

Yeah, that one was worth remembering.

A DC Anecdote

April 5 2014

...Because I am entirely too tired for a long one. My best moment so far on this trip has been at the White House. As you may know, there has been a long running continuous protest against nuclear weaponry going on outside the White House for well over 30 years. Upon being told what it was and what was going on, the vast majority of my students virtually ignored the White House to go over and speak with the protester for a while. Some of them even had pictures taken with him, and asked a number of good questions. He talked with my group for nearly 10 minutes while hundreds if not thousands of other people walked past him, scoffed, or otherwise ignored him. And he complimented me personally on how well engaged and polite they were after I had to shoo them away so that we could go to our next place.

I don't say it enough, but I'm really really proud of my kids.

Wet Teenage Girls

April 15, 2014

One of the problems with my career is that I am occasionally forced to act as somewhat less than a decent person because I am a teacher.

This is one of those stories.

For the first time, the hotel we stayed at on the DC trip had a pool, and a pool with reasonably late hours so that the kids stood a good chance of being able to swim both nights we were staying there. They had a couple of *hours* during the first night, as a matter of fact. The chaperones just went downstairs and chilled next to the pool while the kids splashed and threw each other around, occasionally reprimanding stupid behavior (true, hilarious fact: after one transgression, one of my chaperones– who is our gym teacher– actually made one of the kids get out of the pool and do push-ups.) but mostly just watching. By the time the pool closed most of them (and the chaperones) had gone back to their rooms and it was just down to me and a couple of kids. Now, the hotel has a rule– which the kids had been informed of– that denizens of the pool need to be wearing shirts while wandering around in the hotel. One of my girls, while getting out of the pool, discovered that one of her roommates had absconded with both a) her shirt and b) her room key. Neither of these are *really* big problems, mind you; I had her drape her towel over her shoulders (large towel, slim girl; no biggie) and I had extra copies of all the keys in my room.

We knocked on their door first; nobody home. Well, fine, I'll go get my key and let you in. I turned and left, not really expecting her to follow me; I didn't even actually notice she'd tagged along until I had my room unlocked and was halfway in. At which point it hit me that the hotel hallway camera was about to record my ass taking a half-naked soaking wet fourteen-year-old girl into *my hotel room.*

I'm still not sure whether making her stay in the hallway counts as an etiquette breach– I suspect it was a bit of an asshole move– but… yeah. No, we're not letting that video get taken, *even just for a few seconds*, even if leaving you in the hallway to *drip* while I go inside and figure out where I tossed the envelope full of room keys seems kinda rude. And then the keys were located and she was let into her room and all was well again.

(Had a similar moment on the way home where several kids tried to get me to add them as friends on Snapchat. Uh, guys? Snapchat is for sending nekkid selfies. Ain't no damn *way* I'm adding you on no Snapchat. Sorry.)

Ah, teaching.

Standardized Testing and Priorities

April 26 2014

I had to waste a day last week giving all of my students the mandatory ISTEP practice test. My Honors kids, due to a smaller number of nonsense behavior/noise issues and a lack of technical problems, finished the test a good fifteen minutes before any of my other classes did, so they got a fair amount of time to screw around on the Internet before the end of class, since bringing them back to the room for half an hour of instruction seemed a) somewhat pointless and b) slightly punitive.

My main job, then, for the last half hour or so of my class, was basically just to wander around and make sure nobody was trying to look for porn. Half of the kids were on Google Maps exploring foreign cities (I love that this is what they choose to do with their time, by the way) and the other half were playing Minecraft, so no problems on that end. At one point I looked outside– one entire wall of the lab is windowed, so I can see anything going on in the hallway– and saw the teacher I've been mentoring all year out in the hallway outside the library with a couple of her kids. Wanting an adult to talk to for a moment, and having a class of kids who I could safely monitor through a wall of glass, I wandered out into the hallway to say hello.

At this point I discovered that the conversation they were having was somewhat more... hmm... *fraught* than I'd suspected from inside the computer lab. One of her girls had just told another student that she was planning on running away from home, and that student had, to her credit, *immediately* told the teacher about it. There are certain protocols that we're to follow under these circumstances, obviously, but generally talking to the kid for at least

351

a *few* minutes before dumping the entire thing into the lap of the school social worker is a good idea, and the teacher was doing just that. I stayed out there long enough to make sure she felt like she had a handle on everything and then went back into the lab, since I could tell the girl wasn't terribly comfortable continuing the conversation with me standing there.

Later that day, once school had let out, I ran into the other teacher in the hallway again and asked her what had been going on with the girl. Turns out she'd just been told, the night before, that she was adopted. Sixth graders not being terribly reasonable creatures, she'd internalized this information not as "my adopted parents love me so much that they picked me to bring home," which I think everyone would kind of have preferred, but as "no one loves me at all, and I should go away."

My first thought, I swear to God, was Why the fuck did they do that to her the week before ISTEP?

Something's gotta fucking change around here.

Okay, You Win

APRIL 27 2014

A student walks up to me. He's got an enormous, wicked grin on his face.

"I'm going to take control of your body and your brain," he says to me, "and then you're going to give me a Jolly Rancher."

The hell you say, I think to myself, but I say "Go for it."

"You are now breathing manually," he says.

He got his Jolly Rancher, the little bastard.

Good Gracious, Ass Bodacious

May 12 2014

Today was a really nice day until around 12:30, when within the first fifteen minutes of my Algebra class starting the temperature in my classroom jumped *twenty damn degrees* and the weather outside took a serious turn toward hellishly humid as well.

Class didn't go as well as it could have.

Entertaining fact: Middle school students are *idiots*. Justification: the *exact same damn kids* who refused to wear coats in the *dead of freaking winter*— and remember we lost several days this winter not to snow, but to *cold*— are now insisting on sweating through the armpits of their *wool jackets* because they don't want to take them off. The *exact. Same. Kids.*

Now, under normal circumstances, I'm perfectly comfortable to simply mock them from a distance. Be an idiot; that's fine. But when I'm damn near *choking on the funk* in my classroom from your sweaty-ass bodies, and, worse, you're *complaining about the heat* while you're wearing that wool sweater... well, it may be that you may be chastised for expressing your opinion.

Mildly. *Lovingly.*

Possibly with something heavy. But maybe not!

And then the phrase "It's getting hot in here, *take off your fucking coat"* floated through my head, with a certain cadence to it, and, well at that point I was done with teaching for the day too.

(Slight detour: Teachers take a fair amount of crap for shifting toward a less academic, more movie-showey style toward the end of the year, and especially past standardized testing. I would like to point out that that is at least partially because it is *hot as hell* inside

Luther M. Siler

these buildings and we hit a point where absolutely no one can concentrate.)

On Honors Classes

May 31 2014

So let's imagine that you're in charge of a school. Or, hell, an entire school district, since for the purposes of this conversation I'd prefer that there be some notion of a wider community that has to be served by your school.

Which is more important: serving the needs of each individual student, or serving the needs of your community as a whole? And what happens if those needs conflict with one another? What if you literally *cannot* serve the best needs of the individual student if you're going to focus on serving the needs of your community?

Think about that while I provide some background and tell a couple of stories. Also be aware that I still have an *intense* goddamn headache and probably should not be staring at a screen or trying to think straight right now, so if this seems incoherent I apologize in advance.

When I was in fifth and sixth grade my school district piloted a new honors program. High achieving students from across the district were pulled out of their home schools and put into two classrooms in the same building. That building, as it turned out, had previously featured some of the lowest, if not *the* lowest, test scores of all of the district's elementary schools. A year later, having literally imported the fifty or sixty smartest fifth and sixth graders available to them (and, presumably, displaced some of their other students to make room for us, although we were stuck in a portable classroom in the parking lot for sixth grade) the district made much hay about how the building had been turned around.

The building hadn't been turned around. They'd just played with the numbers a bit. The classes were supposed to be

357

educationally innovative, piloting all sorts of new ways to teach. I do not recall learning much in fifth and sixth grade. I do recall my mother constantly struggling with the principal– who, incidentally, is one of my district-level supervisors now. For whatever it's worth, she appears to have positive memories of *me*.

This was an early lesson for me on 1) how to lie with statistics, and 2) the cynicism embedded into standardized tests. Note that this was in the mid eighties and thus *way* predates our current obsession with standardized testing.

Note also that my parents enthusiastically registered me for this program when the opportunity became available and that I, furthermore, was *super* psyched about being in it, despite having just had what was probably the best year of my school career in a school I loved in fourth grade. Nobody had to talk anybody into anything here.

Fast forward to now: my district has an honors academy at the middle school level. This is the program I was in in fifth and sixth grade writ large. Note also that the "honors academy" is the *largest middle school in the district*, with, I believe, nearly twice the students that my building has. Note that again, since these kids are all at the honors academy, that means that they're *not* in my building or any of the other schools.

I could complain about this building quite a lot, if I wanted to. As an educator, I *hate them*. They win virtually every district-level competition that exists; it turns out that if you pack a building with high-functioning kids with active, engaged, and generally *wealthy* parents, you get things like great sports programs as a side effect. Nobody else can compete. The entire rest of the district is basically competing for second place.

Now reflect upon the fact that my building (and every other building in the district) is still expected to pass the same number of kids on the ISTEP as every other school in Indiana, despite the fact that, give or take, 20% of my highest-functioning, highest-scoring kids are taken from my building and sent to this other school, and that furthermore we lose additional kids to this school *every year*. Last year, for example, *nineteen* kids from my school with passing or high-passing ISTEP scores transferred to this other building.

We are, effectively, expected to achieve average results– but with the top 20% of our distribution sliced off and sent somewhere else. And it happens every single year. And they are *expanding* this other school, adding new classrooms every year for the next three or four years— so it's only going to get *worse*.

Note that I cannot challenge the decisions of *any* of the individual kids or the individual parents. My parents, and I, made the *exact same decision* when I was in fifth and sixth grade, and frankly would probably do so again.

Note that this individual decision, made enough times, basically means that achieving "average" results becomes *mathematically impossible*.

(One of the solutions to this is to work with a growth model rather than caring about pass rates. I've talked about this before; I don't think the ISTEP should even *have* a passing score. But that's not the world I live in at the moment.)

In the last couple of weeks, I've gotten both my ECA (End of Course Assessment) results and my ISTEP scores back. I was initially a little depressed with my ECA scores— a high school graduation test that is given to my honors 8th graders— until I looked at previous scores for my building and realized that I'd managed the *highest pass rate the school has ever had*. I literally passed three times as many kids as a couple of years ago.

My ECA scores, in other words, make me look like a genius.

I got my ISTEP scores back yesterday. ISTEP scores are tricky; an essential part of the scores (the growth model part) don't get released until a bit after the raw scores, and the raw scores can be a bit misleading if you're not careful about how you look at them.

My honors kids— the same kids that had the record-setting ECA scores— did great, and were more or less in line with the improvement numbers I've seen in years past. Keep in mind that in the last two years I had the best improvement numbers in the building one year and either took second definitively or tied for second, depending on the metric you're using, in the second year.

My regular ed kids did *terrible*. My seventh graders barely moved *at all*. I have a couple of pockets of success here and there— I had four kids who I was *really* hoping for passing scores out of, who have never passed before— and I got two out of the four and the third kid held on to what was frankly a staggering score increase from last year, but still didn't quite pass. But on average my seventh graders were basically *exactly* where they were last year. (This phenomenon doesn't appear to be limited to me, by the way– everyone I've talked to is shocked by how poorly the 7th graders did.)

So, I'm gonna be evaluated on these test results, right? Do we look at the honors kids, and conclude that I'm a stellar educator? Do we look at the seventh graders, and conclude that I'm terrible? Or do we look at an average of both, and conclude that I'm merely mediocre?

Here's the problem with honors classes: by concentrating the kids who do best into individual classrooms, you by definition *take them out* of regular ed classrooms. Which has the effect of concentrating special ed students, low-functioning but not quite special ed students, kids who could do well if they wanted but simply don't give a shit, and– worst of all– *behavior problems* into all of your other classrooms. Which means that the kids who either don't care or are actively invested in being destructive have a *much easier time* of taking over and destroying your class for the kids who *do* care.

I had two different results with these two classes. My first and second hour, while the kids are mostly bright (although some of them clearly don't want to be) is overrun with behavior problems and has been all year. My third and fourth hour kids are mostly– understand that this is not an exaggeration– either special education kids or *criminals*. Fully 20% of third and fourth hour spent some time this year either expelled from school or wearing ankle monitors. I have *four different students* in that class with sub-60 IQs. My best students in that room wouldn't even qualify as *average* in my other class.

It turns out that I'm a *much better teacher* when I get to, y'know, *actually teach*. My third and fourth hour *cratered* on the ISTEP. It turns out it's really goddamn difficult to get math concepts through to kids when half of them don't give a shit and the other half require individual attention. That class had other adults in it for the entire school year but even with three people in the room there are simply *too many kids who need help* for us to be able to actually do our jobs adequately with all of the kids– particularly when there are three or four at any given time who will literally do *nothing* if an adult is not standing next to them monitoring them at all times.

Now, none of these kids *change* if I introduce our honors kids back into the classroom with them. But you know what happens? They actually *see success*. I can ask questions of the classroom and have somebody who is going to *answer*. The number of times I've asked 3rd and 4th hour *simple shit* this year and gotten nothing but blank stares because half of them don't know, half of them don't care, and 2/3 of them are waiting for *someone else to answer* beggars belief. And, furthermore, it increases the resources available to the kids who need help– if you can ask TJ how to do a problem and expect to receive a coherent answer, rather than him just saying "it's 3″ (and honors kids generally *want* to be helpful to other students rather than just letting them copy) then you *don't have to ask me*. I can concentrate my efforts on fewer kids, which means that *more of them actually get educated* on any given day. Which means that, overall, my building looks better and more of our kids are getting the educations they deserve.

What I can't do as well in those circumstances– and maybe this means I'm just not good enough at differentiating my instruction; don't get the idea that I'm trying to put all the blame on the kids here– is push the honors kids. See the problem? Getting rid of honors classes requires a collectivist mindset from both the parents of those honors kids *and the students themselves*. If I don't have that honors Algebra class, well, I can't teach anybody honors Algebra, now, can I? I can do individual enrichment but that's not *remotely* the same as an entire directed class.

Which means that those parents and those kids have to *decide* that the education for *everybody* is more important than *their own* education. And I cannot criticize anyone for not being willing to make that decision.

After all, I didn't make it myself, did I?

Bah.

An Actual Conversation with My Son

June 14 2014

...who, remember, isn't yet three.

SETTING: The boy has just gotten up, and I'm getting him changed and dressed.

HIM: Daddy, are you a teacher?

ME: Yes.

HIM: Why?

ME: I have no idea.

HIM: But you're a teacher?

ME: Yes.

(Several minutes pass; various early-morning toddler things happen. I ponder the chain of events leading up to that question; I have never said the words "Daddy is a teacher" to my son, and I'm not sure he knows what the word means. He decides he wants a chocolate graham cracker for breakfast, a request which is denied until other, more appropriately breakfasty foods are eaten.)

HIM: Chocolate graham cracker!

ME: No.

HIM: But I want chocolate graham cracker!

ME: No. You can have a chocolate graham cracker once you eat some cereal or a squeeze pack.

HIM: But I want chocolate graham cracker!

ME: Do you remember asking me if I was a teacher a few minutes ago?

HIM: Yes.

ME: This means that I am used to disappointing children who want things, and that I don't care even a little bit when I do it anymore.

363

Luther M. Siler

(He contemplates this for a moment.)
HIM: ...I want raisins.
Exeunt.

On Teacher Pay, Again

August 21 2014

We went to Taco Bell for dinner. Taco Bell is hiring. They have a big sign– that I couldn't get a picture of on account of I was driving– in their drive-thru, indicating that assistant managers can make up to $38,000 a year and building managers– they called it something else, but I don't recall what– can make up to $50,000 a year.

Meaning that an *assistant manager at a fast food restaurant* can make $500 a month more than a starting licensed teacher– a job that, mind you, *requires* a college degree, which I doubt (correct me if I'm wrong) assistant managing a fast food restaurant does– and that a *manager* manager can make more than I did teaching last year, with *two Master's degrees* and *twelve years of teaching experience*. And that, furthermore, the teachers will never *reach* those salary levels, because it is effectively illegal to give us raises. I mean, they can be tied to student test scores and evaluations and things like that, but the way the laws work it is trivially easy for districts to simply declare that they don't have the money to pay us more– and the governor and the legislature are *also* trying to starve public schools of funds any way they can, so the districts are more often than not telling the truth.

And I'm not trying to denigrate fast food employees here– I've done that job, and I have tried to never treat a fast food employee with anything less than perfect respect since, and keep in mind that I have a second job where I work behind a register *right now*— but god damn it you should make more *teaching* than you do at fucking *Taco Bell.* Fucking society *depends* on our asses. This is *bullshit.*

365

Part Four: Administration

2014-2015

I changed buildings, but not districts, for the 2014-15 school year. This job ended up being administrative in nature— I was basically an assistant principal, but with a different title and not quite as much authority, and was no longer actually teaching every day. I took the job thinking that a year outside the classroom might help get a bit of my mojo back.

You'll see, I suppose.

On Why I will Never Be a Principal

October 4-5, 2014

Thursday.

My day starts at 6:00 AM. I wake up and, as I do every morning, grab my phone off of my nightstand and check my messages, notifications, and other digital distractions while I'm waiting for my wife, who gets up earlier, to get out of the shower.

I discover that my principal and AP are going to be out of the building for the morning, and that myself and another staff member have been named designees for the day– basically, it means I'm the principal until they get back. (Important note: for the majority of this story it is necessary to remember that there is another adult who is working just as hard as I am for the entire morning. At times we are together and at times we are dealing with different stuff simultaneously. In other words, even though this story is going to be a mile long, this *isn't everything*.)

I make sure to dress nice.

I get to work around 7:15 AM. The office is already full. There are already two parents with kids in tow, two or three kids at the counter, and another kid with his fists clenched and breathing heavy standing over in the corner with two staff members surrounding him and trying to keep him calm. I point at him. "My office, now," I say, because he's making a spectacle of himself. The other staff members usher him away. I speak with the secretary for a moment and determine that one parent is there because of a bullying issue and the other is needing a re-entry conference for a student who has been suspended. These will be the day's first tasks. The three kids at the counter are there because of something connected to Swingyfists McBreatherson.

By the time I get to my office to drop off my laptop– a journey of perhaps 25 feet– it has already been determined that DCS needs to be called for Swingyfists. Our social worker is called from his other building (which he hasn't even gotten to yet) and another staff member with an administrative license and a counseling background is called down to help with him. They're in my office with the door locked.

I try to unlock my door– which has never been closed with me outside of it in the entire time that I have had this job– and discover that I was given the wrong key when they were handed to me and I never noticed. I have literally never locked or unlocked my own door.

My assistant principal waves me over. You're not supposed to be here today! She tells me that she is not, in fact, actually there and that I'm imagining her, and that she's just picking up some stuff for the meeting she and the boss are going to spend the morning in. She hands me a stack of referrals from the day before. "These kids have been spoken to and just need to be told about the consequence of whatever they did," she says, showing me where that information is recorded. I need to call them down, tell them what's happening, and then, depending on the kid and the consequence, inform parents, ISS, or our lunch detention supervisor to expect the relevant kids.

I get someone to let me into my own office. Swingy is crying; everyone else is congregating around him.

Five hundred and sixty-five words in, and I'm just now putting down my bag.

I leave more experienced staff to deal with the DCS issue and call back the parent with the re-entry conference so we can get that kid back to class. These are pretty simple; we go over whatever got the kid suspended, make sure everyone understands our behavior expectations, and outline consequences should behavior continue. They are supposed to be fast.

Dad comes back with his two kids. Two? Sister is with the kid I have a folder on. Whatever, I think, and go through the conference. It's pretty straightforward, actually; without context it appears that the kid either mouthed off to the principal while he was originally dealing with the issue or the referral itself is being understated. My spiel basically boils down to "You're being a shithead in class. Stop."

Dad does not say a single word during the conference.

I finish my bit and ask if either of them have any questions. They do not. I give the kid a paper he needs to give to his teachers to prove he had the conference (he can't be readmitted to class without it) and send him off, expecting Dad and sister to get up too. Neither of them move.

"Huh?"

Turns out sister was suspended too, this time for hitting somebody. They didn't tell the office staff they were there for two reentry conferences. So I gotta go find her paperwork. On the way, I run into the 7th grade special ed teacher, who tells me that she's pretty sure that the kid I just talked to isn't actually supposed to be back until tomorrow. I stop him before he leaves the office and double-check; she's wrong. I have the same conference with sister, except a bit more severely, because her suspension involved violence. Dad still does not say a single damn word. Off to class.

I call back the parent with the bullying issue and her kid, who turns out to be her granddaughter. Here is the entire story: 1) Two weeks ago somebody's phone was stolen; 2) That person thinks granddaughter stole her phone; 3) She didn't; 4) other kid isn't convinced. At one point she threatened to call the police about it but didn't.

Anybody in the same classes together? No. Are you being harassed about it by either the other girl in class or online? Other than this Facebook message from a week ago, no. Anybody threaten to hurt you or beat you up for stealing the phone? No. Are you getting hassled about it by other students? Sometimes they ask if I stole the phone. What happens when you say no? They go away. What happens when you walk past this other kid in the hallway? Nothing.

I am going to spare you the bullying rant. This is manifestly and clearly and obviously not bullying in any way. Note that grandma isn't prodding the kid to give me additional details; it's not like she's clammed up. This is the whole story.

It takes half a damn hour to convince grandma that I'll look into it but right now this is not a bullying issue in any way that I'm aware of. Off to class!

By this point, Swingy and his cohort are out of my office; I know not to where, and I figure it's not my business.

Eleven hundred twenty-six words; it's probably just barely 8 AM.

Luther M. Siler

We start calling the kids from the previous day down. A few of them go smoothly. "You fucked up. Lunch detention." "You fucked up. Go to ISS; stay there today." That sort of thing. The few who I have to call parents for have no numbers that work in the system; the kids give me phone numbers and they don't work. (This is a major issue in schools in poverty-stricken areas, by the way; there's an essay that's been rolling around in my head for months about phone service as a civil rights issue that I keep not writing.) I can't get ahold of goddamn anybody.

One pair of knuckleheads is brought down by their teacher, who gives me a note from a third kid about how the pair of knuckleheads and another kid have been threatening to beat him and his cousin up after school. Knucklehead A and B are already in ISS for the day; that's the reason we brought them down. We speak with Knucklehead C and determine that he is only tangentially related. We read the riot act to A and B and send them off, but– importantly– do not call their parents, because our thought is that the bullying issue (and this really is a bullying issue) changes the game a bit and we don't want to have to call them twice. We table this until after the real administrators get back.

MEANWHILE: While I was dealing with the three parent conferences, Goofus and Goofuser have gotten to school, half an hour or so late. Goofus and Goofuser are both eighth graders. Goofus is Goofuser's uncle. Goofus, at fourteen, has gang tattoos on the back of both hands and up and down his arms.

They have arrived at school high as fuck, which is clearly apparent to everyone who interacts with them for more than a minute or two. My counterpart has been waiting for our SRO (basically, the building cop) to get back to him about what to do while the kids cool their jets in ISS. At some point around now, the SRO gets back to us: the kids are both to be searched for contraband. If drugs are found, the police are to be called; if no drugs are found, the kids' parents are to be contacted and the kids are to be sent home.

We pull Goofus and Goofuser from ISS and have them dump their pockets and their shoes. Goofus is clean; Goofuser inexpertly attempts to hide two lighters in his hand. Lighters, by the way, are an expellable offense all by themselves. They are not drugs, though, so we don't call the cops, but it does mean we have more paperwork to do. We start calling parents and get ahold of Goofuser's mother, who is Goofus's sister. She is with Goofus's mother, who is also her

372

mother. They need to come get the boys. They're in Elkhart, apparently, so it's gonna take a minute. Fine; G&G go back to ISS.

Right around here, somewhere, is when we got the "SECURITY TO THE ART ROOM RIGHT THE HELL NOW" call over the radios. My compatriot, who is in better shape than me, runs. I do not.

The story: there has been some back-and-forth "your momma"-ing between two kids, which was started by Student A. Student B, who I'll call Gasbag, has knocked Student A out of his chair and started kicking him. The two students were separated and pulled into the hall by the teacher and a para, at which point Gasbag broke away from the para and punched Student A once or twice more again.

Now, I know Gasbag. Gasbag is one of the most cold-bloodedly remorseless kids I've ever encountered, and is badly in need of a psychiatrist. I've watched staff members walk him though the consequences of his life decisions right up to the point where he gets killed in jail and he just shrugs. This kid cannot be in school. On a better day, I have sympathy for him. Today– both in the sense of the story and right now as I'm typing it– is really not that day. This kid has been enrolled in our building for something like fifteen days and has been suspended for over half of them, all of those suspensions for fighting. He's about to be put out for five more and this time I'm now pretty sure we're going to expel him.

It might be 10 AM by now; this is the second expulsion-worthy offense of the day.

I cannot put Student A and Gasbag in ISS together, because Gasbag will attack him again. (Remember, Student A started the verbal altercation and the insults; he just picked an incredibly bad person to insult. He got his ass kicked, but that doesn't make him innocent.) Student A is bleeding from his hand and is complaining about rib and chest pain, so I send him to the nurse first, with instructions to the nurse to refer him to ISS until I can get ahold of a parent. Gasbag is planted in my office. I ask Gasbag if there is any point to talking to him about what he just did.

"Nope. He deserved it. Go ahead and expel me."

Okay!

Another factoid about Gasbag: he came to us after being kicked out of– wait for it– an online homeschooling program. I leave it as an exercise to the reader to determine how such a thing is even possible, as these things are notorious for being nothing but cash grabs that give no fucks about actually educating anyone. His mother works at the closest Subway to our school, and has made me many sandwiches. I like her.

I try several numbers on his emergency card and his little sister's (sister, incidentally, is an angel) before deciding fuck it and just looking up his mother's work. It's close enough to lunchtime that she's probably there; she seems to always be working whenever I go get lunch from there. Weird fact: the Subway website has no idea that that restaurant is actually there! When I call the number listed at another address on the same street, that number is dead. I cannot get ahold of anyone for any reason today.

I don't have time for this right now; I put our attendance secretary on the task of getting ahold of his mom and finding the number and go deal with something else that, right now, I can't actually remember. She finally finds Mom. I fill her in. She sighs, explains that she can't leave work right now, and says that she'll send his older sister to pick him up, but it may be a bit. I say fine. He's already sleeping in my office. Whatever, fuck it.

(Mom, incidentally, has eight children, only one of whom is causing her any trouble, and again: the sister is an angel. Left as an exercise to the reader: how to support eight children on a job at Subway.)

Right around now two different things happen at about the same time: one, sister-mother shows up to pick up Goofus and Goofuser. She goes back to a conference with my compatriot that leads to forty-five solid minutes of weeping and crying about how awful her life is and how she's the only one in her family with a job and how awful it is that she can't trust her brother to be around her son because of what a bad influence he is.

Again: A better me has an enormous amount of sympathy for and empathy with this woman, who is visibly younger than me and has mentioned her two grandchildren, one three months old and one a year and a half, several times. She's apparently trying to get custody of them. She's in a godawful situation to be in. I am, at this moment, unfortunately not that better me. Luckily, my compatriot is better at this than me and he handles the majority of this conference, which includes referring her to our social worker to see if he can get her some help.

Right about now, a teacher drags down… Swingyfists McBreatherson! He's gotten into a verbal altercation with a girl in

the hallway and she's dumping both of them on us. No punches
thrown, just a bunch of yelling.

What the hell is he doing in class? I think to myself, and then
figure whatever, somebody higher up on the food chain than me
decided to put him there, and put it out of my head. Keep in mind:
other than knowing about a DCS referral, I have no idea what this
kid's story is, and I haven't asked.

I am smart enough, though, even in my current massively
misanthropic state, to realize when a kid is having a magnificently
shitty day, and this kid certainly qualifies. I speak with him and the
other girl. This doesn't seem to be a big deal, just a flare-up from
one kid that the second kid didn't decide to back down from.

"You two pissed off at each other?"

"Nah."

"If I send you back to class, are there gonna be any further
interruptions from you?"

"Nah."

"Are you sure? Because you're going home if there are."

I watch DCS kid very carefully when I say this. There's a brief
flash of fear in his eyes, but it goes away quick. I file that away for
later.

I take them back up to class and talk to the teacher. She's
aware of the situation from in the morning, and I tell her that my
theory is just that Swingy's having a shitty day, flew off the handle,
and that the girl didn't back off, but that it's not going to cause
additional issues. I ask her if she's okay with me just putting them
back in her class and she says she is. Off you go!

Back downstairs! I see the same teacher from the bullying note
in the morning outside the office. She has two more kids with
her! One, a tall heavyset kid (a sixth-grader an inch or two shorter
than me) is bawling. The other is a little shrimpy kid. He is angry.

Short version: big kid is a Jordanian immigrant, and neither
speaks nor reads English very well yet. Little kid has been picking
on him– making fun of the way he talks and reads, poking him in the
shoulder, shoving him, bumping into him, all sorts of shit. The other
kid finally snapped in the bathroom just now after the first kid
shoved him while he was at the urinal and swung his arms behind
him to push him away, at which point the little kid punched him in
the neck.

The fact-finding part of the story takes twelve seconds, as everyone involved agrees that that was what happened. I tell the teacher to write up the little dude, send him to ISS, and send the other kid to the nurse. I turn around. There are two high-school aged girls standing behind me in street clothes.

"Can we use the bathroom?"

I blink a couple of times. Why do you want to use the bathroom in a middle school why the hell aren't you in class what the hell is going on who the hell are you people anyway what the hell is happening oh wait I know one of you.

And I do not like her very much.

Hmm. What to call this young lady? Eh. It doesn't matter. I had her for at least three years, one of which she was actually in my classes, at my other building. During that time she was expelled twice; she is horrible. She ought to be a sophomore at this time; why she isn't in school is beyond me.

I made some sort of *why are you here and why are you asking* kind of sound at them; I'm not generally the type to refuse someone access to bathrooms, but there's something to be said for the whole *wait what the fuck* reaction I was having at that time.

Now, by this time, Goofus and Goofuser were both in the office again, and sister-mother is sitting out there with them for some reason. The girl I don't know nods toward the office and says "That's my sister." They've apparently been waiting in the car all this time. Okay. Doesn't explain why neither of you are in class, but I suddenly feel better about letting you use the bathroom. I raise an eyebrow at the one I don't know.

"I got a baby by his brother," she says. She might be sixteen by now. She fails to specify whether it's Goofus or Gasbag's brother who impregnated her; it occurs to me that one of the two grandchildren that sister-mother has been talking about is probably her kid, which explains why she's trying to get custody, because a live, hungry alligator and a thousand angry bees would easily be better parents than this child is going to be. I wave them toward the bathroom and go check on the kid in the nurse's office who got punched in the throat.

And I immediately *fall in love with the kid*, who is the sweetest kid I've ever met, and by the end of hearing his story about what happened I'm ready to plant the other student *underneath* the building. I tell him and the nurse that he can go back to class when he feels ready to, because he's not in trouble, find out whether the nurse is going to call his parents (that's my call; I tell her I'll do it) and go back to the office, where I discover a conundrum has presented itself. Sister-mother can take her son home. However, inexplicably, she's not on her brother's emergency card, which means we can't legally release him to her. We tell her if she can get ahold of her/their mother and get verbal permission from her for us, that will work just fine, because everyone realizes that the policy is in this case a bit of an unnecessary inconvenience.

Oddly, she excuses herself to the hallway to make the phone call, because "the office is too loud." She comes back in and hands the phone to our attendance secretary, who types a few words into her computer and then, in a rather pointed tone, asks the person on the other end of the line what Goofus's birthday is.

"No, that's not it. That's not it either. Sorry, bye."

And she hangs up and hands the phone back to sister-mother. Sister-mother, you see, has just called the two girls in the parking lot and told them to pretend to be their/her mother, only they don't know Goofus's birthday. Our attendance secretary has apparently spoken to Goofus's mother before and she has a very distinct voice, so she knew from the jump that that wasn't her on the phone.

So sister-mother has to leave without Goofus, who is returned to ISS, but takes Goofuser with her. Why their mother is unavailable is never explained.

My assistant principal finally returns! It is noon! Note that it has taken nearly four thousand words to get to noon. I take some time to fill her in on everything that has happened, which takes a very long time, especially since we keep getting interrupted.

We hit the point where I send Swingyfists back to class. She blows up, stunned and horrified that I would do such a dumb thing. I point out again that that's where he already was, at which point she blinks and realizes that no, she's not mad at me, but she is *really* mad at our social worker. I'm going to deliberately omit details of the rest of the conversation but let's make it clear that she was not happy about that particular turn of events.

At some point it occurs to me that I still have Student A in ISS and Gasbag in my office. I am, amazingly, quickly able to get ahold of Student A's grandmother, who tells me she'll call his mother at work and have her get back with me about whether they're going to come get him or just let him walk home at the end of the day. A few minutes later, a young woman in nurse's scrubs who looks a lot like Gasbag walks into the office. It's the sister! At the exact second I wave her over, Student A's mom calls, and I have a brief moment of *shit which one of them do I talk to first*. I choose the person who is physically present over the person on the phone and ask for her to leave a number and that I'll call her right back. I explain the situation to the sister, who luckily understands what her brother is and does not argue or fight, even when I mention the high likelihood of an expulsion. I take her to my office. Gasbag is curled up in a chair, where he's been for the last couple of hours, asleep. She wakes him up with a rather impressive roundhouse slap to the back of his head, hitting him hard enough that she has to be hurting her hand in the process, and just about drags him out of the office.

Well, okay, bye.

I call Student A's mother back. Her main concern is whether her son was fighting. I say that he did not actually land or throw any punches to the best of my knowledge and make it clear that he's been in ISS for starting the confrontation. As it turns out, they live nearby, and after making sure that the other student is out of the building and can't chase him home or anything she tells me that he can go home on his own. Okey-dokey.

I go to McDonald's, buying a triple cheeseburger and a large fry. On the way back, I manage to cough up an enormous wad of phlegm, which is rather unpleasantly in my mouth now. True fact about me: I don't spit. Which means that I don't know that if you spit a huge loogie out of a car window at speed, it's going to bounce off of the moving air outside the car and end up all over the expensive sport jacket you're wearing and yes you just managed to spit on yourself while driving back to work.

So that happened.

(Oh, I forgot: at some point early in the morning, the secretary made a run and brought me coffee. We had to pull the lids off to figure out which coffee was mine and which was hers, and in my brief conversation with Gasbag, I had taken the first sip from the nearly-cold cup of coffee and spilled half of it all over myself, because we hadn't put the lid on right. This is thus the second time that something connected to McDonald's has led to foreign liquids on my clothing.)

I get back and eat in a hurry. It suddenly hits me that we never contacted the parents of the two boys from earlier in the day, the ones who were involved in the bullying issue and the threats to the other kids. Then it hits me that I don't remember talking about them with the assistant principal. I stick my head in her office and ask if she remembers talking about them. She doesn't. I look through the stack of write-ups she has.

They're not in there. Neither is the note.

What the fuck.

Me and my co-principal tear my office, his office, the main office itself, and the conference room apart looking for these write-ups and, most importantly, that note. Nowhere to be found. I have been being very careful over the course of the day to keep track of all of my paperwork, so this is *insanely* aggravating that I can't find the documents that I most need for my boss to see at this point.

So pile some extra aggravation on everything else at this point, with a nice little dose of incompetence. I really do not like feeling incompetent.

For reasons that aren't interesting, our building is dismissing today in a different way from usual, one that demands that all the televisions in the building be tuned to the same channel and that all the VCRs be on. We do not have time for there to be technical glitches while this is going on, so my co-principal and I have been planning all day on going around to the classrooms and pre-testing everything before crunch time. It is now *way too close* to crunch time, and we abandon the search and rush out to get the classrooms set up properly. At some point we get dragged into the sixth grade team meeting, and they spend time I don't have interrogating me about some details about our testing and data collection process, details that I only barely have to begin with.

We are down to our last grade hallway when I get a call over my radio that there is a parent to see me in the office. The parent wants to talk about "the bullying issue from this morning." I spend a moment thinking *how does he know about that already*, thinking they're referring to the boy who was being picked on *shit I lost that paperwork and we haven't found it*.

Nope. Remember Phone Girl, my second conference of the day, 21000 hours ago? I was talking to her grandmother. This, now, is her *father*, who is telling me that he's going to keep his daughter out of school until "this is resolved."

379

I'm still, at this time, not entirely sure what the hell "resolved" even means, because it's been two weeks and the girl's phone hasn't been found and I can't just snap my fingers and produce the damn thing, nor can I tell her to stop thinking that this other girl has stolen her phone because her thinking that makes the other girl's parents upset. There is, in short, really not a thing I can do about this, short of magically producing the phone. I nonetheless promise to do some investigation tomorrow, having correctly predicted to his mother earlier in the day that I would not have time to deal with it during the day today. He says he is not sending his daughter to school tomorrow. *Fuck it, it's Friday*, I think, and tell him that's fine. I promise to call him after I talk to the other girls and send him on his way.

I walk out of the office to go back to tuning televisions and VCRs and discover that the father of Neck-Punch is outside, collecting Neck-Punch for a previously scheduled doctor's appointment.

Fuck I never called him and told him his kid got punched in the neck.

I am in the middle of asking him if he has a few minutes to talk to me about his son when my radio bleeps. There's a fight in ISS, or there's about to be, and they need security. *Shit*. I give him the most apologetic look I can muster, ask him to hold on for a few minutes while I deal with this new bullshit, then race off to deal with ISS. Luckily, by the time I get there, the principal and a couple of other staffers have already gotten it under control. Guess who was fighting? If you said Goofus, you win. I don't know who he was going after, though.

I mentally mark that Not My Fucking Problem, come back, apologize profusely to Dad, and explain the situation from earlier in the day to him, continuing to tell him how sorry I am for not getting in touch with him earlier– my meeting with the AP had completely driven his son out of my head and I'd forgotten about it. Luckily (again) he is as wonderful as his son, and after I bring up another couple of (unrelated) issues that my talk with the boy had brought up and explain what our options are for dealing with them, dad thanks me (I take a risk and reply "shukran," which gets me a big smile from both of them) and they leave.

My compatriot comes to me with a huge smile on his face. He's found the paperwork! He'd set it down in the AP's office while looking for something else; entertainingly, it was in the room it was supposed to be in, just on a different shelf. Unfortunately, at this point, there's no time to talk to the boys any more, much less call their parents, before dismissal. It hits me that we also haven't done anything about the neck-puncher other than sock him in ISS for the day. All these, as well as official suspension decisions for the various other things I've dealt with throughout the day, will have to be finished after school.

Dismissal happens.

I have a few more conversations with my AP and then head home.

Here's the thing, chirren.

Thursday was a day from hell. There is no damn doubt about that at all. And it is amazing to me just how much I didn't know about how *difficult* being a principal was prior to taking a job where I work in the office.

I didn't have to deal with teachers.

I didn't have to deal with the union.

I didn't have to deal with downtown.

I just had to deal with *discipline*, and it produced a day busy enough that it produced over five thousand words of writing.

And here's where this ties in with my other educational obsession: my school added a hundred and twenty-five new transfer students this year. We acquired those kids because we're a good school and parents are pulling their kids from other crappier schools and sending them our way. And the first month or so of school has been rough as hell because a lot of those transfer kids, as well as a gaggle of kids from Chicago and Michigan City, aren't necessarily getting with the program on how things work around here. My boss begins nearly every conversation with "Where did you go to school last year?" because nearly every kid who lands in the office is a new student. All three of my major trouble kids, plus about 2/3 of the rest, were new to the building.

When these kids, who have been in failing schools for years, drag down our test scores– as, inevitably, they will, because that's how math works— our teachers will be blamed, and our school's ranking will go down.

Because we succeeded, and other parents sent their kids to us.

Let that roll around in your head a little bit.

Luther M. Siler

2015 Luther edit: I also feel compelled to point out just how few students this entire odyssey encompasses. It's easy to read something like this and conclude that I work in a nightmare school again. Literally hundreds of kids came to school that day and did exactly what they were supposed to. The problem was that I saw each and every one of the ones who didn't.

On School Clothes

October 12-13, 2014

I have spent the last couple of hours going *I will not write about dress codes* in my head, like a mantra.

It has failed.

A couple of words of warning: first, I currently expect this to be a bit on the long side, and second, I think I'm probably just going to stream-of-consciousness the whole thing rather than try and organize it in a way that makes sense, because it's Sunday night and this is a complicated subject and I still don't feel like thinking as hard as it probably deserves. So if you catch me contradicting myself or something doesn't seem quite consistent, that's why. Like I said: complicated subject.

You may not be aware that every school I've ever taught at has at least nominally had a uniform. I started off at a Catholic school, of the jumpers-and-skirts variety, moved to a Chicago Public Schools school that had a loose one, and then to my current district, where we've always had uniforms of some sort but of a looser definition than the Catholic schools do.

I have been to many, *many* faculty meetings about dress code in one way or another. I have made an ass of myself at many, *many* faculty meetings by trying to address some of the questions that I'm going to raise here. No one but me is ever interested in discussing them. Which is stupid, because you *shouldn't have a dress code* if you don't have some idea of *why* you have a dress code.

Here, for example, are several reasons to have a dress code:

1) Control. You want to be in charge of the decisions of your students, and to let them know that you, as the administration and the teachers, are in charge. One of the ways you let them know

383

that you run their lives is by controlling what they are allowed to wear.

2) Modesty/"Distraction". Note that this one is generally girls-only, and is closely related to #1. Girls' bodies are inherently dangerous, particularly to boys, and the best way to make sure that the boys' days aren't ruined by the girls' bodies is to cover up the girls' bodies as much as humanly possible. It is critical to make certain that at no time is it possible for a girl bit to make a boy bit any more rigid than it ordinarily is. Note that "distraction" is not always sexual in nature; things like pink hair or piercings can be deemed "distracting."

3) Professionalism. Going to school is a kid's *job*. Adults are expected to dress in certain ways for their jobs; kids may as well get used to this idea right now. Also something about promoting habits of mind to go with the orderly atmosphere you are creating by requiring everyone to dress similarly.

4) Social leveling. If the kids are all wearing the same thing, it makes it more difficult for the rich kids to show off their money or for the poor kids to look like they don't have as much. Also, conformity issues: it's harder to single out kids for not joining the crowd and wearing the New Cool Brand (which they may or may not be able to afford) if everyone has to wear the same shirt.

5) Gang affiliations. This only applies to certain schools, obviously, but if you have a gang presence in your neighborhood frequently you want to do your best to make certain that kids can't outwardly display gang affiliation. This is hideously tricky; keep reading.

You may have already figured out from my phrasing that the two I have the most comfort with are #3 and #4; #1 is wildly unnecessary and #2 doesn't always *have* to be problematic but very frequently is, particularly when you add religion into the mix. #5 is essential if you're in a school with a gang problem but requires an ever-evolving list of things to ban as the symbols and signs evolve. Most of the school uniform drama-outbursts that make their way into the media is from people trying to shove the first two in where they don't belong; for example, a chaperone father being turned on by a prom dress and trying to slut-shame the girl wearing it.

In fact, let me make this crystal clear right now: women are not, under any circumstances, responsible for the reactions of men or boys to their clothing.

Period. Point-blank.

See, nearly 800 words already and I've barely gotten started.

Anyway: your *reasoning* for why you're controlling your students' attire should inform the *level* of control that you're exerting over that attire. If you are interested in controlling your students, and control *itself* is the virtue, then you're going to be worried about things like belt buckles and shoelaces and hairstyles and all sorts of nonsense. You're also setting yourself up for an *immense* number of fights. If you just want your kids to look clean and whatever the fifth-grade equivalent of "professional" is, then maybe the fact that Brittany has pink shoelaces on one shoe and green on the other isn't a problem.

So let's talk about how you control clothing. There are two ways. A proscriptive dress code is a *thou shalt not* dress code. Don't wear this, don't wear that; you can wear this in *this way* but not in *that way*. These dress codes tell you what *not* to do or, frequently, what not to *show*, and are often actually referred to as "dress codes." A descriptive dress code specifically *tells the kids what to wear,* and is less concerned with "nots." The most extreme version of this is the classic Catholic school uniform, where every boy and every girl in the building are going to be basically wearing the exact same thing, often bought from the same vendor. These are often *not* called dress codes; they're called *school uniforms.*

These things can bleed into each other, obviously, but the more alike the kids look when you walk into a building the more likely it is that you're dealing with a descriptive dress code rather than a proscriptive one.

I don't like proscriptive dress codes. The reason: the more rules you have for what *can* and *can't* be done, the more fights you're going to have with your students, and every *second* of arguing about dress code is a second I'm not spending instructing. Just for example: yoga pants. I'm a grown-ass man, right? And I don't have a daughter, and my wife prefers to wear jeans.

I don't know what the fuck a "yoga pant" is, I have no intention of *learning*, and I'm *not* about to waste my time arguing with a twelve-year-old about whether she's wearing them or not. Kids become lawyers *awful goddamn fast* when they think their pants are capris and you think they're yoga pants. (Is that combination possible? Hell, I have no idea, but one school I worked at officially laid down a rule that if the pants had rivets *anywhere on them* then they were jeans, regardless of color, fabric, fit, or any other consideration. Rivets=jeans=against dress code, period.)

Any and every rule can be made obnoxious in this way. For example: say you don't want your kids dyeing their hair. So you make a rule saying you can't dye your hair. Then Brittany, who was a blonde last year, starts the year as a brunette. Do you make her go change her hair back to her normal color? No, that's ridiculous, and you'd have to *ask her* what her natural hair color is. Maybe she was breaking the rules all last year!

Okay, so you modify the rule: you can't dye your hair *unnatural* colors, because kids with blue hair are distracting. You just made it against the rules for every black and Hispanic kid in your building to go blonde. Did you mean to do that? Or do you ban specific colors, and then get into bullshit about whether someone's hair is mauve or turquoise or blue, and this *specific shade of blue* isn't actually prohibited on your list of "unnatural" colors.

(The solution is to not give a fuck about hair color. Yes, Damien's blue hair will be distracting– for an *hour*. So will his next haircut. So will *your* next haircut. I shaved my beard off once and was fending off questions about it for a *week.*)

I find that the best way to handle a dress code is to set general rules that are clear and easy to follow and to expect the kids to stick by them– if you *make* a rule, it is *critical* that you *stick by* that rule. If not, *get the hell rid of it.*

For example, I see no reason at all to ever care about any of the following things: hair, ears, noses, lips, feet, shoes, shoelaces, belts, accessories of any kind, including necklaces, rings, bracelets, or other forms of jewelry. We once mandated that all students wear belts. It was pointed out that some kinds of girls' pants don't have belt loops. Okay; we modified the rule that if your pants *had belt loops* then you had to wear a belt.

Can you guess what happened? The kids started *cutting off their belt loops.*

This is fucking ridiculous.

And, see, again: I'm coming at dress codes from #3 and #4. I want the kids to look reasonably clean and neat, because they're *at work*, and I would like there to be *some* social leveling going on. #4 never *really* works, but it does help a bit. The kids just find other things to signify status with. This is a particular problem with gang affiliations; you'll discover midyear that all the kids who are 2-6ers have been wearing a rubber band on their left ankle or something like that. Ban that, and they start wearing their collars a certain way. You can never really get rid of it.

Here, to my mind, is how to do a dress code: either go whole-hog, like the Catholic schools, and specify a certain shirt, pants, belt, skirt, jumper, and type of shoe for *every kid in your building,* and then provide a specific local vendor who provides those items at a reasonable cost and vouchers for your families who can't afford the uniforms, or go descriptive but simple, and *don't stress out* about the things you don't cover in your dress code.

For example, if I wrote my school's dress code, it would look like this:

1) Polo or button-up shirt with a collar (boys and girls). Long or short sleeve, colors to be determined by the school. Most in my area have settled on blue, with some allowing other colors.

2) Dress pants. Dress pants do not have rivets, are not made from denim, and are not form-fitting. (Note: *never* ban a specific style of clothing. You will fight for years about what cut of a pair of pants are or whether pants are "yoga pants" or "stretch pants" or "leggings" or "jeggings," which I think might *actually be a thing*, and whether that matters.)

3) In colder weather, a plain one-color sweater (define colors as necessary) may be worn. The sweater must be one piece and not have a zipper.

4) Skirts of XXX color may be worn by either gender. Skirts above the knee should be paired with leggings of XX color. (Skirt length rules are hideous and horrible. I'd honestly just insist on everyone wearing pants all the time just to avoid debates about skirts. This is the best I can do; I'll get more into it later.)

5) Shoes must have a back to them; IE, no flip-flops. (I know I said earlier that I don't care about shoes. This rule could be rephrased as "Shoes should actually *be shoes.*")

6) Shirts shall be tucked in at all times, and pants shall be worn at the waist. ~~Shoes with laces should be tied.~~ Y'know, screw

that last rule. I mean, it's *true*, but it doesn't need to be part of a dress code.

      7) And that's *it*. I give no shits about anything else. Everything else is up to the kid. Glory in yo' spunk, as BB King might say.

      That's already 2000+ words, and I haven't gotten into talking about sexism yet.

      I'll start with a story. I don't feel like sagging pants was a *huge* thing when I was in middle school and high school, but it was certainly a thing that was around and that some people did. I have, in fact, one story about sagging pants that dates to seventh or eighth grade.

      Actually, this isn't much of a story: one of the kids in my class was sagging, and the teacher's response was to call him out in front of the entire room with the words "Mark, I don't wanna see the color of your underwear." Now, she was a Japanese immigrant, so to properly enunciate it you have to say it with a Japanese accent and stretch out *Mark* into *Maaahk*.

      It's actually the quintessential "you had to be there" thing– but people I know who were in the room at the time *still say that to each other* every once in a while despite the fact that I haven't seen the Mark involved since graduating high school. I'm pretty sure he's a pastor now, which is *hilarious*.

      So let's begin our discussion of sexism and gender in the middle school with what I'll call the Maahk rule: *I don't want to see the color of your underwear.* This is, refreshingly, a gender-neutral rule: it means that the boys have to keep their pants at their waists (and I don't know if I pointed this out, but telling boys to pull their pants up and boys and girls to tuck in their shirts are *easily* my #1 and #2 uniform corrections, and they are *miles* above whatever #3 might be.) and it means that if the girls wear skirts, they have to wear them long enough that flashing isn't going to be an issue.

      If it were up to me, I'd simply ban skirts entirely unless a family could provide a bona fide religious requirement to wear them– if only because those families never *also* produce length-of-skirt issues. Why? Skirts are hideous, not in terms of how they look or the function they provide but because *everything involved in dealing with them* quickly becomes either unfair or creepy as hell. Monitoring skirt length *sucks*. The fingertip rule depends on how long a girl's *arms* are, which seems stupid. "Knee length" requires you to define where the *knee* is. I have actually seen staff members (none male, thank God) *require girls to kneel* in order to determine whether their skirts are the right length.

Uh-uh. No. Never. Under no circumstances, this sucks and it's shaming and fucked up and it should *never ever happen in a school,* particularly and *especially* if it's a male staffer. When I worked in the Catholic school I made it perfectly clear to both the principal and the pastor that there were *no circumstances* under which I was ever saying a *single word* to a student about the length of her skirt. Period. Surprisingly, I got no pushback on that. Are there girls who just really like wearing skirts? I'm sure there are. I like wearing jeans. Can't wear 'em to work. Too bad. This is where the "professional atmosphere/this is your job" aspect of dress codes kick in.

The other problem with skirts? Teenage and tween-age girls have a habit of *growing.* Which means that a skirt that was entirely appropriate at the beginning of sixth grade might be *oh holy shit* short by the *middle* of sixth grade. More on this in a bit.

So, yeah: the Maahk rule. I don't want to see the color of your underwear. And if it were up to me, we'd just do away with skirts altogether.

Alternatively, one could choose to allow skirts, but require *all skirts* regardless of length to be paired with leggings. The main thing is, I *never* want to get sucked into the skirt-length debate. I'd much rather just ban the damned things.

On to the other sexualizing aspect of dress codes: tight and/or revealing clothing.

Actually, let's get this out of the way first: I don't think there's ever much of a reason to have dress codes before fifth grade or so. If you *do* have a dress code before fifth grade, *none of this should matter,* because a nine year old in a sundress is *not* trying to attract male attention by showing her shoulders and you should stop being a creepy asshole if you think so. Have a descriptive dress code if you like, but the idea that eight-year-old girls should have to worry about clothes being tight or revealing is *ridiculous* and if you are worrying about that yourself as an adult there is something wrong with you.

Here are some reasons why a young woman might wish to wear tight and/or revealing clothing:

1) It's comfortable; to hell with what anybody else thinks. As a fat man, I can't relate to this, because it is

impossible for me to be comfortable in tight clothes. However, I'm willing to believe it's true. Aren't I charitable?

2) You want people to look at you. True of many girls. Also true of many boys, obviously, but in boys this rarely leads to tight or revealing clothes. Important: it is *okay* to want to be looked at. It just may not be *appropriate for school.*

3) Picking a fight. This is closely related to #2, but adds a level of aggressiveness to the whole thing. There exists a subset of young women who appear to wear tight clothes specifically so that they can bark "Why are you *looking?*" at the first staff member to challenge them on it. In some ways, it's garden-level predetermined insubordination, with a nice soupçon of creepiness and assholery to go with it.

4) You have no idea that you're even doing it. And here, you see, *especially* at the middle school, lies the problem.

I don't give a single shit about the "distraction to boys" angle of the dress code, folks. Boys need to grow into *men*, and part of growing into a man involves learning how to not turn into a slavering halfwit every time a bare shoulder or a bra strap floats across your field of vision. If you're *really concerned* about the girls' clothing screwing up the boys' ability to learn, well, allow me to introduce you to a little thing called *gender based education.* You don't solve the distraction issue, assuming that is even possible, by corralling the girls. You solve it, if you care to do so, by corralling the *boys.*

Also true: there's literally *no level to which women's clothing can be controlled* that will remove sexual distraction from teenage boys. It's *fucking impossible.* Boys that age– probably girls too, to at least *some* extent, but I've never been a teenage girl so I can't be sure– are *perpetually distracted by sex.* It's fucking unavoidable. Much like Shaquille O'Neal, you cannot stop it, you can only hope to contain it.

Even if you remove the girls *entirely* you will *still* have seventh grade boys adamantly refusing to stand up every once in a while and will have to deal with the *oh shit he has a boner* moment as a teacher and decide what to do about it. That would happen if you put him *alone in a room,* too. Welcome to puberty.

(HA! That's a reason for *boys* to not wear tight clothing! Boner prominence!)

The reasons that dress codes *should* worry about tightness and/or revealingness are Reasons 2 through 4 up there. Why? Because *intent matters*. Because we *do* need to worry about people who are going to school for reasons other than academics– and *intentionally* dressing to "show off the goods," so to speak, *is a problem*– and because one important aspect of dealing with particularly middle-school aged girls is that they frequently have *no idea what they're doing.*

This is where I start dancing around violating the "women are not responsible for men's reactions to their clothing" rule, but I really do think there's a difference here: if you're wearing yoga pants because they're comfortable, I don't have a problem with you. If you're wearing them to get Billy in 3rd hour (or, for that matter, Jenny in 4th) to look at your ass, you're *deliberately disrupting* the educational process– or at least aiming to– which is an actual and *distinctly different* problem. This is *not the same* as demanding girls be responsible for boys' reactions. It's expecting girls to be responsible for *their own* actions. You aren't at school to catch a boyfriend. You're at school to *learn*.

This may be a distinction without a difference. It does mean that schools *do* have a non-sexism-related reason to police tight and/or revealing clothing– because it's not as if you can institute a rule that if you think something is comfortable it's okay.

And, honestly, I'm much more concerned with #4 anyway. The maturity level of middle-school aged kids in a single cohort (and this is true for boys and girls) is *incredibly variable*, and can vary insanely over the course of the year.

Ask any sixth grade teacher, in particular: they are, by and large, teaching *children* in August and September and right around March they start getting caught making out and grabbing each other's asses. And frequently they have *no idea* that something is showing off too much chest or too much butt or too much leg. Why? Because those legs have grown six inches in the last five months, because those boobs *weren't there* a year ago, and because *what do you mean I have a butt*. Go into any middle school in America and you will find eighth grade girls who look like they're ten and eighth grade girls who could walk into a bar and not get carded until they opened their mouths. And just because a girl *looks like* she could walk into a bar and not get carded does *not* mean that she has *remotely* the emotional, physical, and, yes, *sexual* maturity to be able to deal with what has happened to her body over the last few years.

Schools take on *a lot* of responsibilities beyond reading and 'rithmetic, guys. One of them is trying to guide these kids through adolescence– trying to *literally* keep them comfortable in their own skins. And rules about tight and revealing clothing *need to be there,* for two separate reasons: to keep the ones who legitimately *are* showing off from *deliberately* screwing up what is supposed to be a professional atmosphere, and to help those who have no idea from doing it *accidentally.* At some point, somebody– and generally it needs to be a female staffer– needs to pull Susie aside and *make sure she realizes* that it might be time to think about a new pair of pants, or to call her parents and suggest that *they* do it. Because it seriously might be that three months ago those pants fit *just fine* and she doesn't realize that they look like they were applied with a *spray can* this morning.

True story: I had an eighth-grade girl walk up to me once while I was at the front of a school bus. I had my hand on the top of the seat in front of her. The girl dropped her *entire rack*– and she was probably a C-cup– onto the top of my hand and my arm. She had *no idea* that she was doing it. If you're sitting at a desk, they'll come over and lean over the desk to show you something, with, again, *no idea* what they may or may not be showing off. If an adult woman lets me look down her shirt, or pushes her boobs into my hands, ten will get you twenty that she's *doing it on purpose.* Teenage girls don't all have that awareness of what they're doing yet; they may legitimately have no idea. Or they *might.* Either is a problem, yes?

Here's the problem (he said, 4000 words in): All of the last, oh, six paragraphs or so can end up in practice looking *exactly like* Girls are Temptresses Who Must Be Controlled to Save the Boys. As I said earlier, a distinction without a difference. And I'm not into that. I think it's offensive and ridiculous. But how do we *insert* a difference in there so that it's clear that this is coming from a place where 1) the most important about being in school is the *learning* part, and 2) when someone breaks tight/revealing dress code rules, keeping the focus on *education*, and making sure that the kids are *aware* of how they might be perceived?

Enforcement, of course. The focus should *never* be on making someone wearing inappropriate clothing feel bad about it. I understand the reason behind, say, making uniform violators wear a bright pink 4XL I'm Out of Uniform shirt, but it's *not my job to make kids feel bad*, and in most circumstances if a disciplinary intervention produces *shame* it's probably one that should be avoided.

And it's here, unfortunately, where I kinda run out of ideas. While I don't much like the Shame Shirt, the advantage of it is that it *keeps the kids in class*. I don't like the idea of keeping Jenny out of class because her pants are too tight or her shirt is too short (left unsaid so far: an operational definition of "too tight," which is virtually impossible) and I *also* don't like the idea of letting her know that if she doesn't want to go to class all she has to do is wear a miniskirt to school and *bam* she gets to sit in ISS all day.

The best solution, it seems, is for the school too keep a *lot* of spare uniform-appropriate clothes on hand, in a wide variety of sizes, and require uniform violators to put those on. Problem is, that's expensive and difficult and those clothes are going to go home and not come back a lot, which is why most schools go with the Shame Shirt solution– or just locking kids in ISS– instead. I suppose schools could go the same route my kid's day care goes with and require parents to send a spare set of clothes to school with their kids, but that's ridiculous on a lot of levels too, chief among which that– yep– they're gonna grow out of the *spare* clothes too.

So, yeah. Here's where I run out of options. I think the best solution is probably something detention-based, with removal from class only an option in the *most serious* of cases. If you have a kid who is perpetually disregarding the dress code, male *or* female, you don't deal with that as a dress code violation. You deal with it as *repeated insubordination*, which is another thing entirely. The focus shouldn't be on the clothes. The focus should be on *you have had this explained to you repeatedly and you are refusing to comply*. That's an entirely different story.

And it can't be solved with a giant pink shirt.

On How Not to Talk to Parents

November 13 2014

So it snowed today.

It snowed rather *a lot,* and rather unexpectedly as well. I had no idea that it was snowing until I opened my garage door. It's a bit of a mystery how I managed to not look through any of the *three* windows in my bedroom, but I did it. I am normally able to leave the house around 7:00 AM and arrive at work with a cup of McDonald's coffee in my hand at around 7:25. I wanted to be in by 7:15 today, so I left ten minutes early, at about 6:50. It took *54 minutes* to get to work. Highways were shut down, cars were spinning off the road everywhere, and, as it turns out, there were a number of minor school bus accidents as well.

Keep in mind: *everyone who lives here* drives in snow for *half the damn year.* Or at least what *feels* like half the damn year. It was *slick as hell* outside; even taking the approach to my school *very* carefully I still managed to miss the damn parking lot, and even at lunchtime my anti-lock brakes kicked in on the very first turn out of the lot. It was *shitty* outside today, people.

Anyway. Back to those minor school bus accidents. The district made the decision very early in the day to cancel all after-school activities and all field trips (I don't know that there actually were any, mind you) and other things requiring transportation *during* the day as well except for that which was absolutely necessary to get kids to and from school. So they decided to do an all-call to every parent in the corporation, because, well, that kind of decision is going to affect a *lot* of kids.

Important: I have not *heard* the all-call, but I've seen the carnagey aftermath, so it's possible that I'm slightly misrepresenting this? But apparently the all-call included, in addition to the cancellation information, the fact that there had been "several" minor bus accidents in the morning but– and this was apparently delivered with a cheery tone of voice, which given the person who I know sent it, doesn't surprise me– there were "no serious injuries."

Guess which words *every fucking parent who got the call* heard? "Bus accident" and "injuries." The goddamned phones were ringing off the hook *all day*. In addition to the usual complement of assholes who don't answer the phone then *don't listen to their voicemail* and just call the number back without knowing who it is they're calling– hearing from people saying "I don't know who called me, and I don't know what they called about, and I think *you* should have that information" is always fun– we got a number of irate phone calls from parents who were mad because we hadn't called them to let them know that their kids were in a bus accident.

Because, see, they *weren't*.

One parent was even angry that we hadn't notified her that her child had been *injured* in a bus accident, and wanted to know what hospital she was at. If her child doesn't pass ISTEP, the *school is blamed*, people.

Not having an "I love my job" day right now, guys.

The Food Drive

November 27 2014

Lots of schools do food drives this time of year, generally trading a canned food item for some sort of prize, like a dress down day or a homework pass or something like that. My school is no exception. The difference is that my school turns around and gives that donated food right back to our own families rather than donating it to a food bank. We pulled together 54 boxes of donated items in all; I have no idea how many items in total but it was a *lot*. A couple of our staffers spent a couple of days sorting everything out and trying to make sure that what was in each of the boxes was roughly equivalent, and on Tuesday a few of us drove to a meat market in Buchanan, Michigan and bought 54 turkeys, one for each of the boxes.

I spent most of yesterday with our librarian, out distributing packages to our families. We went out in pairs, most teams going to 10 or 12 houses. The librarian and I had a double run and hit 21.

It was... sobering. I've lived in this town for most of my life and taught in its public schools for the last eight years, and I've always known that there were pockets of severe poverty throughout the town– hell, I've talked about the effects poverty has on our kids any number of times in any number of venues. But this was the first time where my job for a day was literally to drive around and find out where my kids live. Our principal, at one of his houses, was greeted at the door by a man with a gun in his hand. The librarian and I didn't have that, but we did have one house that we didn't leave food at on account of the place looked like it had been abandoned for years, only to get back to school and discover that, yes, that was the right address and more than one of our students *still live there*.

397

I can't properly describe how bad this place was. Suffice it to say that my job today was to drive around and deliver donated food to families who are poor enough that they need such assistance. These people, as you might expect, don't exactly live in beautiful, well-maintained homes. Nonetheless, the rest of the houses were *mansions* compared to this one. There is *no way* they have electricity or heat. They didn't have *knobs on the doors*, for God's sake. The front door was held shut by a padlock. The librarian looked in a window and said that the place was full of trash. I got back to school too late to do anything about it, but I'll be calling DCFS on Monday. I *have to*.

Across the street was what looked like a $300,000 house. Literally exactly across the street.

We got back to school in time to discover that three of our kids were being removed from their father's home, also by DCFS. It is absolutely the best decision for everyone involved.

Be thankful for what you have, folks.

I Hope This Is Funny

December 18 2014

I don't know how to write this. I've been working on it in my head for over a week now, and in *none* of the versions in my head have I hit the tone I like, but this story is either funny enough or weird enough to deserve telling– I just don't know how to do it *right*.

Also, here's a phrase I've never used on the blog before, but this is important: Consider this your trigger warning, if you're partial to such things. This will end well, but it will not *start* well.

I was out of the office for a good chunk of last Tuesday. When I got back the guy who had been acting as our principal designee (because the principal and AP were both also out of the office) said that there had been a really weird spike in sexual harassment issues during the time we'd been gone. These things happen in middle school, but they're not super common, so for multiple things to happen in the same day is odd. I'm not around for the explanation or the ensuing phone calls; I just know Stuff has Happened.

The next day, I walk into a parent conference with the designee and the assistant principal because I need to talk to my boss for a few minutes, and end up sitting down and being part of the meeting. Mom is the parent of a fifth grade boy, and he appears to be in *grave* trouble. She is expressing two emotions: the first is horror and the second is an almost *craven* sense of apologia. She's so sorry for what he did that it almost hurts me to listen to the conversation.

She keeps saying that when he used "the word" or "that word" that he didn't really mean what the word *actually meant,* that they are immigrants and "that word" is used differently in their country. She looks Hispanic, and so does the boy, and he has a unique first name that really doesn't scan to any particular ethnic group or nationality

399

that I'm aware of, so I assume "their country" is somewhere in South America. Then I hear her speak to her son in whatever language they speak at home and it's *clearly* not Spanish, but she doesn't talk long enough for me to get past *hey wait that isn't Spanish* and start listening for whatever the language actually *is*. The general mood in the room is solemn; I consider leaving but she begins addressing her remarks to me as well as the other two as if I belong there so I don't.

Eventually, she leaves, insisting that not only will she tell her son to stop using "the word" but that *she* will stop using "the word" herself, because she knows that the reason this happened is that she's been setting a terrible example for their son and that she realizes that this is not how things are done in America.

One guess on what I think the word is, right? There's only one word in the English language– well, two, *maybe*— with enough power that someone would refuse to even say it while *talking about it*. So he's called someone the N-word, right? But that's not sexual harassment. It's a lot of things but it's not sexual harassment. So... huh? Weirdly, though, there's talk about how she's pretty sure her son *likes* the girl he used "the word" around, and... huh.

They leave. The AP and the other guy exchange a look, both take a deep breath, and then *crack up laughing*.

"What the hell happened?" I ask. "What was the deal?"

"He threatened to rape a fifth grade girl," the AP says, practically wiping tears from her eyes. The boy, remember, was *also* a fifth grader.

My eyes widen. *What the fuck are you assholes laughing about?* This is, as you might imagine, a *big* deal. I've literally never had to deal with a *rape threat* in a school before. That's *major*.

I express that sentiment. They laugh harder.

"They're German," the AP says, as if that explains it. I give her a *yeah, so the hell what*? sort of gesture.

Apparently there is, and if you are German or speak German better than I do *please* feel free to enlighten me here, some sort of German proverb, or slang expression, or figure of speech, or *something,* that basically means "stop bugging me" or "leave me alone," meaning *mild,* possibly even affectionate harassment– that, when translated into English, comes out as *rape*.

This woman has been using this phrase, translated, around her son, for *years*. She has apparently, and at this point my AP does a picture-perfect impression of this lady, one that causes *me* to lose it and crack up out of sheer disbelief, on multiple occasions said the phrase "I'm busy, go rape your father" to her son.

Her son, in saying "I'm going to rape you," to a little girl in his class, meant "I'm gonna get on your nerves."

And, understandably, this has caused *all sorts of merry hell* to break loose. Apparently Mom is fully aware of the word's connotations in English– how could she not be?– but hasn't managed to purge the word from her vocabulary, to the point where American friends of hers have actually called her out on it and asked her to stop using it. You can imagine how this would go, right? You don't just drop a loaded term like *rape* into a conversation without causing a little bit of a hitch here and there. And, *God,* if she's seriously said "Go rape your father" to her son while on the phone with someone else? What the fuck *I don't even.*

This all sounded deeply weird to me, of course, even a little unbelievable, until it hit me that I use the phrases "Are you fucking with me?" and "Are you shitting me?" on a fairly regular basis, and in *very much the same way* those phrases would be hugely opaque to anyone with no understanding of colloquial English. This is, presumably, more or less the same phenomenon, only through another filter where it's been translated.

So… yeah. I have no idea if anyone reading this is laughing right now, or if you just think that's an insanely weird conversation to have to have. I hope you at least understand why I felt like I had to write about it.

Another Actual Conversation with a Parent

January 16 2015

Hi, Mr. Smith? This is Mr. Siler, I'm the <job title> at <school>. I have your daughter Sally with me right now. Do you have a moment?

No, sir, she's not in trouble. In fact, she asked me to call you. Yes, that's correct.

Well, this morning she found me in the cafeteria and let me know that another student who sits near her had been smoking on the bus that morning. She reported that he was smoking marijuana, but as it turned out it was just cherry-flavored tobacco.

Yes, we've concluded our investigation and the situation's being dealt with.

Yes, I'm quite happy that she spoke up. She did the right thing. But that's not why I'm calling. Yes, this happened this morning. Several hours ago. I sent her to class right after she told me about it, but she's only just now come back downstairs to my office.

Well, you see, Sally is very concerned that it's possible that her clothing might still smell of this young man's tobacco. She... uh... well, she says that you tend to smell her clothes before doing the laundry, and she's very upset at the possibility that you might smell the tobacco on her clothing and think she's been smoking.

Yes. She doesn't want to get in trouble. She wanted to call you herself, but I told her I thought the story might be more convincing coming from me.

Yes. Really.

403

No. I smelled her sleeve– she, uh… she actually insisted that I do that. And I need you to understand that smelling a student's clothes is not exactly a day-to-day job task around here. In fact I've been teaching for thirteen years and this is the first time a student has insisted that I smell them. I can't smell a thing. Honestly, sir, I think she's a little nuts.

Yes, she's right here. She's laughing, in fact. Would you like to talk to her? Okay. I'll send her back to class, then. Thank you. Enjoy your weekend.

Well, That's New

January 20 2015

"He tried to pull the gas lines out on the stove and then he ejaculated all over everything" is not a sentence anyone has ever said to me at work before.

In Which DO NOT WANT

JANUARY 30 2015

For reasons that I can't get into, I had to call a couple of seventh grade girls out of class and into my office toward the end of the day today. I picked them from a list of kids I *could* have chosen because I know both of them fairly well, relatively speaking, and because as near as I've been able to tell they're both relatively smart and honest kids. They both happened to be in the same class and so came down together.

They walk into my office and one of them asks if they can shut the door. "I don't want to talk about this with the door open," she says.

I raise an eyebrow. There is literally *no way* that she can have any idea what I want to talk to them about. It's flatly impossible.

"You two are in *so much trouble,*" I say. I am doing this to fuck with them. They're not in the tiniest *shred* of trouble, but I know they're both good kids and they're going to temporarily freak out if I tell them I'm mad at them.

And they don't react.

Um.

"So, uh, why do *you* think I called you down here?"

"The Ellie Mae thing," one of them says. Now, I don't know who Ellie Mae is, and that's not her name, but it's close enough in a way that entertains me.

I look at the other one. "You're both involved in this, right?" She nods.

Note that I didn't even know the two of them were friends. This is hilarious.

"Tell me your side of the story," I say.

407

Two minutes later, having been led through a dizzying shitstorm of names and social media accounts and a web of cousins and aunts and uncles so thick that I halfway want to start drawing a *map*, I halt the conversation and tell them why they're actually down in my office. "We will deal with this other thing afterwards," I say, parts of my brain screaming at other parts of my brain to run. Because this has every sign of a Sally told Sherry that Susie told Sammie that Sharon saw Shayna say to Shalynn that Sally's sister's boyfriend's third cousin was a slut, and I want nothing to do with it.

But, because I am a rockstar, I sort everything out and issue instructions for what is to be done on Monday. Only problem is that what was supposed to be a five-minute conversation ended up taking 25.

But I *love it* when they accidentally rat themselves out like this.

In Which You Don't Need to Know This

February 9 2015

I stopped at McDonald's for coffee on the way *home* from work today, if that tells you anything about my day.

This story is going to be a little different, and you may want to bail now. I'll give you a blank line as a warning.

Okay.

There are two adult bathrooms at my new place of business. One of them is a one-seater and is effectively a private men's room for the office. That bathroom has two problems: 1) it is *directly* outside the principal's office and 2) I am one of only three men who might ever use it, and one of the other two is frequently not *in* the office, so not only is there a theoretical chance that my boss might hear me in there but if I power bomb the place everyone is going to *know it was me*. This cannot stand.

I am actually covering classes today, because we have *that many teachers absent*, and it is my prep period. I am in my office frantically trying to get some of my own job done before I have to go do someone else's for a while. I have, as it happens, already *had* a cup of coffee this morning. Now, for most people, coffee is a diuretic. For me, it has rather more... *substantial* effects, if you know what I mean and I hope you do.

...

Coffee makes me shit, is what I'm trying to say here.

So, yeah. As it works out, *both* of the other men in the office are not currently *in* the office, meaning that I can basically do whatever I want in My Other Office with no worries. I become aware of Impending Pressure and head off to do my business.

Meanwhile: the assistant principal is next door. We have recently had a very serious bullying issue on one of our buses that she's been straightening out, and she's been using varying levels of severity depending on the level of insistence of the various children involved that they had nothing to do with it. As it turns out, there is video. Fairly a *lot* of video. So each and every one of these lil' sweethearts is busted; it's just a matter of how long they're gonna lie before a hammer gets dropped on their heads. The kid currently in her office is being *very* insistent that he's done nothing and said nothing and at the moment the AP is simply sitting there calmly categorizing his lies for use later.

This will, as it turns out, not go well for him.

So, back to me: I'm doing my business. I'm doing *quite a lot* of my business, as it turns out, and it occurs to me partway through that I ought to be really glad that there's no chance anybody else is gonna be trying to get in here anytime soon.

I finish. I wash my hands.

Thank *God* I washed my hands.

Because when I open the door, my assistant principal is standing *immediately outside the bathroom, with the student,* who has clearly spent my entire time in the bathroom bawling his eyes out. I do not know how long they have been waiting.

"Go on in there and clean yourself up," she says to him.

I have two choices at this point. This bathroom ain't fit for human habitation, and there is *no escaping the fact* that I am the one who has ruined it. I can either admit it and suggest that the boy use the ladies' bathroom (which, much like ours, is a locking one-seater) or I can just shrug and let this boy enter into the bowels (see what I did there?) of Hell, where the sulfur in the air will surely blind him before he's able to wash the tears from his face.

Instead of doing either of those things, I just died of shame on the spot.

You gotta do what you gotta do sometimes, y'know?

In Which My Day Starts Off Weird

February 26 2015

I should have taken this and gotten a picture on the spot; I apologize for my failure as a writer.

My day began with an irate parent in the office– before I was even able to get to my desk and put my stuff down. She's mad that a teacher has sent a note home without any "useful" information on it, including her signature, and is furthermore angry that her daughter was prevented from leaving the gym at the end of the day so that she could go to said staff member and acquire this all-important signature. She's demanding to speak to the teacher in question immediately.

Right away I smell a rat, for several reasons, not least among which is the fact that the teacher in question has *gym duty* at the end of the day and would, therefore, have been *in the gym.* I ask to see the note. The parent hands me two pieces of paper: her daughter's progress report, which has every single grade carefully scratched out with what appears to be *both* black pen and Sharpie, and the handwritten note from the teacher.

Note that the parent is mad at the *teacher*, which means that I don't help her mood any when I immediately start laughing and tell her daughter that she has exactly *one* chance to tell the truth before we have a serious problem. Because this is basically the note:

MS WHATSERNAME:

YOURE DAUTERS GRADES ARE INCORRECT THESE IS THE REAL ONES:

1) A

2) B-

3) A

411

4) B
5) B+
6) A-
7) A

SHE IS DOING A LOT BETTER LATLY PLEASE CALL US IF YOU HAS ANY QUESTIONS.

I didn't memorize the motherfucker; I remember there was definitely one word in there that had a superfluous "e" in it somewhere, but you get the idea. Furthermore, every letter on the page has been gone over at least two times in a way *absolutely no adult anywhere* writes but is currently a popular affectation among teenage girls.

Note also that the students have *eight* classes, not seven.

What's Mom mad about? That the classes aren't *labeled*. She apparently hasn't noticed the… uh… *various other issues* with the note. She then proceeded to get mad at me for declining to punish her daughter at school; sorry, lady, this one is *clearly* your problem. I'm not doing *anything* about it.

And, say it with me: if the daughter doesn't pass ISTEP, it's *my* fault.

People who are Qualified to Teach

February 5 2015

This is not actually my story. It's put together from various things people have told me in my capacity as building designee over the last couple of days. I also know the student in question pretty well, because she was at my other school before moving to my current one, with a year or so off in between where her parents were "homeschooling" her. Keep that lil' detail in mind while you're reading this; this child's parents think they can homeschool her, and are legally allowed to by the state of Indiana. I also know her older sister, who is high school age; no part of this story would be any more or less surprising coming from her.

Tuesday: I hear from our social worker. The student has been referred to him by a teacher, and he's keeping me in the loop. She has reported, apparently with a giant smile on her face (a sort of cheery obliviousness is characteristic of this family) that she hasn't been able to sleep in several days because 1) she and her older sister have been sleeping on the floor in the dining room of her house because someone else is using their bed (it's unclear how many beds we're discussing) and 2) in addition to sleeping on a linoleum floor, she's being kept awake by the *mice* constantly running over her body all night and waking her up.

And then there's 3) the ghost. She reports the ghost, apparently, in *exactly* the same tone and facial expression as the sleeping-on-the-floor and mice-all-over-me story. The ghost is named Wanda or Wendy or something, wears a long white dress, carries a *scythe*, of all things, and keeps waking her up by leaning over her and staring at her face. So, she's sleeping on the floor in the

413

kitchen, the mice are running all over her, and she wakes up and there's the ghost staring at her.

Hell, if I've *ever* had a *what is this I don't even* moment in teaching, this is it; half of this story is *clearly* problematic as far as the chances of it being true; the rest of it, given what I know about the family, would not surprise me a bit. I tell him I'll notify the principal and he should continue with his investigation and get anyone involved that he needs to get involved.

Wednesday: I hear from the *nurse*. This kid— the same kid, only the nurse doesn't know the story from yesterday— has come in and requested a menstrual pad. The nurse hands it over and waves her to the bathroom to... put it on? Install it? Use it? What the hell is the correct verb here?

Anyway, one way or another the kid comes out a minute later and tells the nurse that she *doesn't know how* to... I'll say "put it on" until someone corrects me. The nurse, somewhat bewildered because the girl is an eighth grader and presumably has been dealing with these things for a couple of years or so, says something like "put it in your underwear," or whatever you might say, hell, I don't wear the damned things.

She tells the nurse that she's *not wearing underwear.*

The nurse, now bewildered *and* horrified, asks if she just started her period or dear jesus god *what have you been doing all day?*

The girl tells her that she's just been bleeding down her legs all day. Apparently every so often she's been asking for a bathroom pass and wiping her legs off with toilet paper. It took until 2:00 in the afternoon before "go to the nurse and ask for supplies" occurred to her. She's wearing dark pants, and she's chubby, so no one had noticed any stains. Whether anyone noticed the *smell* and didn't do anything about it is, as yet, an unanswered question.

At this point the DCFS referrals have been somewhat expedited.

Remember: this kid's parents were allowed to homeschool. Also remember: when this child doesn't pass the ISTEP, Indiana law says it's my fault.

On This Week, pt. 2

May 23 2015

The health app on my iPhone tells me that I walked ten miles–
over twenty thousand steps– yesterday, and that is without a single
second of anything that I could accurately describe as "exercise." It
was just *that busy* of a day.

Every so often it hits me just how ridiculous my job can be,
right? Thursday, in particular, was like that. On Wednesday evening
the sister of two of our seventh graders, who has been missing for
several weeks, was found dead in a field a couple of counties south
of here. My understanding is that the man who murdered her turned
himself in and led the cops to her body. Thursday morning, as we
were putting our heads together and trying to figure out what we
should do about that, we had one fifth grade student brought down to
the office whose *nine year old* cousin had just committed suicide the
night before. She had just confessed to a teacher that she was
thinking about killing herself as well.

Within five minutes of *that,* we had two fights in two entirely
different parts of the building, including one between two kids whose
families have literally been feuding since they were in *second
grade.*

Within five minutes of *that,* the kid who got put up for
expulsion for shoving me earlier in the year was back in the office
because *he* blew up at somebody– an event that turned out to
legitimately not be his fault, but he claims nothing is *ever* his
fault. On the rare occasions he's actually telling the truth– which
isn't the case most of the time– we still need to do an investigation to
verify it independently.

415

I tried to send him home on a home isolation(*) anyway, because generally once he gets his blood up he's incredibly difficult to calm down even if whatever happened really isn't his fault. His mom's response was to tell me that she wasn't coming to get him, that we should put him in ISS, and that if he messed up in ISS– which everyone involved knew he was going to– we should call the police.

He's 12.

I got to the office around 7:25. By 7:48 AM, my morning was *done*. Right there. Done. Before 8 AM.

And y'all think I should be worried about *test scores?*

So. Right. The ridiculousness part. That was my morning. Other stuff happened, but I had enough student issues on my plate before eight in the morning to keep me busy until well after noon. What did I spend the afternoon doing?

I spent the afternoon building radio-controlled sharks, learning to fly them, and then teaching 8th graders how to fly them. And worrying about *inflatable pools* and *popsicles.* We had our post-ISTEP celebration at the end of the day yesterday, and the theme was "beach party." And my boss is not the type to do *anything* half-assed, so there was *extensive* setup required to get everything right. So there were games and competitions in the gym for a while at the end of the day, and then two dances– one for 5th and 6th graders, one for 7th and 8th, in separate parts of the building.

At the end of the 5th and 6th grade dance, something amazing happened. There were, I dunno, 250-300 kids in the room, and maybe 12-15 adults or so. We cut the music and the adults all raised their hands. That's *all we did.* I was looking around while all this was going on, and *none of the adults were talking to anyone.* The kids all did one of three things:

> 1) Some went to stand next to their teachers;
> 2) Some went and stood against the wall;
> 3) Some went and sat on the bleachers.

But *every kid in the gym* was moving with purpose and to a destination, and they were all doing so quietly, with *none of them* being told what to do. We somehow managed to dismiss *half the building* at the end of a dance on a Friday before a three day weekend, in– well, not *silence*, but manageable quiet– without *talking to the kids.*

And then I did a six-hour shift at my other job, which featured my high school co-worker not bothering to show up until an hour and a half after the start of his shift, a visit by a dozen or so special-needs adults, a group that comes by all the time and who I really enjoy having with us but who generally require about three times as much, uh, *hospitality* as any similar group ought to, and the immense, "well, this may as well happen" fun of having to clean up a pool of what was clearly menstrual blood on one of our picnic benches toward the end of the shift. A pool that no one informed us about, and I only found because I was checking the gameroom.

It's been a long goddamn couple of days, is what I'm saying.

(*) Not a suspension, but functionally indistinguishable from one and frequently used for emotionally disturbed special ed students who are out of suspension days for the year.

417

Stuff They Don't Train You For

May 27 2015

I mentioned earlier that we discovered late last week that a close family member of two of our boys was recently found murdered. The guy who killed her went to the cops and confessed and then led them to her body. (Fun fact: he's pleading innocent. Figure that out.)

Bad enough, right?

Found out today that we *also* have relatives of the *murderer* in the building. And that the various parties are reacting to each other… *predictably.*

When you take classes in ed school, they do not tell you what to do when the uncle of one student has murdered the sister of another student.

That's kinda heavy, so let me leave you with this: have you heard of the Charlie Charlie Challenge? If not, stop reading this immediately, because you don't need stupidity of this magnitude in your brain.

You're still here, aren't you? Last warning.

Okay, fine. The Charlie Charlie Challenge works thusly: Divide a piece of paper into four quadrants. Write "Yes" in two of them and "No" in the other two. Balance one pencil atop another in a roughly perpendicular fashion. Ask the "Mexican demon" known as "Charlie Charlie" a question.

This part's critical: Be too stupid to remember that gravity exists.

Then scream.

419

Luther M. Siler

We had eight fucking kids in the office across three different incidents about this fucking nonsense yesterday, and from what I'm hearing, it's nationwide.

Teenagers are *morons*.

The Most Embarrassing Thing Possible

MARCH 26 2015

I did not know that I was looking, but I have found it. I have discovered what the literal most embarrassing situation imaginable is.

It is when you are a thirteen-year-old girl and your mother, with your father also in the room, describes your recent bout with vaginal itching to your male principal.

There is no way to be more embarrassed than when that happens. It is impossible.

Trying to Fight Off a Long Rant

January 28 2015

The State of Indiana, in their infinite wisdom, has had the ISTEP test redone for this year. And they have let us know that this one will involve High Standards! And Rigor! Lots of Rigor! You can sprinkle it on stuff, like cinnamon sugar.

We take three practice tests over the course of the year so that we can get some idea of who might pass the ISTEP, because there are no other ways to figure that out other than testing.

The results of the second test are (mostly) in, and I've been looking at them all week.

Currently perhaps a *dozen students* in my building are expected to pass the ISTEP. In the *building*.

That is not a typo or an exaggeration. Historically we've been passing, oh, 70% of our kids or so, give or take a couple standard deviations.

But, hey, what do you want us to do? Make excuses?

(Luther 2015 edit: At this writing, October 2015, we STILL do not have ISTEP results from the final test. The state board of education met last week to determine cutscores and declined to do so. It will be 2016 before we see the results, at which point they will be substantially more useless than normal, and that's hard to do. We may well have started this year's ISTEP before we see the scores from last year's, the way they're going.)

423

I Can't Tell If this Is Sad or Funny

April 17 2015

And the answer may very well be "both."

A couple of months ago one of my sixth grade boys attacked me in the office. I didn't mention it here. It wasn't a big deal. The kid was in the midst of a massive emotional meltdown and he has trouble controlling his temper on the best of days. I wasn't mad. We had to put him up for expulsion, but when a kid's special education disability can be found to have *caused* the behavior that led to an expulsion, that kid is frequently sent directly back to school and everyone involved knew that that was exactly what was going to happen and it did.

(I understand that this policy may prove controversial. I'm not super interested in defending it or denigrating it at the moment. It's just how things work in our current system. Roll with it.)

At his expulsion hearing, I went over what had happened and spent a few minutes talking with the kid about things he could have done to make the situation work better. I made it very clear to both him and his mother that if he's in a situation where he feels like he's about to lose his temper, I want him to come talk to me if he needs to, and that under most circumstances my office door is going to be open to him whenever he needs it to be. Since he came back, I've checked in with him on my own two or three days a week, and he's been referred to me once or twice a week as well.

Basically what I'm saying is I see this kid every day for one reason or another, and I spend a fair percentage of my copious spare time talking him off of ledges. But! He hasn't gotten into a fight or hit anyone since he came back. In fact, to the best of my recollection

425

he hasn't even had a day of home isolation since he came back. This represents *incredible progress*.

He needs a name. We'll call him David.

So today I got a phone call from one of the special ed teachers that David had been sent to her room by another teacher on a time-out and that he was insisting on talking to me. I went to the classroom and found him in the hallway about halfway to meltdown mode– hands clenched into fists, breathing heavily, pacing around, the works.

I got the story out of him fairly quickly, and this is the part where telling this story gets a bit difficult, because I don't quite know how to describe this other boy, who we'll call Jonathan. Jonathan is *probably* gay. He certainly acts the part; he's noticeably effeminate and he *plays up* his effeminacy (is that a word?) to a degree I have literally never seen from a twelve-year-old before. He gets picked on by the other kids from time to time, which will surprise no one, but what *may* surprise you is that we've had to deal with *him* for sexual harassment issues before. For example, we had a big kerfluffle on Monday *just this week* because Jonathan was blowing kisses at several of the other boys in the room– a fact that they did not react to with calm equanimity.

Put the pitchforks down. As I've said *many, many times*, bullying is an infinitely more complicated issue than society is ever willing to admit, and frequently what people might want to point at and screech "bullying!" is actually a situation with multiple bad actors. This is *absolutely* one of those situations.

At any rate, David has gotten into an argument with Jonathan, and rather than punch Jonathan in the face he's left the room, gone somewhere else, and asked to talk to me. He's upset with Jonathan because he doesn't like "that gay stuff" and blah blah blah garden-variety middle-school homophobia. Am I happy about it? No, absolutely not. Am I willing to pass over GVMSH because at this precise moment with this precise young man right now we're working on *don't punch people in their faces,* a lesson that he seems to actually be learning? Yes. Yes I am. Judge me as you see fit.

I get a description of what has happened out of him. As it turns out, what specifically set him off was Jonathan telling him, loudly, in class, that he was going to "do a booty porn" with him.

You read that right. *Booty porn*. Jonathan wants to do a booty porn with David! But David does not want to be in a booty porn! In fact, he quite badly wants to punch the faces of those who suggest that he should be in booty porns. But he has been told not to punch faces, so instead he left the room.

I deposit David in the office, tell the office to sit on him and let him calm down for a few minutes, and go find Jonathan. I have a problem here; I can calm David down easily enough, especially given a few minutes. What I *can't* do is put him back in the classroom with this kid, and if Jonathan really suggested he was going to fuck this boy in the ass and videotape it– because hell if I can figure out what else "do a booty porn" might mean– then we're right back to sexual harassment issues from *Jonathan*, and my day, much like an erect penis, has just gotten longer and harder.

(I'm very sorry.)

I talk to Jonathan in the hallway. A bunch of the boys realize immediately why I'm there and a bunch of hands shoot up from kids who want to tell me what happened. I wave them off. Jonathan comes outside. His story is largely the same as David's in terms of the mutual harassment and name-calling that started the dispute, and then he says something that stops me dead.

"I told him I was gonna do a bully report, and then he got mad and left the room."

Say "bully report" a few times really fast. Now say "booty porn" a few times really fast.

oh what the hell am I doing with my life.

Now, here's the thing: Jonathan is *just clever enough* that he could be lying. And David, as much as I like the kid, is *just volatile enough* that he could have put the worst possible spin on what he *thought* Jonathan was saying.

Do you see where this is going?

I had to pull, one by one, and at random, about half of this poor teacher's class into the hallway, to ask them if they heard the words *bully report* or *booty porn.*

The results? 50/50.

And then I had to go talk to my boss, and say the words *booty porn* to him a bunch of times, and explain to him why I was resigning immediately and refusing to deal with any of this nonsense any longer.

The end.

Mosquitoes

April 17 2015

In my first act of the day, seconds after walking into my office, I had to have a parent/teacher conference with a parent whose son had been suspended for two days for stopping outside of a classroom full of girls, blatantly and obviously scratching his balls, and then loudly announcing that he had crabs.

Mom told me that the reason his crotch itched was that he'd been wearing loose shorts yesterday and working in the yard, and there had been issues with mosquitoes.

It is April. I do not believe this story.

But the conference was *hilarious.*

Afterword: Searching for Malumba

October 2015

The man is elderly, hawk-faced, wearing a neatly tailored black suit. He reminds me of no one so much as a white-haired, crew-cutted Peter Lorre, right down to the slight German accent. His lips are contorted in a scowl.

"TAKETE!" he shrieks, raising his arms above his head, his hands curled into claws. The consonants in the word are harsh, the sound fierce, almost violent.

His face relaxes, the scowl replaced with a broad smile. His eyes, formerly piercing and angry, are now a warm, friendly blue.

"MALUMBA!" he says, spreading his arms wide, drawing out the vowels. "Maaah-looooooom-baaaaaah!"

Malumba is nice. Malumba is soft. Malumba is welcoming. I like Malumba more than Takete.

It is 2005, and I am within a month or so of my first job as a fully certified classroom teacher. This man is a consultant who is presenting at a faculty meeting. It is Thursday, and everyone in the room is visibly exhausted. Tomorrow, he will be visiting some of our classrooms and providing feedback to us on how we might improve the environment in our classrooms.

It is 2015. I do not remember the man's name; I likely had forgotten it within a few weeks of his "professional development," and he did not visit my classroom. Repeated Internet searches to try and determine his identity have come up empty. If I am being honest, I only vaguely remember the point of using made-up words to illustrate, respectively, chaos and peace. I will remember the

431

visual of him saying those two words for the rest of his life, and
Searching for Malumba was the title of my book about teaching
before I really even had a career to write about. The first incarnation
about this book was just about my *first year* as a teacher. There have
been many years since then; hundreds if not thousands of students,
perhaps a dozen classrooms, and untold thousands of pieces of paper.

I do not know if I ever found malumba. It was there from time
to time, certainly, with the right students, on the right days, but
certainly never with the consistency that I had always hoped for.
Sadly, I found takete in my classroom far more often.

Books are supposed to end with happy endings. This one,
unfortunately, probably does not. I am back in the classroom again,
teaching fifth grade this time, and I am looking almost frantically for
another job. It may be— I *hope it will be*— the case that by the time
you read this, I am no longer a teacher. I fought the good fight for
fourteen years, and I hope that through all the cynicism and the anger
that are very much a part of this book my readers see some hope and
some caring and perhaps some love as well. I cannot do it any
longer; the fire in my belly is no longer there, and I cannot come
home to my own son feeling angry or upset from work any longer.

I hope that I helped. I hope that the children in my classroom
are better off for me having been there; I hope that those of them
who are adults now remember me fondly. Some, surely, do not; I
only hope they are outnumbered by those who do. I could not find
malumba in my classroom; it now falls to me to create it in my life
instead.

Thank you for reading, and thank you for— I hope—
understanding as well.

Thank You

...for reading *Searching for Malumba*. I hope you enjoyed it. If you did, please feel encouraged to review it at the website of your choice.

Luther M. Siler

About the Author

Luther M. Siler was born in 1976 and currently resides in northern Indiana. Sharing his house with him are his wife, his four-year-old son, a dog and a cat. He has been a teacher since 2001 and has been named Teacher of the Year twice in that time.

In addition to writing about teaching, he writes science fiction novels about space gnomes and Mars.

You can follow Luther at his blog at http://www.infinitefreetime.com, or on Twitter at @nfinitefreetime.

Also by Luther Siler

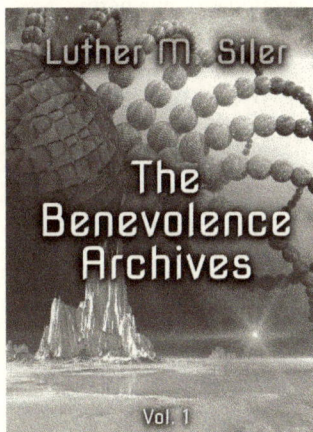

THE BENEVOLENCE ARCHIVES, VOL. 1:

Troll evictions! Dwarf pirates! Daring rescues! Angry gods! Impossible technology! Oversized bars! Pissed-off ogres! Disrespectful spaceships! All this and a mild disregard for proper wound treatment!

THE BENEVOLENCE ARCHIVES, VOL. 1 is a novella-length collection of six short stories set in a common universe. Combining elements of space opera-style science fiction and high fantasy, THE BENEVOLENCE ARCHIVES tell the adventures of Brazel, Rhundi, and Grond, a gnome/halfogre team of smugglers.

435

THE PLANET IT'S FARTHEST FROM: A simple job in a saloon goes poorly for Brazel.

THE CLOSET: Brazel and Grond are hired to teach someone why gambling can be a bad idea.

YANK: Dwarven pirates. 'Nuff said.

REMEMBER: Brazel and Grond are hired by one of the galaxy's most powerful people for a suspiciously easy job.

THE CONTRACT: Rhundi tries to get through a simple business negotiation without anyone being shot.

THE SIGIL: Brazel and Grond encounter something horrifying on a frozen rock in the middle of nowhere.

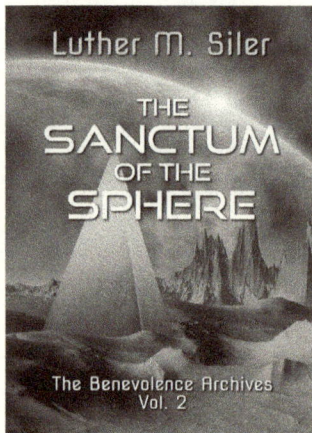

THE BENEVOLENCE ARCHIVES, VOL. 2: THE SANCTUM OF THE SPHERE

"Go rob that train." Nice, normal. An everyday heist.

But nothing is ever normal for Brazel, Grond and Rhundi.

A simple act of motorized larceny quickly explodes into a galaxy-spanning adventure for the two thieves. Blade-wielding elves, a fast-moving global war, a secret outlaw space city, incomprehensible insectoids and one impossibly lucky human are just the start of their problems. And that's before they learn that someone from Grond's past has gotten the Benevolence involved...

What is happening on the ogrespace moon Khkk?

Who are the Noble Opposition?

And what is the secret of THE SANCTUM OF THE SPHERE?

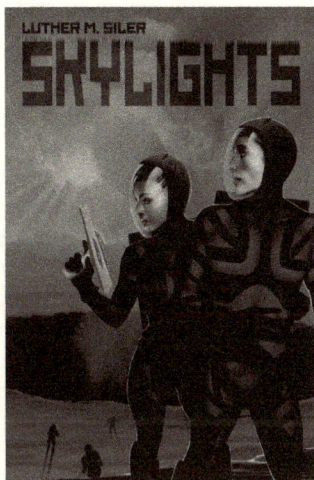

SKYLIGHTS

August 15, 2022: the *Tycho*, the most advanced interplanetary craft ever designed by the human race, launches from Earth on an expedition to Mars. The *Tycho* carries four passengers, soon to be the most famous people in human history.

February 19, 2023: The *Tycho* loses all communication with Earth while orbiting Mars. After weeks of determined attempts to reestablish contact, the *Tycho* is declared lost.

2027: Journalist Gabriel Southern receives a message from a mysterious caller: "Mars." Ezekiel ben Zahav isn't talking, but he wants Southern to accompany him for something— and he's dangling enough money under his nose to make any amount of hardship worth it.

SKYLIGHTS is the story of the second human expedition to Mars. Their mission: to find out what happened to the first.

Read on for an excerpt: the prologue to SKYLIGHTS.

Flashbulb memory, they call it. It's when you remember exactly where you were when you first discovered something or saw something happen.

If you're younger than me, which a lot of you probably are, then your first flashbulb memory is probably related to terrorism somehow. Anybody in, say, their early thirties or older probably remembers exactly where they were on September 11, 2001. A little younger than that and your first flashbulb memory is probably one of the bombings in Chicago in 2018.

I was six years old when the space shuttle *Challenger* exploded. It was January 29, 1986, at exactly eleven thirty-nine in the morning. I was in first grade. For some reason— I could look this up if I wanted, I suppose, but my first-grade self didn't know, so I'm not going to bother— NASA had decided that it would be great if they put a schoolteacher on the Space Shuttle. Her name was Christa McAuliffe, and she'd been a middle school teacher, her students not a lot older than I was at the time.

There was a ton of publicity about her presence on the shuttle. Come to think of it, that might have been the reason that NASA put her there in the first place. Every single kid in my school was watching the flight launch on television. The *Challenger* took off, and we all clapped. Seventy-three seconds later, an O-ring failed on the shuttle's right Solid Rocket Booster. There was a little puff of smoke from the side of the ship.

Some of us were still clapping.

I remember noticing it and wondering, for the split second that I had, what had happened. And then the *Challenger,* with me and millions of other people around the country watching, silently blew apart. There were a few seconds of shocked silence in the room, and then every kid in the class— every one in the building, probably— started crying at once.

You know what? Writing that just now, I wondered what my teacher must have done afterwards. I can't even remember her name. I can remember the wood surface on my desk, because I dug my fingers into it so hard that day that they scratched it and I got splinters. I can remember the wood-grain on the television set they had us watching. I can remember being surprised that Rachel Douglas, the biggest butthead in the entire first grade, was crying as hard as I was. But I can't remember a single thing that our teacher did to try and bring everybody back to sanity after watching that happen. That's how flashbulb memories work; you'll remember the event itself forever, but that doesn't mean you'll remember anything else that happened around it.

Seventeen years and two days later, it happened again. This time, it was the shuttle *Columbia*, and I was twenty-four and no longer sitting in a classroom. In fact, when the *Columbia* was falling apart in the morning sky over Texas, I was stuck in traffic and late to work. I found out about it about ten minutes after I got in, when the smarmy dope from the office next door made some sort of comment about it to me. We had the Internet by then— yes, there was Internet back then, although I think we might have still been calling it the World Wide Web— and I saw the entire thing on CNN's Web site. This time there weren't any tears, just a dull sort of ache in the pit of my stomach. I spent the rest of the day on the computer, chasing down eyewitness reports and trying to devour whatever little bits of actual news managed to leak out. It was funny; I hadn't spent much time thinking about space flight since the first grade, but suddenly the families of the men and women on that shuttle were all I could think about.

I was working for the *Indianapolis Star* at the time, splitting my time between a biweekly column in the science section and general reporting on local news for the rest of the paper. It was a good job; I was happy enough, and making enough money, but I wanted something different from my life.

I decided to write a book.

A year later, I'd completed *Nothing to Bury: the Martyrs of the Space Race*, a look at the lives of the astronauts who had died on the *Challenger* and the *Columbia*, as well as a host of other lives lost in the pursuit of space, and a look at the culture of NASA in between the two disasters. I was pretty proud of it as a piece of work; I wasn't expecting it to necessarily sell well to the general public, but it was a good piece of writing. It did better than I'd expected, enough that I've been able to be comfortable with freelance writing since then. I'm still working for news sites and some of the few print papers that are left, mind you, but I can pick my own assignments and do my own reporting now as opposed to having people assign my projects.

You know where this is going, don't you? I imagine you do.

On August 15, 2022, after years of technical and political delays, the space shuttle *Tycho*, carrying four astronauts, launched on a six-month journey to Mars. They were to remain in orbit around

Mars for thirty days, during which they would land on the planet's surface for the first time in human history, then to return to Earth. The run-up to the launch was the biggest public relations bonanza NASA had ever seen. Everything just *stopped* the day the *Tycho* launched. It was just like it had been for the *Challenger,* only times a hundred. They just weren't as good at hype in the eighties, I guess.

I was watching at home, with a couple of friends— I actually had a little party for the launch. I didn't realize how tense I was until I looked at my hands afterwards. There were furrows in my palms from my fingernails. Then the shuttle took off, soaring into a perfectly blue sky, and I held my breath for a few moments.

The launch went off without a hitch, though, and pictures of the *Tycho* blanketed every website and print doc on the planet over the next few days. For the next six months, everyone was obsessed with Mars. The astronauts provided regular updates on what they were doing. You could get daily blink messages from them if you wanted to, and progress along their flight path was updated live on a map running at the top of CNN.com for the entire duration of the trip. Those six months, I'm convinced, inspired a whole generation of new astronauts, astrophysicists, and pilots. I've never in my life seen America more excited about science. It was amazing.

And then, on February 19th, 2023, when the long voyage was finally over, we ... well, we don't actually know what happened. The *Tycho* was supposed to aerobrake into orbit around Mars, stay in orbit for a day or two, and then the astronauts were going to leave the ship to descend to the planet's surface in a lander. They were going to stay on the surface for two weeks or so, doing experiments, exploring the Martian surface, and making history.

There wasn't anything resembling photo evidence, not good evidence at least— NASA had been sending a steady diet of pictures and video from cameras affixed to the outside of the *Tycho* for months, but they failed at the same time as the audio feed. But we were getting audio beamed back from inside the cabin. Right up until the point where the flight commander, a decorated Marine pilot by the name of Alondra Gallegos, spoke the last words that the *Tycho* sent back to Earth.

"Is that ..." was all she said.

After that, nothing. No sound, no signals, no big explosion to be played on the news over and over again. Just nothing at all, and what started off as mild concern slowly morphed, over the next few days, weeks, months, into the certainty that, somehow, the ship had been lost. There was hope for a while that there had just been some sort of global communications failure, that the *Tycho* was still out there but had lost the ability to talk to us. Sadly, those hopes didn't make much sense in reality— the *Tycho's* communication capabilities were among the simplest systems on the ship, something a talented twelve-year-old would have been able to repair, *and* there was a redundant backup system. Anything catastrophic enough to have completely crippled the ship's ability to talk would have caused fatal damage to the rest of the ship as well. We just couldn't figure out what. Conventional wisdom eventually decided there had been some sort of asteroid or meteorite impact, something like that.

There was no flashbulb moment for the *Tycho*. The families of the four people lost on that mission— Alondra Gallegos, Harrison Brown, Kassius Newsome, and Ai-Li Wu— will never be able to move on. Many of them are convinced that their family members are still out there somewhere. There was no national mourning like there was for the *Challenger* and the *Columbia*. It was as if, after three high-profile ship losses, this time the country just wanted to forget about it.

I got a few calls for interviews after the *Tycho* lost contact, and a few more a few months later, once NASA officially stopped trying to reestablish contact with the ship. I turned them all down, though; I didn't want to base any more of my career on profiting from the deaths of people more heroic and important than I was. I didn't want to write about space any more.

Little did I know.

www.ingramcontent.com/pod-product-compliance
Lightning Source LLC
Chambersburg PA
CBHW031824090426
42741CB00005B/115